SPLENDOURS OF ANCIENT CHINA

MAURIZIO SCARPARI

Thames & Hudson

虞帝舜

帝舜二妃娥
皇女英

周

Text *Maurizio Scarpari*
Editorial production *Maurizio Scarpari,*
Valeria Manferto De Fabianis, Giulia Gaida
Graphic design *Luana Gobbo*
Drawings *Roberta Vigone*
Translation *A.B.A., Milan*

*First published in the United Kingdom in 2000 by
Thames & Hudson Ltd, 181A High Holborn, London WC1V 7QX*

© 2000 White Star S.r.l.

British Library Cataloguing-in-Publication Data

A catalogue record for this book is available from the British Library

ISBN 0-500-51024-5

Printed and bound in Italy

CONTENTS

(Note: numbers of captions refer to the page on which illustrations appear.)

1 Made of gilded bronze, this statuette of a kneeling servant girl is in fact a lamp. The sleeve of her garment acts as a chimney and falls so that the girl and the lamp blend into a harmonious composition. [Western Han]

2–3 A safe-conduct issued by the ruler of the southern kingdom of Nanyue: the inscription of four gold characters on the back of this inlaid bronze tiger reads 'permit for carriage by order of the king'. [Western Han]

4–5 Nü Ying and E Huang, daughters of the legendary emperor Yao and wives of his successor Shun, are portrayed with their husband on this lacquered wooden screen. The scene, taken from Lienü zhuan (Biographies of Exemplary Women) by Liu Xiang (78–8 BC), is painted in the style of famous artist Gu Kaizhi (c. AD 345–406). [Northern Wei]

6–7 The dragon occupies a very important place in Chinese mythology. While in the West it is often regarded as a force of evil, in China it is considered a propitious, just and benevolent creature, and it became the symbol of imperial authority. [Six Dynasties]

8–9 Companions in eternity: terracotta figurines such as these women, dancing with graceful, elegant movements, were frequently placed in magnificent Han tombs to entertain the deceased in the afterlife. [Western Han]

中
國
古
代
明

PREFACE

China has one of the oldest civilizations in the world. Covering a huge territory crossed by great rivers, it was perceived by its inhabitants as the centre of the world, *Zhongguo* (the 'Middle Kingdom'), from where culture spread throughout East Asia. Social organization was generally based on a system of kinship that guaranteed the most powerful families the loyalty of immense clans. Various dynasties ruled one after another, in accordance with a tradition that told of mythical rulers who had discovered all the inventions fundamental to human life, such as fire. Their ambition was to conquer and unify *Tian Xia* ('everything under the heavens'), but they had to contend with the continual threat posed by barbarian incursions as well as the power of the local lords, who attempted to undermine central authority.

The dream became a reality in 221 BC, when the ruler of the Kingdom of Qin defeated all his adversaries and founded a vast empire which, with varying fortunes, lasted until 1911. Deified as *Tian Zi* (the Son of Heaven), the emperor, was worshipped as the mediator between the divine and human realms. Prosperity and abundance were interpreted as a sign of his rectitude, while famine and calamities were attributed to his decadence.

Although the Silk Route saw continual trade between China, India and the countries of Central Asia, the great civilizations of the Mediterranean basin had no significant contacts with East Asia, with the result that for the West, China long remained a fabulous, distant world. Its civilization proved to be far more complex, and even more fascinating, when scholars gained access to its documentary sources, and, increasingly, when archaeologists began uncovering the testimony to the magnificence of China's past.

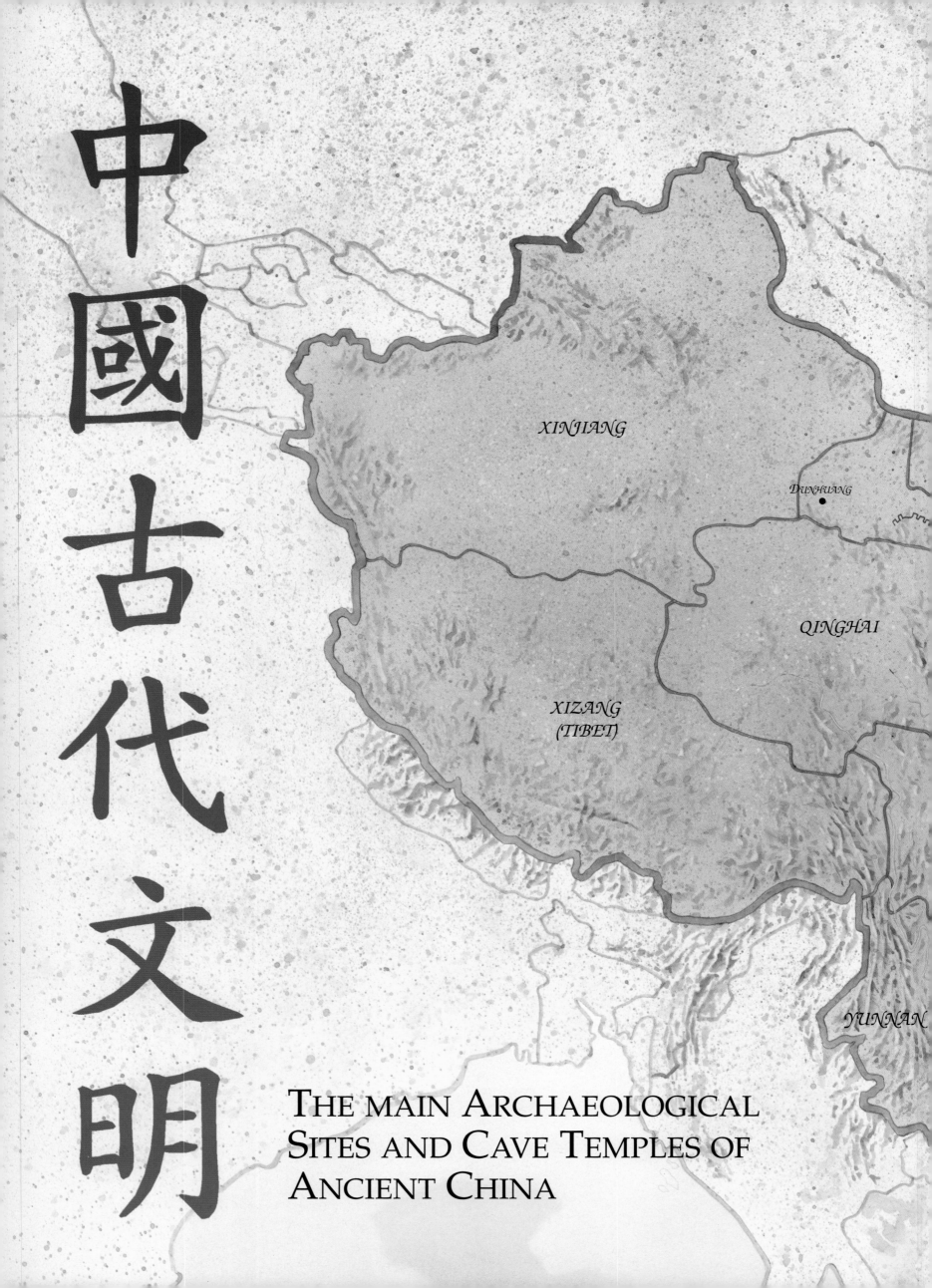

中國古代文明

XINJIANG

DUNHUANG

QINGHAI

XIZANG
(TIBET)

YUNNAN

THE MAIN ARCHAEOLOGICAL
SITES AND CAVE TEMPLES OF
ANCIENT CHINA

HEILONGJIANG

JILIN

INNER
MONGOLIA

NIUHELIANG

LIAONING

Yellow *River*

DATONG
YUNGANG
BEIJING

YING XIAN
MANCHENG
PINGSHAN

HEBEI

NINGXIA

SHANXI

SHANDONG

HOUMA
ANYANG
QUFU

GANSU

BANPO
LUOYANG
ERLIGANG

MAJISHAN
FUFENG
LINTONG
KAIFENG

XI'AN
LONGMEN
ZHENGZHOU

SHAANXI
ERLITOU
JIANGSU

HENAN

ANHUI

NANJING

SICHUAN

SUZHOU
SANXINGDUI
SHANGHAI

CHENGDU
CHONGQING
PENLONGCHENG
WUHAN

HUBEI
HANGZHOU

Yellow
Sea

Yangzi *River*
LIANGZHU

East
China
Sea

ZHEJIANG

CHANGSHA

MAWANGDUI
XIN'GAN

GUIZHOU
HUNAN
JIANGXI

FUJIAN

GUANGXI
GUANGDONG

Taiwan *Strait*
TAIWAN

CHINA THROUGH THE MILLENNIA

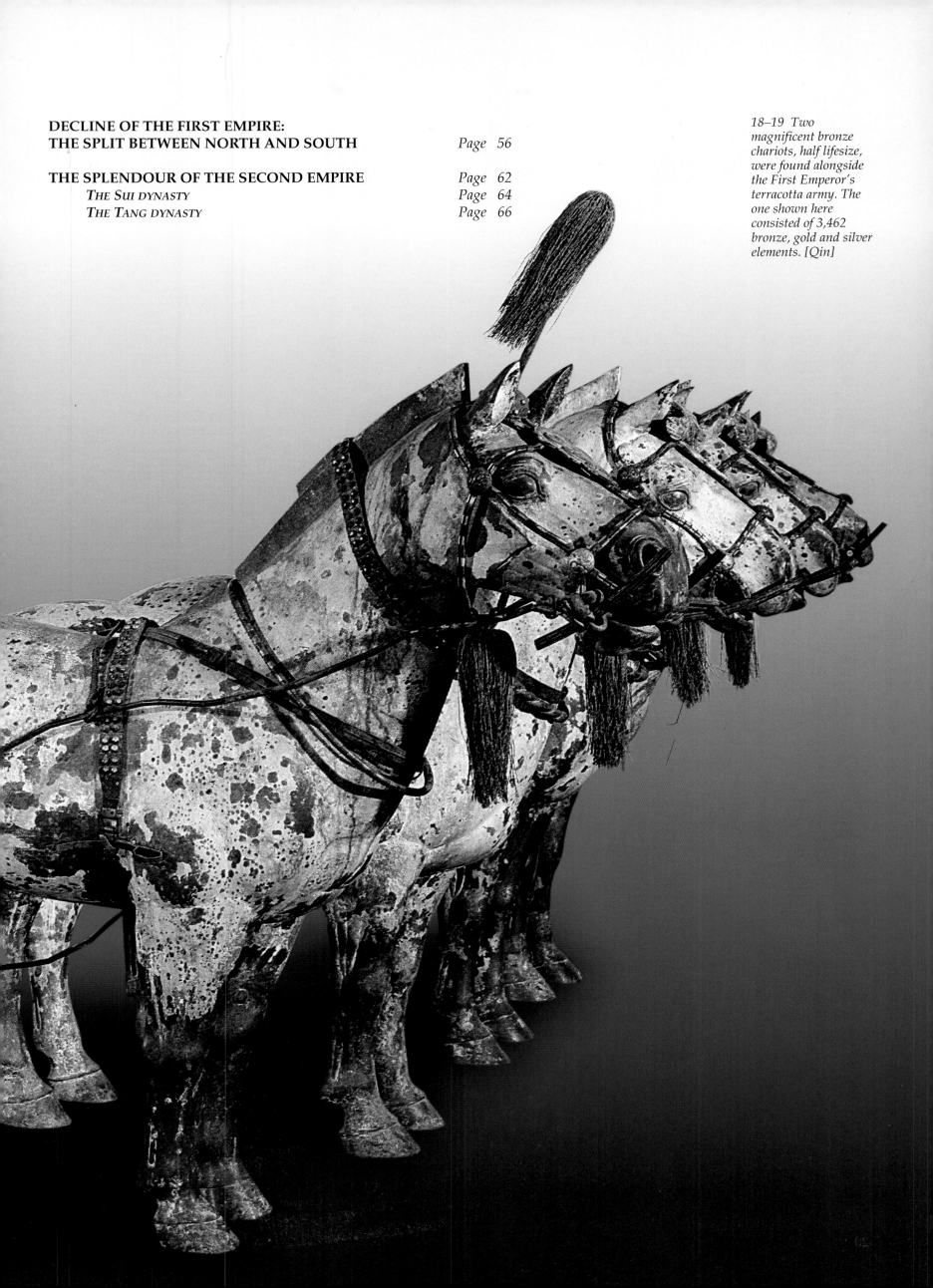

18–19 Two magnificent bronze chariots, half lifesize, were found alongside the First Emperor's terracotta army. The one shown here consisted of 3,462 bronze, gold and silver elements. [Qin]

THE NEOLITHIC

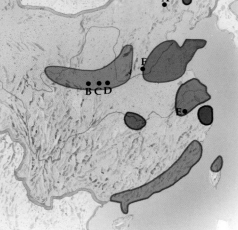

Main sites

A Niuheliang
B Banpo
C Miaodigou
D Yangshao
E Fanshan
F Dawenkou

Main cultures

▨ Xinle - Hongshan
▨ Yangshao
▨ Dawenkou
▨ Daxi
▨ Majiabang
▨ Hemudu - Liangzhu
▨ Dapenkeng

China is one of the areas of the globe that has been inhabited by humans from the earliest times, as demonstrated by the discovery of hundreds of Palaeolithic sites and fossil deposits. The large quantities of stone tools and bone fragments found have enabled scientists to trace the evolution of the earliest hominids, who were descended from *Australopithecus*.

Homo sapiens appeared during the last Ice Age, some 40,000 years ago, long after his remote ancestors, Yuanmou Man (*c.* 1.6–1.7 million years ago), Lantian Man (700,000–650,000 years ago) and Peking Man (500,000-400,000 years ago). Dramatic changes in conditions began in the 10th–9th millennium BC, when gradual improvements in climate caused the glaciers to recede; fertile river valleys formed and coastlines grew, creating an environment suitable for permanent habitation.

20 (above) The design carved on this jade, consisting of a face rising menacingly above the head of a monster with huge eyes and flaring nostrils, is typical of the Liangzhu culture. The function of this and similar objects and the significance of the images are still unknown. [Liangzhu]

20 (right) Blocks of jade pierced with a tubular hole are known as congs; *they were probably connected with religious beliefs of which nothing is now known. The anthropomorphic and zoomorphic designs carved on this* cong *are characteristic of the Liangzhu culture. [Liangzhu]*

21 (left) The jade discs found on the bodies of the dead, known as bis, are just as mysterious as the congs. These ritual objects, which seem to have been of great importance to the Neolithic populations of the east coast, are less frequently found in the early dynastic period, but came back into fashion later. [Liangzhu]

21 (below) During the Neolithic, jade was the most prestigious symbol of political and religious power, forming an intermediary between the human and divine spheres. The working of jade was known from the earliest periods, but was particularly advanced during the 3rd millennium BC.

Communities of hunter-gatherers and fishermen, which up to this time had been nomadic, began to settle in permanent villages. They started cultivating the land, raising domestic animals and produced pottery and stone tools in what is often known as the Neolithic Revolution. Numerous sites in China have produced evidence of these early cultures, which have been named by archaeologists after the place where the major discoveries were made, and are largely classified on the basis of the type of pottery produced. It is often difficult to reconstruct the relationships between various settlements and their chronological order, as regional differences and common elements coexist, indicating the existence of a trading network and continuity of development. Dates proposed for these numerous Neolithic cultures vary, and sometimes even conflict.

Chinese civilization gradually developed within this context of territorial interaction, and the formation of the empire in 221 BC can be viewed as the political consolidation of a long, complex process of integration, beginning with the first primitive communities, which led to a widespread cultural style.

The earliest Neolithic sites are found in the southern provinces of Fujian, Jiangxi, Guangdong, Guangxi and Guizhou (10th–9th millennium BC) and in the eastern regions of the north, along the Liao river (8500–7000 BC, Xinglongwa culture; and 7000–5000 BC, Xinle culture). There is also much evidence for the development of settlements in the central, northern and coastal regions from the 6th millennium BC. The most highly developed areas comprised the basins of the Yellow river (Huanghe) and its tributary the Wei and, further south, the Yangzijiang valley. Agriculture was largely based on millet-growing in the northern regions, which had a dry climate, and rice-growing in the wet, rainy southern areas.

The northern cultures that developed in the provinces of Henan, Hebei, Shaanxi and Shanxi are called Cishan-Peligang, after the two type sites (6500–4900 BC). According to some researchers, a number of even older settlements belong to these cultures. Their characteristic features were stone objects made with highly advanced techniques, a rather coarse reddish or brown pottery, and an economy based on dog and pig raising and the cultivation of

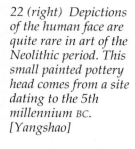

22 (right) Depictions of the human face are quite rare in art of the Neolithic period. This small painted pottery head comes from a site dating to the 5th millennium BC. [Yangshao]

22 (below) Reliefs and attachments in the form of human heads, such as this one which seems almost to be forcing its way out of the body of the vessel, may depict shamans, the political/spiritual leaders of Neolithic communities in China. [Majiayao]

the *Setaria italica* and *Panicum miliaceum* varieties of millet. Grave goods found in some burials suggest a form of religious belief. The Yangshao culture, which developed later in the same area (5000–3000 BC), is the best documented and best known, with over 1,000 sites scattered over a huge area that stretches east from Gansu and Qinghai provinces along the Yellow river valley.

Banpo (4800–3600 BC), a village in Shaanxi built on a huge circular site surrounded by a deep defensive ditch, is representative of the early phase of the Yangshao culture. The arrangement of the dwellings, which have sunken floors, and the animal enclosures suggests that there were no major distinctions in rank between the members of the community. The huts, like the tombs, were similar in shape and size, except for a large building that held a central place in communal life. Red pottery bowls, jugs and vases of various shapes were made without the fast-wheel and are decorated with geometrical patterns, human faces, fish and deer, and marked with signs resembling a primitive form of writing. Stone and pottery spindle whorls, together with impressions of textiles on the bases of pottery vessels, indicate the development of spinning and weaving. Patterns on pottery consisting of bands of wavy lines and open spirals prevailed at a later stage: Miaodigou (3900–3000 BC).

The Majiayao, Banshan and Machang cultures emerged between 3300 and 2050 BC from the Yangshao culture in the western provinces of Gansu and Qinghai, in an area that includes part of Inner Mongolia. The Qijia culture (2250–1900 BC) and the Huoshaogou culture in west Gansu (c. 1800–1600 BC), characterized by the production of objects and jewelry of copper, bronze, gold and silver, may have developed from the Majiayao culture.

The Dawenkou culture (5000–2500 BC) spread through Shandong and some parts of Jiangsu, Anhui, Henan and Liaoning. The pottery, now made on the wheel, is of various colours, depending on the clay mixture and the firing process used. The wealth of grave goods found in some tombs, which contained wooden coffins and dozens of stone, bone and jade objects and jewelry, demonstrates the existence of a highly stratified society.

The economies of the eastern cultures of Majiabang (5000–3500 BC) and

23 (top) Wavy lines and scroll designs are the dominant themes in the rich decorative repertoire of the Majiayao potters, who were masters in the art of creating vortex effects with bands of parallel or undulating lines. [Majiayao]

23 (left) Highly stylized fish and human faces decorate this pottery basin typical of the Yangshao culture of Banpo. These basins were used as lids for children's funerary urns. [Yangshao]

Hemudu (5000–3300 BC), in Jiangsu and north Zhejiang, were based on fishing, rearing dogs, pigs and water buffalo, and the cultivation of numerous aquatic plants, the most important being the *Oryza sativa* variety of rice. This may have been domesticated as early as the 7th millennium BC according to recent research – believed to be the oldest evidence of rice-growing in the world. Remains of houses built on stilts have been found at the site of Hemudu. Majiabang pottery was reddish-brown, while that made at Hemudu was black.

The Songze culture (4000–3000 BC) and the Qinglian'gang (4800–3600 BC), the direct descendants of the Majiabang and

24 (right) Although stylized, this vessel in the form of a small bird stretching its open beak upwards to be fed, demonstrates a close observation of nature. [Hongshan]

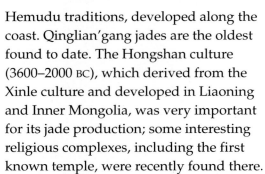

Hemudu traditions, developed along the coast. Qinglian'gang jades are the oldest found to date. The Hongshan culture (3600–2000 BC), which derived from the Xinle culture and developed in Liaoning and Inner Mongolia, was very important for its jade production; some interesting religious complexes, including the first known temple, were recently found there.

Jade production became highly developed during the Liangzhu culture (3300–2200 BC), which also flourished along the east coast, in Zhejiang and Jiangsu. The beauty and technical perfection of the objects made may reflect the existence of an élite which held political and religious power; their tombs were filled with immensely valuable objects, many of which were created in accordance with a precise funerary iconography whose meanings are unclear.

The first early territorial states developed along the east coast during this period. Large numbers of jade ritual objects, mainly found in tombs of the Liangzhu culture, represent the insignia of élite groups which held political, religious and administrative power. The jades were symbols of their authority and status.

Rice growing and the manufacture of stone objects and attractive red, black or dark brown pottery were the characteristic features of the Daxi culture (5000–3000 BC), which flourished along the Yangzijiang valley in an area between Sichuan, Hubei and Hunan. The Dapenkeng culture (5000–2500 BC) and the Shixia culture (2865–2480 BC) – mainly

important for the production of finely worked jade – developed further south.

The Longshan culture (3000–2000 BC), which in some areas (Shaanxi Longshan and Henan Longshan) derived from the Yangshao culture and elsewhere (Shandong Longshan) from the Dawenkou, spread along the Yellow river basin from the 3rd millennium BC. It was the progress made in manufacturing techniques by the Longshan culture that marked the evolution from the Neolithic to the Bronze Age.

Metallurgy developed and the potter's wheel facilitated the production of particularly attractive pottery with a uniformly brilliant black colour achieved by firing in kilns low in oxygen. The vessels, often undecorated, were made in a great variety of shapes. Some were too delicate for daily use, suggesting that they had a purely ritual function.

The complexity of the wealthiest burials and finds of animal bones used for divination demonstrate the existence of social hierarchies and a dominant class that held religious authority. The cultures that were to dominate the regions of central China during the Bronze Age derived from the Longshan culture in the 2nd millennium BC.

24 (opposite below) This Neolithic funerary urn is exceptional because of the striking images painted on it. Various interpretations of their meaning have been put forward, but the message conveyed by the stone axe and the crane holding a fish in its beak remains a mystery. [Yangshao].

25 (above) The fabric of this elegant black high-stemmed goblet is known as the 'eggshell' ware because of its extreme thinness – only a fraction of a millimetre at the rim. [Longshan]

25 (right) This three-legged pottery vase in the shape of a bird was discovered in a woman's tomb dating from the 4th millennium BC. It is an object of rare beauty, and nothing like it has been found at other sites dating from the same period; it may indicate the high social position of the deceased. [Miaodigou]

Current archaeological information relating to the development of metallurgy in China demonstrates that the Bronze Age coincides with the period in which written tradition places the Sandai – the Three Dynasties, Xia, Shang and Zhou – which ruled in turn over huge areas of Chinese territory from the 23rd to the 3rd century BC. Ancient Chinese historians idealized this remote period as a time of great wisdom and social order; they attributed inventions crucial to the development of human civilization and the creation of perfect government to mythical wise kings, who were unparalleled examples of virtue and moral rectitude. Legends recount the epic feats of heroes with supernatural powers: Fu Xi, who invented writing, music, marriage, hunting, fishing and animal-breeding techniques; Sui Ren, the inventor of fire; Shen Nong, who promoted medicine and farming techniques; Huangdi, the Yellow Emperor, who created the wheel, the calendar and the compass and invented navigation; Zhuan Xu, who separated Heaven from Earth; and Yao and Shun, lauded as outstanding models of devotion and morality, who are supposed to have reigned until 2208 BC. Yu the Great, Yao's Minister, who was skilled in flood control, is said to have founded the Xia dynasty on Shun's death in 2205 BC, after the traditional three-year mourning period.

As the legends suggest, the second part of the 3rd millennium BC was indeed a period of great innovation, and the change from the Neolithic to the Bronze Age involved fairly continuous development. The Longshan culture had become widespread, and a thriving trade was conducted between its settlements. Rule by a class of shaman-priests became

established within the context of an increasingly differentiated society. The political dominance of the magical-religious sphere influenced the use of resources, so that technological progress was directed towards producing exquisite ritual items rather than improving farming techniques.

Metallurgy and the first forms of organized government developed against this background. The state took shape when the distinct cultural entities fighting for control of the Central Plain won political and military victories. The Xia, a development of the Henan Longshan culture, gained control of the central part of the Yellow river basin. They ruled until the 16th century BC, when they were defeated by the Shang, the descendants of the Shandong Longshan culture.

The Shang, who originally settled to the east of the Central Plain, maintained their supremacy until the 11th century BC.

The Zhou, inheritors of the Shaanxi Longshan culture, settled in the westernmost lands and ruled, formally at least, until the foundation of the empire.

A far greater quantity and variety of objects cast from tin and copper alloy were produced in China in the Bronze Age than in comparable cultures in other parts of the world, although the representation of the human figure was not common (so far, only one sculpture of a man and some gold-plated bronze heads have been found buried at Sanxingdui in Sichuan, at a site dating from the 12th century BC). Some idea of the scale of the bronze production of the period comes from tombs: one Shang tomb of 1200 BC contained over 1,600 kg (3,527 lb) of bronze objects, and nearly 10 tonnes were found in a burial dating from the 5th century BC. Finally, a single *fang ding* ritual vessel from the Shang period weighs no less than 875 kg (1,230 lb).

THE XIA DYNASTY

Traditional Chinese histories have never doubted the existence of the Xia dynasty. Sima Qian (*c.* 145–86 BC) the greatest historian of ancient times, listed 17 kings who succeeded to the throne in turn after the death of the last of the pre-dynastic rulers, Shun, although he does not give the sources of his information. According to him, the dynasty, which began with Yu the Great in 2205 BC, ended in 1751 BC (according to a historical tradition using what is known as the 'Long Chronology', rather than 1994–1523 BC in the 'Short Chronology'). Although the Xia dynasty was once considered legendary by modern scholars, its existence may now have been confirmed by the discovery of one of its capitals, traditionally said to have been nine in number.

In 1959, the foundations of a palace covering a total area of over 10,000 sq. m (107,640 sq. ft) were found in the middle of a large residential area at Erlitou, near the city of Yanshi (Henan), on a site consisting of four layers dating from between 2010 and 1324 BC. The palace consisted of a large room with interconnected roofed passageways leading off it. A structure on such a scale may have been the palace of Zhenxun, last capital of the Xia dynasty, and suggests the existence of a highly advanced political and economic organization with developed social stratification. This is further confirmed by the contrast between different types of dwellings and variations in grave goods, which reveal the importance of religious beliefs. Human sacrifice was practised.

As the palaces and houses were built entirely of wood, excavations have only brought to light the stone foundations and the bases for the columns which supported the roofs. Wood has always been a very popular construction material in China. According to some, this choice of such a modest material is related to the way the concept of power was perceived by the ruling class: prestige was based on the strength and size of the clan rather than the erection of monumental constructions. In fact, the remains of the

28 (below) This three-legged jug (gui), made of grey terracotta using a sandy clay mixture, was designed to contain alcoholic drinks. It was found with another container, of the jiao *type, and a lacquered wooden goblet in a niche inside a tomb. [Xiajiadian]*

28 (above) This jue *container for wine is one of the earliest cast bronze vessels. The workmanship is still fairly clumsy – the surface looks uneven, and casting residues are visible at some points. [Erlitou]*

palaces and cities suggest that even the most magnificent buildings were not built with durable materials.

Numerous tools, including a rudimentary plough, pottery with incised marks denoting some advances in the evolution of writing, precious ritual jades, simple bronze objects such as awls, augers, fish-hooks, edged weapons and arrowheads, and musical instruments have been found in the third layer of the Erlitou site (c. 1700–1500 BC), identified by some archaeologists as Xia, as well as at other contemporary sites in Henan, Shaanxi, Shanxi, Hebei and Hubei. Cast bronze vessels used as containers for food offerings or alcohol made from fermented grain which was drunk during ceremonies, have also been discovered. These are the oldest bronze vessels yet found in China, and are indications that the Xia culture coincided with the beginning of the Bronze Age, although the level of workmanship suggests that the casting technique had already undergone a lengthy process of development. Small copper and bronze objects found at sites of the Majiayao, Qijia and Huoshaogou cultures in Gansu and sites of the Longshan culture in Shaanxi, Henan and Hebei demonstrate that craftsmen had been familiar with metals to some extent at least since the Neolithic period.

Nearly all the ritual bronzes dating from the Erlitou culture are undecorated. They were made by casting rather than hammering, as in other parts of the world, and their shapes imitate pottery vessels. The casting technique involved the use of clay piece-moulds; the lost-wax technique was only known in China from the 5th century BC. Successful casting depended on the construction of high-temperature kilns and the availability of large quantities of metal ore, requirements which were fulfilled as a result of both the experience inherited from the Neolithic potters and the wealth of ore deposits in Chinese territory (mines have been found which were in use 3,000 years ago).

A Erlitou
■ Area of Xia influence
■ Xia territory

29 The precise ritual significance of the image that appears on this bronze plaque inlaid with turquoise is unknown. It appears to be a monstrous animal seen from above, with piercing eyes that stare coldly at the observer. [Erlitou]

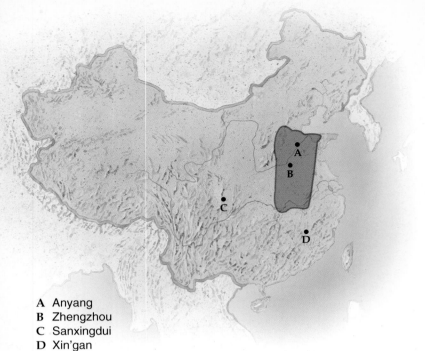

A Anyang
B Zhengzhou
C Sanxingdui
D Xin'gan

According to tradition the Xia dynasty, which had ruled by divine authority, lost the favour of Heaven because of the irreverence and incompetence of the last sovereign, Jie, who was dominated by a cruel, dissolute concubine. The unworthy behaviour of someone who held such a sacred office provoked the wrath of Heaven, with serious repercussions. Jie was the cause of such terrible disasters and such violent social disorders that he was deposed in favour of Tang, a man of great virtue who was considered worthy of receiving the divine mandate; thus began the Shang dynasty.

Shang was originally the name of the ancestral capital of the people who defeated the Xia. Later, it came to indicate the shaman-kings who ruled a kind of confederation of tribal groups, each with different traditions and customs, for over seven centuries. The historical existence of the Shang dynasty was confirmed by excavations from 1928 onwards in

30 (below left) Two crested birds surmount this elegant jia vessel, with slender tripod legs, combining to form a harmonious design. [11th century BC]

30 (below) This huge fang ding was cast in one piece: an eight-part mould was used to make the outer section; the handles were directly cast in a double mould, while the legs required one inner and two outer moulds. [Erligang]

31 (below) Containers for liquids in the shape of animals, called *gongs, were popular* from the 13th to 9th centuries BC. The example shown here, one of the finest and most richly decorated, represents a cross between a feline and a bird. [Shang]

31 (bottom) Wine played an important part in the numerous ceremonies at the Shang court. It was consumed in large quantities from flat-bottomed bronze goblets (gu) with tall stems, which tapered towards the top and ended in a trumpet-shaped spout. [Shang]

Anyang (Henan), which brought to light remains of the last capital, Yin, inhabited from *c.* 1300 BC. The ruins cover a total area of 24 sq. km (9 sq. miles), including both the city (Xiaotun) and the cemetery (Xibeigang), on opposite banks of the Huan river.

The enormous disparity between the splendour and complexity of the political and administrative organization of the Shang civilization as manifested at Anyang, and the modest remains of Neolithic cultures previously discovered, led researchers to search for evidence of the early Bronze Age in China in order to refute theories of a massive migration of populations or the assimilation of knowledge from the Middle East.

It was not until the 1950s, when remains of various settlements of the Xia culture (Erlitou) and the early part of the Shang dynasty were found, that archaeologists were able to demonstrate the continuity of indigenous development and the reliability of the traditional accounts. Foundations of a massive city wall, 20 m (66 ft) deep and 7 km (4 miles) long, made of rammed earth, were found in Erligang near the city of Zhengzhou (Henan). Palatial buildings stood inside the walls, and houses, warehouses, craftsmen's workshops, foundries and burial complexes were found outside. The concentration of wealth in the city, which must have had a majestic appearance, is far more evident than at Erlitou. Some archaeologists believe that this may have been Ao or Xiao, the second dynastic capital. Later, numerous settlements discovered in Shanxi, Shaanxi, Shandong, Hebei, Anhui and Hubei were linked with the Erligang settlement, especially the 4th layer of the Erlitou site.

Another archaeological event that revolutionized knowledge of the Shang dynasty was the discovery of a huge quantity of written documents (nearly 200,000) recording in minute detail the divinatory practices and activities of shamans in religious ceremonies at court. When this material, dating from the reign of the last nine rulers, was deciphered, the nature of the Shang-Yin civilization became much clearer. The records take the form of inscriptions on oracle bones (*jiaguwen*), huge numbers of which were found in the archives at Anyang. These animal bones, mainly the shoulder blades of cattle but also sheep bones and tortoise shells, were exposed to heat after appropriate rituals. The cracks produced were interpreted by the shamans as answers from the ancestors who were invoked during the divinatory rite.

This practice was already known in the Neolithic but it was only in the second part of the Shang dynasty that the number and order of each crack, the questions posed, and often the answers, were recorded by incising them on the bones. These are the first known Chinese

texts of any size and are an invaluable source of information. Divination using oracle bones and tortoise shells was a common practice in Shang China; and predictions based on divination by fire were also respected. Such activities were considered an essential first step in the court and state decision-making process.

The Shang dynasty can be divided into two chronological phases: the first is known as the Erligang or Zhengzhou phase (*c*. 1500–1300 BC), and the second is the Anyang phase (*c*. 1300–1050 BC). Sophisticated bronze manufacturing techniques flourished in the Erligang phase; bronze vessels were used by the aristocracy in religious ceremonies and placed in tombs as grave goods, alongside valuable jades. Although there is some evidence that the forging process was not unknown, the vessels were invariably made by casting in clay moulds (over a thousand have been discovered at a single foundry). During the Anyang phase, ritual vessels featured more realistic portrayals of animals and more expressive, stylized masks. Short inscriptions, mainly indicating the owner or recipient of the vessel, also appeared and, in the later phase, the event that was being celebrated.

Thirty Shang kings are believed to have reigned, acceding to the throne in accordance with a complex system of succession based on kinship within the dominant clan. The royal line was constituted by a class of shaman-priests; the ruler (who held political, military and religious power) and his clan derived their power from their acknowledged ability to communicate with the ancestors and deities who lived in the spirit world. The direct relationship with the ancestors, whose influence on earthly life was considered vital, gave the ruler and his

32 (opposite) This rare inlaid ivory goblet belonged to queen Fu Hao and features decorative motifs typical of ritual bronzes of the Shang period: delicate inlaid turquoise taotie masks and thick spirals incised on the body and the handle, shaped like a bird of prey. [Shang]

33 (left) Two distinctive features of this jade statuette of a kneeling woman are her complex hairstyle and the large knot at the belt. It was part of the sumptuous grave goods of queen Fu Hao. [Shang]

33 (below) Communication with the deities and the ancestors was achieved by means of complex divinatory practices, often using animal bones. The eight inscriptions on this tortoise shell relate to hunting expeditions. [Shang]

lineage a divine character, legitimizing their dominant position in society.

Ancestor worship was at the core of religious beliefs. Religion and politics were closely linked, with rites and ceremonies playing a vital political role. Worship of the ancestors of the royal family, governed by a complex ceremonial including divination, could only be celebrated by their direct male descendants.

The rich decoration on the ritual bronze vessels included a variety of animals, some depicted more realistically than others, which were closely linked with the rituals. Large quantities of wine were consumed during such ceremonies to help produce the state of trance required to make contact with the beings of the other world.

The Shang rulers engaged in frequent military and diplomatic expeditions to maintain and consolidate their supremacy over, or alliances with, other states, and maintained powerful armies equipped with war chariots. The core of the state was the territory directly administered by the royal family. Other regions were administered by governors linked to the central authority by kinship or subjection. On the edges of the Shang territory were other populations, considered barbarians, from which slaves and sacrificial victims were often taken (an astonishing number of human victims has been found in royal tombs).

Archaeology has demonstrated the existence of some advanced cultures not mentioned in oracular inscriptions and unknown to traditional historians. Objects found in two sacrificial pits at Sanxingdui near Guanghan (Sichuan), of the 12th century BC, demonstrate highly developed religious beliefs and customs, independent of what became the dominant centre of Chinese civilization.

In the traditional histories, the Shang dynasty fell for the same reasons as its predecessor. The last ruler, Di-xin (or Zhou Xin), a debauched and corrupt ruler, is said to have committed such terrible crimes that he incurred the wrath of Heaven, which decreed that he should be deposed. Thus the Mandate of Heaven (*Tian ming*) was once again invoked to legitimize the overthrow of a dynasty. According to this concept, Heaven (*Tian*), the supreme deity, transfers the divine mandate to one who possesses particular moral strength and charisma (*de*), and proves himself capable of restoring law and order. The reprehensible conduct of kings was constantly invoked by historians to justify the decline of a dynasty. In reality, towards the end of

Shang rule, the tensions between central power and peripheral interests that influenced much of Chinese history was becoming increasingly evident.

The Shang aristocracy began to distance itself from Di-xin, weakening his power. Wu (1049/45–1043 BC), king of the Zhou, took advantage of this situation, not only to shake off the authority of the Shang once and for all, but also to gain supremacy over the territories controlled by them. The kingdom of Zhou was to the west, along the Wei river basin. Its capital Feng, near the present-day city of Xi'an, had been transformed by the last predynastic ruler Wen (1099/56–1050 BC), Wu's father, into a powerful, organized state, able to rival Shang. Relations between the Shang and Zhou dynasties

had been strained for some time, and Wen was imprisoned at Youli, near the capital Yin, in an attempt to neutralize the serious threat posed by his military power, which was now sufficient to overthrow the Shang dynasty. Wen's son achieved this after his father's death. Wu took over the leadership of an impressive army that included not only Zhou troops but also soldiers of other ethnic groups such as the Shu and the Qiang, which had always been enemies of the Shang. He was also supported by large sectors of the Shang aristocracy.

Around 1050 BC (opinions differ as to the exact year, but 1045 seems the most likely date), an epic battle was fought at Muye, near Yin. The Zhou won a decisive victory. Di-xin was killed but Yin was not

34 This magnificent bronze pan *was used as a finger bowl in sacrificial ceremonies and the accompanying banquets. The fish, dragon and bird incised inside it symbolize the animal world and the spirit world, placed in communication by the rituals enacted. [11th century BC]*

A Hao
B Feng
C Luoyang

destroyed, and Wugeng, the son of Di-xin, was allowed to rule under the supervision of three of Wu's brothers. A new capital was built at Hao, near the previous one, which maintained the role of religious capital and site of the royal temples.

Thus began the Zhou dynasty, which was to rule until the foundation of the empire. Historians divide this era into two main periods: the Western Zhou, until 771 BC, and the Eastern Zhou, from 770 to 221 BC.

Wu was succeeded by his son Cheng (1042/35–1006 BC). In view of Cheng's young age Wu's brother, the Duke of Zhou (1042–1036 BC), was appointed his regent. Wugeng felt that the time had come for revenge and rebelled, perhaps with the support of part of the Zhou aristocracy. The Duke of Zhou intervened, defeated the rebels and divided the new territories into principalities, which he assigned to his brothers. A second capital was built at Luoyi, near present-day Luoyang (Henan), to control the eastern regions. When Cheng reached his majority, the Duke of Zhou stood down. Later historians, influenced by Confucian philosophy, held up kings Wen and Wu and the Duke of Zhou as models of virtue and wisdom.

The historical events and deeds of the early Zhou kings are told in a number of works, though the only surviving versions were compiled or rewritten several centuries later. Parts of the *Shujing*

(Book of Documents), a collection of historical texts, and the *Shijing* (Book of Songs), a collection of poetry, appear to date back to the Western Zhou period.

Inscriptions on bronze vessels, some of which are hundreds of characters long, form invaluable historical documents. They represent a direct source of information, not mediated by tradition, and provide the best method of checking the reliability of historical and literary accounts.

35 (above) The pattern of entwined dragons or snakes, usually confined to the decoration of textiles or to minor parts of bronze vessels (such as handles), is the dominant theme of this hu *dating from the 9th century* BC. *[Western Zhou]*

35 (above) Of the thousands of bronze vessels dating from the Shang and Western Zhou period only about 40 are in the shape known as jiao. These ritual vessels for wine drinking were not found among grave goods in later periods. *[Western Zhou]*

36 (right) The distinctive shape of the hands of this small bronze image dating from 900 BC, found at Baoji, is similar to that of the large statue found in one of the sacrificial pits at Sanxingdui, dating from 12th century BC; its significance is a mystery. [Western Zhou]

Although no great progress was made in agricultural techniques during the Shang period, under the Zhou dynasty the practice of crop rotation was introduced, so that exhausted land no longer had to be abandoned, and the cultivation of soya began. Craftsmen held a relatively high position in society, due to the great religious prestige of jade and bronze objects and vessels.

The Western Zhou period is divided into three phases. The first (*c.* 1050–957 BC) comprised the kingdoms of Wu, Cheng, Kang and Zhao; the middle phase (*c.* 956–866 BC) saw the rule of the Mu, Gong, Yi and Xiao; and the third (*c.* 865–771 BC) was the period of the rule of kings Yi and Li and, after the regency of Gong He, Xuan and You. The dynasty's decline began under king Xuan (827/25–782 BC), and was accentuated when the next king, You (781–771 BC), came to the throne. In 771 BC the Quanrong, a barbarian population not subject to Zhou rule, struck up an alliance with part of the Zhou aristocracy, killed You and expelled the Zhou from their western capital, Hao.

36 (below) Both the shape and decoration of this glazed earthenware jar are based on bronze vessels from the Eastern Zhou period; at this time, the ornamentation was purely for aesthetic reasons, having lost its religious significance. [Eastern Zhou, Warring States]

The Zhou kings took the title of Son of Heaven (*Tian zi*), and this name was used by all subsequent rulers. They were no longer attributed with the divine nature of the Shang kings and their families, by virtue of their relationship with the ancestors and other deities; instead they were the representatives of Heaven on earth, and ruled only as the executors of its will. This change of perspective had important repercussions on all aspects of society. Ceremonies and rituals underwent radical transformation, and the huge amount of material and human resources used to aid communication with the other world was drastically reduced. Divination also slowly lost its central place in worship.

The structure of the state, now more complex than in the past, was still based on kinship. The distribution of power was governed by a set of rules inspired by religious values, and was based on the hierarchical relationships within the clan, governed by a system called *zongfa*. The position held by each member depended on whether he belonged at birth to a main or secondary branch of the clan. Rituals and traditions served the function of confirming and sanctifying these distinctions, which were thus evident on all occasions.

THE EASTERN ZHOU DYNASTY

A Zhou

37 (left) This magnificent goblet with ear-shaped handles has survived for 23 centuries thanks to the special process of lacquering that made it waterproof, resistant to acids and able to withstand heat. The lacquer was applied to the wooden base, left to dry, polished and covered with a new layer; this procedure could be repeated up to 30 times. [Eastern Zhou, Warring States]

37 (below) The gold inscriptions inlaid on these bronze permits in the form of bamboo canes indicate that they were issued by the King of Chu to the lord of the small but strategically important kingdom of E in 323 BC, to authorize the transit of goods along the rivers. [Eastern Zhou, Warring States]

Warring States

The Eastern Zhou dynasty (770–221 BC), divided by historians into two phases, began with the transfer of the capital to a site near modern Luoyang. The first phase is known as the Springs and Autumns period (770–475 BC) after a work dating from the 5th century BC, the *Chunqiu* (Springs and Autumns [of the Principality of Lu]), the official annals of events that took place between 722 and 481 BC in the small kingdom of Lu, the birthplace of Confucius. The second phase, known as the Warring States period (475–221 BC), is named after a historical work compiled in the 1st century BC, the *Zhanguo Ce* (Intrigues of the Warring States). It consists of a collection of texts dating from the 3rd–2nd centuries BC recounting the history of various principalities in the 4th and 3rd centuries BC.

The political and institutional order that had characterized earlier periods gradually disintegrated. The Zhou royal family, which no longer had sufficient military strength to hold and defend the territories under its rule, had lost every vestige of political authority. It merely retained the role (albeit an important one) of supreme religious authority, as it stood at the head of the *Tian Xia* ('that which is under the heavens'), i.e. the civilized world. A multitude of kingdoms and principalities, large and small, governed by descendants of the heads of lineages which had received their investiture from the Zhou kings in exchange for tributes and military aid, fought to assert their independence or supremacy. When the local lords gained power, they unlawfully took the title of *wang* (king), which until then had been reserved for the Zhou rulers, who looked on powerless, merely legitimizing annexations and usurpations carried out without their consent.

In the 7th century BC the outlying kingdoms gained increasing influence on the political scene, and soon became a serious threat to the regions of the Central Plain. First the kingdom of Qi, then Jin, to the north, and the kingdom of Chu to the south, fought long and bloody battles for supremacy, which continued until the 5th century BC before any of the combatants gained the upper hand. In 453 BC Jin was

split into three parts, which became the kingdoms of Zhao, Wei and Han.

During the Warring States period, seven kingdoms (Zhao, Wei, Han, Qin, Qi, Yan and Chu) fought for supremacy. The process of integration entered a troubled, obscure phase, which was to have a decisive influence on later balances of power. Continual battles, changing alliances, frenetic diplomatic activity, betrayals, surprise attacks and brutal murders were the ingredients of a rapidly evolving political situation from which the kingdom of Qin emerged triumphant, aided by its favourable strategic position to the west of the Yellow river in Shaanxi, protected by strong natural defences.

Major institutional and administrative reforms inspired by the theories of Shang Yang, a leading exponent of the Legalist (*fajia*) school who lived in the 4th century BC, had been carried out in Qin. As a result of the rigid application of these reforms, a strict domestic policy designed solely to strengthen the state, and a ruthless foreign policy intended to unify *Tian Xia*, the entire civilized world, Qin had become an unrivalled military power. The ascent to the throne in 246 BC of Zheng, a man of great talent and exceptional organizational skills, proved to be the turning point. Under his leadership, the Qin armies defeated all their adversaries one after another between 230 and 221 BC. Thus the first great empire in Chinese history was born.

Individual kingdoms, under constant pressure from external threats, had introduced a system of power which guaranteed the maximum political and military strength. In a period of rapid change, the kinship system no longer reflected the social hierarchies; military valour and wealth instead led to the emergence of a new ruling class, while the impoverished and lower branches of noble families had formed a class of intellectuals. Ministers, reformers, thinkers and philosophers tried to reformulate a concept of society that explained the ideological and cultural crisis which had accompanied these

38 (left) This bronze bird with the antlers of a stag stands 143.5 cm (56½ in) tall and was found next to the coffin of Marquis Yi of Zeng. Its position suggests that it had an important ritual function, which is not known for certain, but it may have been a stand for a musical instrument. [Eastern Zhou, Warring States]

39 (opposite above) This container (dou), consists of a long-stemmed bowl and a lid in the shape of an upturned cup; it is decorated with a cloud motif, embellished by exquisite gold filigree. [Eastern Zhou, Warring States]

39 (opposite below) A handle in the form of a fantastic animal – a hybrid feline – and legs in the form of creatures with a menacing appearance resembling griffins or birds of prey decorate this bronze and copper container for alcoholic drinks. [Eastern Zhou, Warring States]

needs of war, unprecedented technological developments took place. Between the 6th and 5th centuries BC the casting of iron (which the West was not to discover for another thousand years) and steel provided armies with more effective weapons, such as the crossbow, and furnished farmers with new tools for tilling the soil. Wood, stone and the few bronze tools, were gradually replaced by mass-produced iron and cast-iron equipment. This allowed huge areas of land to be ploughed, and led to a considerable increase in productivity.

Bronze, once reserved almost exclusively for ceremonial functions, was used increasingly for everyday objects. Manufacturing techniques underwent major changes and new processes were introduced. Trade intensified, boosting the economy and leading to the accumulation of great wealth. Huge irrigation projects were implemented, canals hundreds of kilometres long were dug, great dams were built to change the course of rivers, and massive defensive walls were constructed.

profound upheavals. In a situation of such material, spiritual and ideological confusion, a value system that could form the foundation of a new order and be useful for social control and practical government became a necessity.

Various models were proposed. Ideas circulated among the intellectuals of the day, and stimulated a variety of opinions. It was against this background that the main currents of thought in ancient China, known as the Hundred Schools, developed. Confucianism, Daoism and Legalism, among others, emerged in this period. This was the age of Confucius, Mencius (Mengzi), Xunzi, Laozi, Zhuangzi, Shang Yang, Han Feizi, Mozi, Gongsun Longzi, Zou Yuan and many other great masters.

Despite the resources expended on continual wars, or perhaps precisely because of the boost provided by the

THE FIRST EMPIRE

By 221 BC, the long and difficult process of integrating the various populations who lived in the vast Chinese territory had been completed, allowing the foundation of an empire which, despite various vicissitudes, was to persist for over 21 centuries, until 1911. The period between 221 BC and AD 220, during which power was held first by the Qin dynasty (221–206 BC) and then by the Han (206 BC to AD 220), was crucial to the formation of the administrative, economic and social structure of the empire.

An unprecedented population explosion and an economic boom were created by the political unification achieved by Qin Shihuangdi (221–210 BC) and consolidated by Wudi (141–87 BC), supported by the impressive civil engineering projects they commissioned.

40 (opposite) Archers played an important part in the First Emperor's army. In pit 1 next to the emperor's tomb, where the majority of the army of over 6,000 statues is buried, they occupy the foremost position, deployed in seven columns of three rows of men. Arrowheads, a bronze sword and the remains of a bow were found next to this kneeling archer. [Qin]

41 (left) This lacquered dish with gilt-bronze inlays bears an inscription on the base which describes the article and specifies the date (AD 4), place of manufacture, and the craftsmen who contributed to its production. [Western Han]

41 (below) For the Chinese, a pair of geese, here in the form of painted terracotta vessels, symbolized marital harmony, as the goose was the emblem of sincerity and reliability. [Han]

42 The lively form and powerful appearance of this bronze horse, in typical Han style, not only reflect a stylistic choice but also reveal the vigour of the real-life models.

To strengthen the imperial cavalry, the emperor Wudi had 'heavenly horses', which were more majestic than Chinese breeds, imported from Central Asia. [Eastern Han]

43 (below) Our knowledge of ancient Chinese textiles and costume comes mainly from the statuettes made of painted wood or other materials found in large numbers in tombs dating from the Han and subsequent periods. [Western Han]

43 (right) Han potters were experts in using lead glazes based metal oxides to produce a range of colours, from brown to amber-brown (iron) and green (copper). Surprising and beautiful results could be achieved, as demonstrated by this elegant lidded hu *vase. [Han]*

High levels of technical skill were achieved in metalwork, carpentry, spinning, weaving and many other areas of production. Flourishing crafts and trade created enormous wealth.

Intellectual activities prospered not only in the fields of literature, history and philosophy but also mathematics, medicine and astronomy. This was the period of great poets such as Sima Xiangru (*c.* 179–117 BC) and Cao Cao (AD 155–220), philosophers such as Dong Zhongshu (*c.* 179–104 BC) and Wang Chong (*c.* AD 27–100), historians like Sima Qian (*c.* 145–90 BC) and Ban Gu (AD 32–92), and authors such as Liu Xin (50 BC–AD 23) and Ma Rong (AD 78–166).

It was also an age of great scientists, such as Zhang Heng (AD 78–139), the inventor of the armillary sphere and the seismograph. The unknown artists of the day, who still held the lowly status of craftsmen, produced works of great beauty, such as finely decorated lacquerware, elegant fabrics, delicate paintings on silk, wall frescoes, glazed pottery and celadons, stone sculptures and wood carvings, reliefs, jewelry and ornaments of precious jade and metal.

The invention of paper, made from silk, linen or hemp, dates to this period. It was widely manufactured from the 1st century AD (the oldest surviving fragment of hemp paper used for writing dates from AD 49), long before it was known to the Arabs (8th century) and Europeans (10th century), who only began to manufacture paper in the 12th century. The technique spread to Korea and Vietnam, and was introduced into Japan in 610 by the Korean monk Damjing (579–631). The oldest surviving paper book is the *Piyujing*, a Buddhist work dating from AD 256, now in Tokyo.

A Xianyang

All the enemies of the Qin were subjugated in just a few years: the kingdom of Han was defeated in 230 BC and Wei in 225; Chu capitulated in 223, Zhao and Yan in 222, and Qi in 221. Never before had such a huge territory been ruled by a single king. The empire now included the Gansu and Qinghai plateaus; to the south, Guangdong and Guangxi and beyond; to the east it reached the sea, and to the north it stretched beyond the Yellow river and the Liaodong peninsula. King Zheng of Qin, aware that he had inaugurated a new epoch, took the title of *Huangdi*. Until then, the names *Huang* and *Di* had been reserved for legendary rulers who had founded civilization; to the Shang, *Di* was the supreme deity. Openly challenging tradition, Zheng proclaimed himself First (*Shi*) August (*Huang*) Emperor (*Di*), the founder of a new dynasty that was to last for 'ten thousand generations'.

Realizing how difficult it would be to achieve the full integration of populations that had fought one another for centuries, Qin Shihuangdi and his prime minister Li Si introduced a series of measures designed to consolidate central power. The Legalist doctrine that had formed the basis of the policies of the Qin kingdom for 130 years, bringing it political and military success, was adopted as the ideology of the empire. According to advocates of the rule of law, only the interests of the state were of importance. They devised and implemented a system of strongly organized, centralized government based on two fundamental principles: the law (*fa*), the essential tool of social control, and tactics (*shu*), which provided a way of exploiting the natural tendencies of man, considered to be intrinsically negative unless used in the service of the state.

The theory held that an efficient legislative system must be impartial, simple, comprehensible and public, so that no one could be unaware of it or

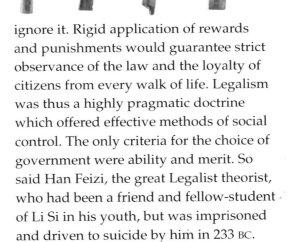

ignore it. Rigid application of rewards and punishments would guarantee strict observance of the law and the loyalty of citizens from every walk of life. Legalism was thus a highly pragmatic doctrine which offered effective methods of social control. The only criteria for the choice of government were ability and merit. So said Han Feizi, the great Legalist theorist, who had been a friend and fellow-student of Li Si in his youth, but was imprisoned and driven to suicide by him in 233 BC.

In order to put these principles into practice, the ancient aristocratic families were deprived of power and forced to move to the capital, Xianyang, near the present-day Xi'an (Shaanxi). The empire was divided into 36 commanderies (*jun*), each of which comprised a variable number of counties (*xian*). In each area the population was organized in districts (*xiang*) formed by groups of 1,000 families (*ting*), which were divided into villages of 100 families (*li*). These divisions were

44 (opposite) The hairstyles of the soldiers in the terracotta army are quite elaborate, though always neat, and consist of number of plaits gathered together at the nape of the neck and tied tightly. [Qin]

45 An increasing number of finds provide evidence of the perishable materials used for writing before the invention of paper in the 1st century AD. Bamboo or wooden strips and rolls of silk were in use until the 5th century AD. The texts were written vertically with a brush on the prepared bamboo strips (each strip forming one column), which were then tied together, to read from left to right. Among the most important finds is a small collection of philosophical books found in a tomb of 350 BC in Guodian, in Hubei. [Eastern Han]

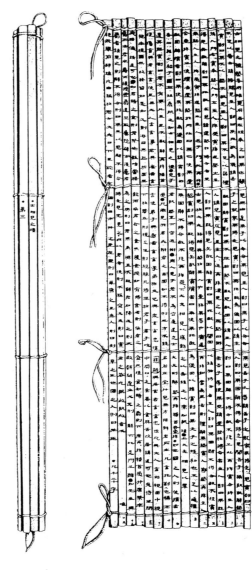

46 *This terracotta footman, associated with the tomb of Qin Shihuangdi, kneels in a position of submission, showing deference in accordance with the protocol customary in ancient China, which survived in Japan. His clothes were originally painted in various colours.* [Qin]

ruled by officials nominated by the emperor and appointed locally. The Legalist principle of collective responsibility was introduced, and applied to groups of 5 or 10 families.

The central government was organized around a triumvirate: the Imperial Chancellor or Prime Minister (*chengxiang*) headed central administration; the Grand Marshal (*taiwei*) was supreme commander of the military; and the Imperial Counsellor (*yushu dafu*) had supervisory functions. The governorates were responsible to the administrative bureaus (*cao*), which reported directly to the prime minister. A body called the Council of the Nine Ministers (*jiuqing*) dealt with the running of the imperial household.

Orders were issued relating to standardization of the writing and monetary systems, weights and measures and the wheel gauge of carts; these orders, most of which had been successfully applied in Qin, were designed to promote the political and economic unity of the empire. Codes were promulgated, some of which we know due to the discovery in 1975 in a tomb at Shuihudi (Hubei) dating from 217 BC of sections written on bamboo strips forming a kind of book. According to tradition, the first code dates to 536 BC when Zichan, prime minister of the kingdom of Zeng, had the criminal laws engraved on bronze tripods.

The kingdom of Qin had introduced a code of law in 513 BC. In the 4th century BC, at the time of Shang Yang, the kingdom had six basic laws. The Shuihudi documents contain a remarkably large number of regulations and represent the first code known to historians. The statutes mainly deal with questions of administrative and criminal law, a characteristic which was to remain practically unchanged during the next legislature. The rules governed not only central and local government, but also many aspects of people's private lives.

As traditions were a serious obstacle to the implementation of his new plans, Qin Shihuangdi issued a decree in 213 BC ordering that historical, literary and philosophical works of the past be burnt, with the exception of the scientific treatises and annals of Qin. A single copy of the destroyed books was retained in the imperial library for the sole use of the authorities. Severe punishments, including death, were imposed on anyone who made criticisms based on traditional doctrines and customs, or who opposed the decree. In 212 BC, 460 Confucian literati are said to have been buried alive for failing to observe the decree, though there are serious doubts as to whether this really happened. For over 2,000 years, Chinese historians reviled the First Emperor for his scorn of culture, exaggerating his acts of arrogance and ferocity.

In reality, public works of great utility were constructed, which were destined to last for centuries. An impressive road network was built to allow rapid travel between distant regions of the empire. Its total length, some 6,800 km (4,225 miles), exceeds that of the road network built by the Roman empire.

Work began on the Ling canal to connect the Xiang river with the Li river, so that the Yangzijiang basin was linked with the Zhujiang (Pearl river) basin, facilitating cargo transport and irrigation of huge agricultural areas. The Great Wall, an immense defensive construction winding for over 5,000 km (3,100 miles) was completed, by connecting, strengthening and extending existing defences erected on the borders of the northern kingdoms of Qin, Zhao and Yan, which were constantly threatened by Xiongnu raids.

Millions of peasants were employed on construction work and also in the many military campaigns conducted to suppress frequent revolts caused by the government's centralizing policy, which was especially hated in the south, and to deal with threats from outside the empire – from the south, across the natural borders of China, and from the north, where nomadic and semi-nomadic populations lived beyond the Great Wall.

The First August Emperor died in 210 BC during an expedition to Shaqiu (Hebei). He was buried at Lintong (Shaanxi) in a mausoleum defended by a terracotta army; some 7,000 warriors, over 600 almost life-sized horses, 100 wooden and 2 bronze war chariots and large numbers of weapons were buried with him.

The dynasty that was to have lasted for 'ten thousand generations' did not survive the loss of its founder. The court and government were riven by power struggles, led by prime minister Li Si and the influential eunuch Zhao Gao. They tricked the Crown Prince into suicide, and crowned Shihuangdi's second son, Hu Hai, Second August Emperor (Er Shi Huangdi).

In 206 BC, having eliminated Li Si, Zhao Gao also had the Second Emperor killed, and gave the crown to Zi Ying, Shihuangdi's grandson, who did not dare to take the title of Third August Emperor. The new ruler, realizing the threat posed by Zhao Gao, had him executed, but it was too late to save the dynasty. While the government was weakened by court intrigue, the population, by now impoverished beyond endurance, was on the point of revolt.

Continual military expeditions and the construction of the public and private works ordered by the First Emperor had diverted millions of peasants from farm work. The imposition of the laws of Qin to newly conquered areas had been too strict and not gradual enough, and had not taken account of local customs. Rioting had broken out in 209 BC and spread all over the empire. In 206 BC, after fierce fighting between the rioters and the imperial army, Liu Bang, a man of humble birth, and Xiang Yu, an aristocrat from the ancient kingdom of Chu, rode into Xianyang with their armies, bringing the Qin dynasty to an end.

The Han dynasty was founded in 206 BC, although Liu Bang only took the title of emperor in 202 BC, when he defeated Xiang Yu, once his most powerful ally. For the first time in Chinese history, a man of humble birth sat on the throne destined for the Son of Heaven. He was to be remembered by the posthumous name of Gaodi, High Emperor, or Gaozu, High Progenitor (206–195 BC).

The new emperor established his capital at Chang'an, near Xi'an, and in an attempt to stabilize his authority he allocated land and titles to those who had supported him in the campaign against Xiang Yu. The new rulers took the title of *wang* (king), as their predecessors had done during the Eastern Zhou period. Apart from the prime minister, who continued to be appointed by the emperor, the officials of the various kingdoms were appointed locally, and the seven kings maintained the right to keep private armies.

As the institutions of the Qin period were retained at a central level, the creation of kingdoms inside the empire led to a dual system of government. Its fragility soon became apparent, and was a source of perennial conflict. The central authority aimed to regain control over the whole empire, whereas the local rulers pursued a destabilizing policy designed to achieve independence. Gaodi put an end to this situation by replacing the kings with princes of imperial blood.

Twelve emperors and a dowager empress succeeded to the throne from 206 BC to AD 9. The most outstanding was Wudi, the ruler who contributed more than any other to strengthening the dynasty. In his 54-year reign (141–87 BC) he introduced a policy of conquest and decentralization. Under Wudi the empire flourished and almost doubled in size. To the north it included South Manchuria and Korea, and to the south various independent kingdoms were conquered.

Governorates were established in the west, in strategic regions for the control of the major trade routes to Central Asia. Chinese armies ventured as far as Xinjiang, the oases of the Tarim Basin,

48 (below) This elegant jade handle depicting the head of a fantastic creature holding a bi disc in its mouth was found in the tomb of Zhao Mo (137–122 BC), the second ruler of the southern kingdom of Nanyue. It was probably part of a box or chest containing the king's exquisite grave goods. [Western Han]

48 (bottom) The precious jades found in the tomb of Zhao Mo include this fine ornament which some scholars interpret as a buckle used to hang a sword from. [Western Han]

48 (top right) The sinuous lines of this graceful jade figure of a dancer, just 3.5 cm (1.4 in) tall, are emphasized by her long garment with wide sleeves that flutter in the air. [Western Han]

49 (opposite) Numerous red pottery statues, some 62 cm (24 in) high, were found in a pit near the tomb of emperor Jingdi (157–141 BC). Their arms were originally added in wood and their clothes were of silk or hemp. [Western Han]

A Chang'an
B Luoyang

three-lane major roads were up to 23 m (75 ft) wide, with the paved central lane reserved for messengers and officials. A canal over 100 km (62 miles) long that connected the river Wei to the Yellow river was completed in 129 BC. Such impressive civil engineering projects and the high level of technology achieved by craftsmen promoted an unprecedented economic expansion. The huge amount of wealth accumulated led to the emergence of a new and powerful political class, which was determined to maintain its privileges at all costs.

The first Han emperors do not seem to have been particularly interested in ideological questions. Wudi, however, felt that obedience to the ideals and principles associated with the earliest ages would constitute the basis of his authority and the cornerstone of the new age he had inaugurated – given the solemn name of *Taichu* (Great Beginning). And the doctrine that seemed best able to meet his desire for legitimization was Confucianism: not so much in its original form as its adaptation by the leading philosopher of the Han period, Dong Zhongshu (c. 195–115 BC), who reinterpreted the philosophy of Confucius in the light of other theories (for instance Legalism and Daoism). Confucianism was therefore adopted as the ideology of the empire – and so it remained, despite fluctuations in popularity and numerous revisions, for over twenty centuries.

The Imperial Academy was instituted in 124 BC to educate the new generation of officials. Its teaching was largely based on the study of the Confucian classics and it soon became the main channel of recruitment to the central and local civil service. The first universal history, the *Shiji* by Sima Qian, dates from this period. This monumental work was to serve as a model for later dynastic histories, and contributed greatly to the formation of the imperial ideology of the Han period. The arts and literature developed and flourished as never before.

50 (above) Han craftsmen displayed some of their greatest imagination and artistic ingenuity in creating lamps, as seen in this magnificent painted bronze example in the form of a goose, holding a fish in its beak. The adjustable cylindrical lamp is inserted into the belly of the fish. [Western Han]

Ferghana and the upper Sir Darya valley, setting up garrisons wherever they went. The frequent missions to the west and the establishment of permanent garrisons in ever more distant areas helped to create strong political, economic and cultural ties with populations which until then had had no contact with Chinese civilization. Caravans of goods and travellers journeyed safely along the Silk Route, from Chang'an to Merv, and from there to the Mediterranean coast or, by another route, to India. Trade with distant countries was also conducted by sea routes to India and Southeast Asia.

The construction of major public works begun by Qin Shihuangdi continued in the Western Han period. The road network was extended; the

In the second part of the dynasty, however, a gradual decline in state institutions and the population's standard of living began. The peasants and small landowners were increasingly burdened by taxes, forced labour and other obligations to the civil and military authorities, and were forced to sell their land. The large landowners, often exempted from the payment of taxes, continued to increase the size of their estates, to the extent that the government endeavoured to confiscate the holdings of the most powerful aristocrats on all kinds of pretexts.

Many aristocrats maintained private armies that represented a constant threat to central authority and the unity of the empire. Towards the end of the dynasty, tensions between the government and the great families increased, and the outbreak of rioting in some parts of the empire gave Wang Mang, nephew of one of the wives of Yuandi (49–33 BC), the opportunity to depose Ruzi (AD 7–9), who was only two years old at the time, and himself take the title of emperor, thus founding the short-lived Xin (New) dynasty (AD 9–23).

東漢

A Luoyang

52 *An ox forms the base of this unusual bronze lamp inlaid with silver. The smoke from the lamp's flame flowed into the body of the animal through the tube curving gracefully from the top of the head.* [Eastern Han]

Although Wang Mang attempted to justify his ascent to the throne according to the theory of the Mandate of Heaven, he went down in history as a usurper, and his seizure of power was regarded as a coup d'état. He introduced a strict centralizing policy designed to reduce the financial privileges of the aristocracy and other powerful families. For this purpose he introduced major reforms such as the abolition of the great landed estates and private slavery, and a ban on buying and selling agricultural land. He initiated programmes of land redistribution and controls on prices and production. His shrewd taxation and monetary policy increased the imperial gold reserves to 140 tonnes in just a few years.

However, these measures met with fierce opposition from the dominant class, resulting in the failure of Wang Mang's reformist policies. Natural disasters, which caused famine all over the country also contributed to the deterioration of the economic situation. Rioting inevitably broke out, often fomented and led by members of the Han imperial family, and the army was unable to quell the revolts. In AD 23 the population of the capital rioted, occupied the imperial palace and killed Wang Mang. Fighting continued until AD 25, when Liu Xiu, a member of a collateral branch of the Han imperial family who led a strong army, proclaimed the restoration of the Han dynasty.

Luoyang (Henan) was chosen as the capital. As a result, the name Eastern (or Later) Han was used to designate the new dynasty, while the previous phase was renamed the Western (or Former) Han dynasty.

The wealthy land-owning families who had grown rich during the Western Han dynasty supported the ascent to the throne of Liu Xiu (Guang Wudi, AD 25–57). Tension between the central power and peripheral interests, which had been constant for the past 150 years,

between 73 and 102, several military campaigns were led by general Ban Chao, brother of the famous historian Ban Gu, who, together with his father Ban Biao and sister Ban Zhao, wrote the second dynastic history, the *Han Shu* (History of the [Western] Han Dynasty).

Ban Chao reimposed imperial authority over the Tarim Basin and along the Silk Route. In AD 97 he reached the Caspian Sea and sent one of his officers, Gan Ying, to seek the ruler of the Roman empire, the existence of which the Chinese had vague, indirect knowledge. The mission was a failure. Gan Ying travelled only as far as the Persian Gulf or the Black Sea because he was badly

53 (below) Mythical beings soar through the air on the backs of winged dragons on this painted pottery lamp for funerary use. The tall, tree-shaped stem rises majestically from the mountain-shaped base teeming with various animals. [Eastern Han]

soon began to ease. The objectives of the imperial government's economic policy changed radically; enslaving the peasants was no longer prohibited, and more and more of them lost their land and found themselves forced to work for the large landowners, while the entire taxation system was overhauled.

In foreign policy, a gradual system of assimilation of the peoples who lived outside the northern borders was introduced. In AD 39 and 44 large groups of Xiongnu were permitted to cross the Great Wall and settle in parts of the empire. The Chinese inhabitants of these areas had to be relocated. But the peaceful situation did not last long. Since the time of Wang Mang, the Xiongnu had regained control of the trade routes of Central Asia. Major interests were at stake, because foreign trade now constituted a significant part of the Chinese economy.

A policy of westward expansion was introduced during the rule of Mingdi (AD 57–75). In a period of 30 years,

53 (above left) Humans, animals, insects and plants crowd the surface of this funerary vessel. The upper part, with the four miniature vessels connected to the main body of the piece, are covered with a glaze of a typical greenish-yellow colour. [Eastern Han]

advised by the Parthians, who controlled the flourishing silk trade and did not want direct trade between the two empires to be established. After the death of Ban Chao the situation degenerated, and relations with Central Asia broke down once more.

Initially, the economy grew healthily. Official figures of the period estimate the total area given over to agriculture at 50 million ha (12,355,000 acres). Farming equipment and many household tools were made of iron or cast iron using a process which meant that objects could be mass-produced; the manufacture of hardened steel weapons also increased.

In pottery, a special lead glaze that could be fired at low temperatures was introduced, and glazing techniques in general were perfected. Celadons, large numbers of which have been found in Zhejiang and Jiangxi, were particularly

55 (below) This bronze vessel used for divination could be transformed into a compass with the aid of a magnet. The square shape represents the earth, while the circular depression, called the Celestial Lake, contained another circular plate (now lost), symbolizing the sky. [Eastern Han]

54–55 (above) In the Han period, tombs of officials and the aristocracy were often decorated with painted or impressed hollow bricks. Geometric patterns acted as the background to depictions of personalities, hunting scenes and episodes from mythology. [Eastern Han]

54–55 (below) The horse-drawn chariot had been known in China since the Bronze Age. Some 20 tombs contain skeletons of horses and the remains of chariots dating from the Shang dynasty, some of which were larger than those used in the Western world. Bronze models of various sizes, often driven by a charioteer, are frequently found among the grave goods of the Han period. [Eastern Han]

attractive, both in shape and because of the smooth, even surface of the glaze.

The nine rulers who held the throne between AD 88 and 220, the year when the dynasty came to an end, were crowned as children. As a result, two factions formed at court – rivals both by nature and in their interests. One comprised the empresses and their powerful families, who had acquired a dominant role not only at court but also in the local decision-making processes through relatives and followers strategically placed in the civil service. The other comprised the eunuchs, mainly of humble birth, whose influence at court increased as a result of the young emperors' irritation with the guardianship exercised by their mothers and relations. The two factions clashed fiercely; first one would gain the upper hand, then the other.

The history of the dynasty was increasingly marked by plots, suicides and massacres. Such internecine strife inevitably had repercussions on public administration, often resulting in the lack of a sound economic policy. As a result of frequent natural disasters, aggravated by the negligence of the authorities, masses of hungry peasants roamed the country, and this, together with the forced migration of whole populations and increasing pressure from the non-Chinese tribes which had settled within the borders of the empire, led to a social crisis of huge proportions. Riots broke out everywhere. The most

dangerous to the stability of the empire were organised by the Yellow Turbans (Huangjin) movement and the sect of Daoist inspiration called the Way of Great Peace (Taiping Dao), which advocated a return to a world in which there were no social distinctions. The rebellions were bloodily suppressed.

The military leaders tried to assert their power in every way, competing for control of the court. As a result of this situation of institutional anarchy, huge masses of destitute peasants flocked to the big cities, and the great landowners' estates were gradually turned into self-sufficient political and economic units. The empire had disintegrated, and was at the mercy of the powerful military leaders: Cao Cao in the north, Sun Quan in the south, and Liu Bei in Sichuan. The Han dynasty officially ended in AD 220.

A Luoyang
B Jianye
C Chengdu

DECLINE OF THE FIRST EMPIRE: THE SPLIT BETWEEN NORTH AND SOUTH

56 (below) This painted terracotta soldier on horseback, from the tomb of Lou Rui, a military commander of

Xiangbei descent buried in 577, was part of the escort that was to watch over the general after his death. [Northern Qi]

The period between AD 220 and 589 was characterized by the decline of central institutions and the fragmentation of the political, economic and cultural unity of the empire. This phase, compared by some to the 'Dark Ages' in Europe, was divided into three: the Three Kingdoms; the Western Jin; and the Northern and Southern Dynasties. Many analogies can be drawn with the situation in the West after the fall of the Roman empire, including the decadence of civilization, the continuation of the imperial ideal at the courts of rulers who considered themselves the legitimate heirs of the tradition, and the spread of universalist foreign religions (Christianity in the West and Buddhism in China) which filled the gap left by a profound spiritual crisis.

Similarly, the 'barbarian' populations first destroyed and then restored the country's cultural heritage. Unlike the situation in the West, however, an alternative institutional system based on feudalism was not created from the ashes of the Chinese empire, nor did the Buddhist religion ever claim power independent of the state. The Chinese

'Dark Ages' instead represented a stage of changeover from a political system that had in the past generated a number of seemingly irreconcilable contradictions to a restoration of the same system, but at a more advanced level, with the contradictions finally resolved.

After the death of Cao Cao in AD 220, his son Cao Pi put an end to Han rule and proclaimed himself emperor of the new Cao Wei dynasty. He took the name of Wendi (220–226), and ruled a territory that stretched along the Yellow river basin and included the northern regions. The capital was established at Luoyang. In the west, Liu Bei, a member of a collateral branch of the Han imperial family, also proclaimed himself emperor in 221; he took the name of Xuande (221–223) and formed the imperial

56–57 The ox and water buffalo were among the favourite subjects of Chinese potters, depicted alone or yoked to carts. When discovered, the wooden parts of this cart were missing and have been restored. [Northern Qi]

57 (opposite above) The camel was the most common means of transport along the Silk Route. Camels are generally depicted laden with goods, as in this case, or ridden by people with Central Asiatic features. [Northern Wei]

Western Jin

A Luoyang

*Northern and
Southern Dynasties*

A Datong
B Luoyang
C Nanjing

kingdom of Shu (or Shu Han) in Sichuan, with Chengdu as its capital. Further south Sun Quan, who had taken the title of King of Wu, also proclaimed himself emperor in AD 229 with the name of Wudi (222–252), and founded the Wu dynasty. His kingdom extended along the middle and lower basin of the Yangzijiang and the southern regions, and his capital was Jianye (Nanjing). Thus began the period of the Three Kingdoms.

The empire was divided into three independent political units, each of which considered itself the sole heir of the Han dynasty. The kingdom of Wei was the most powerful, and in AD 263 Yuandi (260–264) defeated and annexed Shu Han thanks to the superiority of his army, which mainly consisted of soldiers from the 'barbarian' tribes which had been encouraged to settle inside the Great Wall.

In AD 265 general Sima Yuan, from a powerful family which had gradually taken political control of Wei, seized the throne and founded the Western Jin dynasty. He ruled under the name of Wudi (265–289). In AD 280 he defeated Modi (264–280), the weak ruler of Wu, who went down in history as a ruthless drunkard, more interested in his harem of 5,000 concubines than in matters of state. With the annexation of the kingdom of Wu, the unity of the empire was temporarily restored.

To strengthen the power of his family, Wudi divided the empire into principalities which he assigned to his many sons and relatives. Predictably, bitter internal conflict broke out on his death. Fierce fighting – evidence of the lack of a central government capable of imposing authority – destroyed the economic and social fabric of the empire. Non-Chinese populations settled in large numbers in huge areas of the north and were the main source of recruitment to the army. In time, the political influence of the military commanders increased. In AD 304, Liu Xiong of the Di tribe founded his own kingdom in Sichuan. Liu Yuan, of the Xiongnu tribe, did the same in Shanxi. In AD 316 Liu Cong, also a Xiongnu, deposed the last Jin emperor, Mindi (313–316), and founded the Eastern Jin dynasty.

The period between AD 304 and 439, known as the Sixteen Kingdoms, was a time of great confusion. The empire split into myriad ephemeral and independent kingdoms with no real economic or institutional organization, often ruled by military leaders belonging to non-Chinese races such as the Xiongnu, Xianbei, Jie, Di and Qiang. This phase was characterized by a marked division between north and south and the migration of huge numbers of people, not only from the steppes into Chinese territory, but also from the north to the south of China. This led to a rapid process of ethnic integration between barbarians and Chinese, and between the populations of the north and south.

The southern regions were ruled by the Eastern Jin dynasty (317–420), founded by a member of the Jin imperial family, Sima Rui (Yuandi, 317–322), who chose as his capital the city of Jianye, renamed Jiankang (Nanjing). During the Sixteen Kingdoms period, over a million northern Chinese emigrated to the south to escape the devastation. Some of the great landowners also moved; with the enormous wealth they had accumulated and the thousands of people in their employ, they took over the best land around the capital and gained powerful positions in the government and army.

Vicious struggles and court intrigues weakened the dynasty and led inexorably to its fall. In AD 420 general Liu Yu proclaimed himself emperor of the Liu Song dynasty (420–479), itself destined to decline rapidly. This was followed by the Southern Qi dynasty (479–501), the Southern Liang dynasty (502–556) and the Chen dynasty (557–589) – known as the Southern Dynasties.

Of the 22 rulers who held the throne in those 170 years, the most outstanding was Wudi (502–549) of the Liang dynasty. A highly cultured man and a supporter of Confucian principles of government and a fervent Buddhist, he promoted the study of the classics and welcomed artists and intellectuals to his court.

Although Chinese historians have regarded the successive governments of northern China illegitimate, it was the north that paved the way for the reconstruction of the centralized empire. In AD 386 the Tuoba, an ethnic group of Turkic origin belonging to the Xianbei, which had settled in Shaanxi in the early

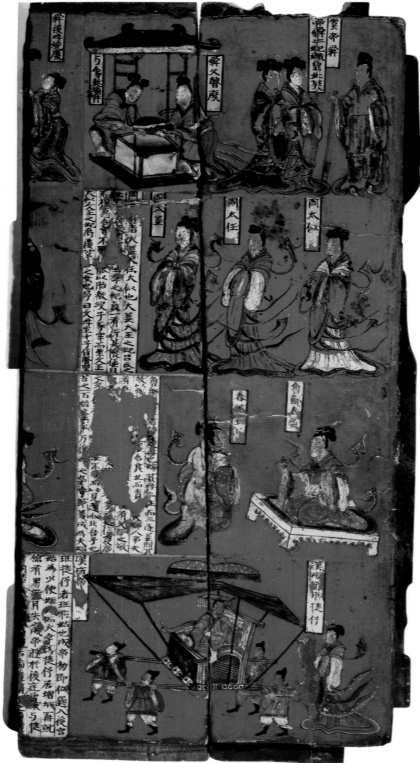

58–59 and 59 Women of particular merit are depicted on this lacquered wooden screen, dating from the 5th century. Among them is Ban Fei, a concubine of exceptional intellect who refused to share a litter with the emperor Chengdi (37–7 BC) so as not to break the rules governing the separation of the sexes. [Northern Wei]

58 (opposite below) This gold seal, weighing over 800 g (28 oz), dates from the Northern Zhou period and is engraved with the name of Dowager Empress Tianyuan. The handles of gold and silver seals were very often made in the shape of an animal. [Northern Zhou]

60 (left) This celadon candlestick in the form of a man riding a mythical animal was produced in the famous Yue kilns in Zhejiang. It was in these kilns that the celadon technique of covering the entire surface of the object with a greenish glaze was discovered. [Western Jin]

4th century, founded the Northern Wei dynasty (386–534), the first of the Northern Dynasties. Within a few decades the Wei extended their rule over the whole of northern China and initiated major economic and social reforms. They introduced a programme to promote the development of agriculture by aiding smallholders and peasants, to whom public land was allocated, and by making the tax system more efficient by restoring central government control over agricultural production. The dominant class, aware of the superiority of the model of Chinese civilization, had begun a policy designed to promote integration between the Chinese and other ethnic groups. After AD 493, when the capital was moved to Luoyang, the Tuoba were forced to adopt Chinese language, customs and surnames, and mixed marriages were encouraged.

Buddhism had been introduced into China during the Eastern Han dynasty and from the 4th century rapidly spread through north and south. The Tuoba rulers, realizing the great potential of the new religion to become the ideological basis not only for racial integration but also for the reunification of the empire, adopted Buddhism as the state religion. Monasteries, sanctuaries and cave temples were built; the Buddhist caves of Dunhuang (Gansu), Datong (Shaanxi) and Longmen (Henan), which date from this period, are famous for the number and quality of their wall paintings and statues. Elements of Indian art were introduced through Buddhism and were adapted, leading to new stylistic forms of great expressive effect.

60 (right) The heads of birds of prey or poultry are the preferred subjects used to decorate this shape of celadon jar, with the light and brilliant glaze giving it an appearance of great elegance. [West Jin]

massed along the northeastern borders, he began a military campaign to unite the northern and southern regions. In AD 588 he launched an attack on Chen, the last of the independent southern kingdoms. He circulated over 300,000 copies of a document denouncing the crimes that allegedly made Hou Zhu (583–589) of the Chen dynasty unworthy of the Mandate of Heaven, and exhorted the population to revolt. Yang Jian seized power without meeting any strong resistance. In 589 the empire, which had survived only as a historical memory for nearly 370 years, was once again a political reality.

The policy of assimilation adopted by the government provoked a reaction by the Xianbei aristocracy, and after a period of relative stability there was another period of upheaval, which did not end until AD 589. In 535 Northern Wei was divided into the kingdoms of Western Wei (535–557), with a capital at Chang'an (Shaanxi), and Eastern Wei (534–550), whose capital was Ye (Henan). The more conservative Western Wei aimed to restore Tuoba institutions, while Eastern Wei continued to encourage the assimilation process. The Eastern Wei dynasty was followed by the Northern Qi dynasty (550–577), founded by Gao Yang, the son of a Chinese general, while after the Western Wei dynasty came the Northern Zhou dynasty (557–581), founded by Yuwen Jue, son of a Xianbei general. The Northern Zhou dynasty conquered the Northern Qi dynasty, and unified the entire Yellow river basin area.

In 581 Yang Jian, who was descended from an aristocratic family of warriors from the north, overthrew the last Zhou ruler, proclaimed himself emperor of the Sui dynasty (581–618) and established his capital at Chang'an in 583. After signing a peace treaty with foreign populations

61 (top) The celestial abode of the Immortals, inhabited by winged creatures and mythological animals and ruled by the divine Xiwangmu, Queen Mother of the West, is depicted on this magnificent white jade zun *vase [Western Jin]*

61 (right) Stoneware vases with green or brown glazes, which were often large and richly decorated with applied floral motifs, medallions and masks of fantastic animals, are typical of 6th-century pottery production. [Northern Qi]

THE SPLENDOUR OF THE SECOND EMPIRE

The reunification of the northern and southern regions and the restoration of the empire were facilitated by the strengthening of bureaucratic, economic and military organization in the Northern Wei dynasty and the period of the Northern dynasties. After centuries of division, the Sui dynasty (581–618), though unable to consolidate its supremacy, paved the way for a great empire which was actually founded by the Tang dynasty (618–907), just as the Qin dynasty had made possible the successes of the glorious Han dynasty eight centuries earlier. The new Sino-barbarian aristocracy of the northwest, which had formed during the centuries of division, had planned the unification with far-sighted determination. Brilliant generals and able rulers emerged from its

ranks, as did emperors of the Sui and Tang dynasties, under whose rule the empire experienced unprecedented territorial and economic expansion and became the greatest power in Asia.

During this period, Chinese culture exerted considerable influence over its neighbours, especially Japan and Korea. It was due to Chinese support that large parts of present-day Korea and Manchuria had been united as the Kingdom of Silla. Under the Sui and Tang dynasties many religions flourished – not only indigenous ones such as Daoism, but also those of foreign origin, such as Buddhism, Manicheism, Zoroastrianism, Nestorian Christianity and Islam. These foreign cults were given varying receptions by the rulers, and were sometimes brutally persecuted. Buddhism, the most popular foreign religion in China, reached its height in this period. Many monks from India travelled to China to spread their religion, and Chinese pilgrims such as Xuanzang (600–664) and Yijing (635–717) travelled widely in Central Asia, India and other countries of Southeast Asia in search of sacred texts to take home and

translate. Buddhism was rapidly integrated into Chinese civilization, giving rise to new religious forms which then spread outside the empire. The repercussions on culture and art were immense; sculptures were almost entirely of religious inspiration, and religious painting developed considerably, as seen in cave temples throughout the empire.

Crafts also flourished, stimulated by the growth of trade, in particular the production of silk and brocade and jewelry. New processes in pottery and porcelain manufacture produced attractive vessels such as the white Xing porcelain and the delicate Yue celadons.

Two major inventions date from the Tang period: printing and gunpowder. Printing derived from the ancient use of seals and the reproduction on paper of inscriptions on stone or metal objects. Its development was fuelled by the desire to propagate Buddhist ideas, as it meant that religious pictures and extracts from texts could be reproduced in large numbers. The use of wooden blocks dates from the Sui dynasty or the early years of the Tang dynasty, while the use of woodcut printing dates from the early

62 (opposite left) The manufacture of luxury objects in gold and silver reached a peak during the Tang dynasty, due partly to influences from other countries, and in particular new techniques imported from Persia. [Tang]

62 (opposite right) This magnificent silver plate with incised and inlaid gold decoration shows the influence of the work of goldsmiths from Persia, from where the techniques and floral motifs derive. [Tang]

63 The camel was used for transport by Middle Eastern merchants travelling along the Silk Route. The female figure riding this camel is a woman from the Hu, a Central Asian people who lived along the western borders of the empire. [Tang]

8th century, and movable type was introduced in the mid-11th century. The first complete known printed text is the Diamond Sutra (*Jingangjing*), translated into Chinese by Kumarajiva in the early 5th century and printed in 868. It was found, with thousands of manuscripts, in a walled-up library in Dunhuang.

Literary and artistic works reached new heights of excellence in the Tang dynasty, with writers such as Wang Wei (699–759), Li Bai (710–762), Du Fu (712–770), Bai Juyi (772–846) and Han Yu (768–824). A huge amount of poetry, some of the best in Chinese literature, was produced: a collection of Tang poetry published in 1707 contains 50,000 poems.

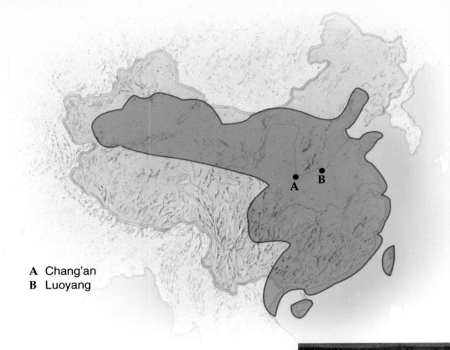

A Chang'an
B Luoyang

THE SUI DYNASTY

64 The characteristic style of sculptures of the Sui period is exemplified by this gilded stone statue of a standing Buddha. The body, with its smooth, rounded lines, is enhanced by the simple, soft drapery. [Sui]

The process of unification begun by Yang Jian (Wendi, 581–604) in 581 and completed in 589 with the annexation of the southern kingdom of Chen, met with considerable resistance in some regions. The imposition of imperial authority by the Sui dynasty stirred up violent reactions, especially in southern China. Law and order were restored by Wendi's son Yang Guang (later Yangdi). He was appointed Governor of Jiangdu (Yangzhou); the city he founded after the destruction of the ancient Jiankang (Jianye) by his father. Here he promoted culture and the arts, encouraged the study of the Confucian classics and the spread of Daoism, and established excellent relations with the Buddhists. Although he is described in official histories as an eccentric tyrant, Yangdi played an important part in consolidating the unity of the empire.

His father, emperor Wendi, a skilled politician and administrator, had appointed excellent ministers and counsellors, with whose help he introduced land and tax reforms; he improved and extended throughout the empire the system of land equalization that had been initiated in the Northern Wei period. He also modified the criteria for the selection of officials, introducing measures designed to assist candidates from the southern regions. He implemented some grandiose public works, such as the reconstruction of the capital Chang'an, the consolidation of the Great Wall and the creation of a huge irrigation system. Over 2,000 km (1,240 miles) of canals linked navigable waterways, forming a huge network that connected the wet, fertile southern countryside with the arid northern plains. Wendi's most ambitious project, carried out by his son after his death,

was the construction of the Grand Canal, which ran from Luoyang as far as the modern cities of Hangzhou to the south and Beijing to the north.

Yangdi (604–617) continued his father's policies but lacked his austere, restrained character and total dedication to matters of state. Yangdi was fond of luxury, and his megalomania knew no limits. Tradition attributes the decline of the Sui dynasty to the enormous sums he lavished on extravagant projects. He had a second capital, Luoyang, built: two million men were employed to give the city the appearance of unparalleled splendour. The imperial park alone covered an area of 155 sq. km (60 sq. miles).

Yangdi built a fleet large enough to carry the whole court down the Grand Canal. His personal ship had four decks, a throne room and 120 finely decorated and furnished staterooms for his concubines. Over 80,000 passengers embarked, including members of the

64 (opposite right) The combination of gold and white jade in this plain but exquisite cup symbolizes the perfect union of wealth and wisdom. [Sui]

65 (right) Buddha flees his father's house at midnight to embark on his spiritual search, aided by genies that lift the hooves of his horse (Dunhuang, cave no. 278). [Sui]

imperial family, ministers, ambassadors, monks, guards, musicians and servants.

The obstinacy with which Yangdi pursued his military campaign against the kingdom of Koguryŏ – modern North Korea and part of Manchuria – also played a part in the downfall of the Sui dynasty. Between 612 and 614 three major expeditions were undertaken, all of which failed with huge losses. Aided by popular uprisings and aristocratic conspiracies, Li Yuan (Gaozu), from a noble family of foreign blood which had settled in China in the Northern Wei period, conquered the western capital Chang'an in 617. Yangdi was forced to flee to Jiangdu, and abdicated in favour of his grandson Gongdi (617–618). In 618 Li Yuan also seized the eastern capital Luoyang, had Gongdi murdered and brought the Sui dynasty to an end, proclaiming himself the first emperor of the Tang dynasty.

64–65 The upper part of this fresco illustrates the Jataka of Sattva, while the lower part illustrates the Sutra of the Field of Happiness. The Sutras or Jataka Sutras are tales of the deeds performed by the Sakyamuni Buddha during his lives prior to his reincarnation as a prince (Dunhuang, cave no. 302). [Sui]

唐

A Chang'an
B Luoyang

of the Buddhist scriptures introduced into China by Xuan Zang. During his reign the Three Faiths – Confucianism, Buddhism and Daoism – became the cornerstone of imperial ideology.

Taizong maintained the tripartite structure of the upper echelons of the imperial civil service, merely introducing some modifications. The Secretariat (*zhongshusheng*), which was responsible for drafting official documents and imperial edicts, controlled the Academy of Sages (*jixiandian shuyuan*), a group of authors who composed literary works under the patronage of the court, and the Bureau of Historiography (*shiguan*), which was responsible for compiling dynastic histories. The Chancellory (*mengxiasheng*), which was responsible for examining the documents prepared by the Secretariat, directed the Bureau for the Progress of Literature (*hongwenguan*), which prepared the emperor's speeches. The Department of State Affairs (*shangshusheng*) controlled the Six Boards and was responsible for implementing decisions. The chief ministers of these three bodies, and other officials appointed by the emperor, met daily in his presence to establish the basic lines of imperial policy.

Under the rule of Taizong, China became a great power once more. After the defeat and submission of the Eastern Turks (630), the rule of the empire extended to the regions of the Ordos and Inner Mongolia, and included the trading and religious centres that had grown up in the Tarim Basin and along the caravan routes of Central Asia, as far as present-day Kirghizstan. Diplomatic relations were established with the powerful kingdom of Tibet, whose ruler

It took time to achieve the full unification of the empire. In 618, when Li Yuan – the emperor Gaozu (618–626) took the throne, the empire was torn by conflicts between some 200 rebel factions whose military power was often formidable. Some controlled huge regions and were led, at least in name, by members of the Sui imperial family. With the aid of his second son Li Shimin, Gaozu put down the revolts over a period of six years, defeated his enemies and restored peace. In 626, after eliminating the true heir, Li Shimin persuaded his father to abdicate in his

favour. Thus began the reign of one of the greatest emperors in Chinese history, Taizong (626–649).

A highly cultured man, educated in the Confucian classics and a talented calligrapher, Taizong appointed excellent ministers and loyal advisers. A skilled commander and shrewd diplomat, he formed a government inspired by the highest Confucian ideals. Unlike his father, who had limited his subjects' religious freedom, Taizong gave Daoist monks an important role in imperial ceremonies and sponsored the translation

66 (opposite) Horses were a favourite theme for Tang potters: this horse and rider are decorated in 'three-colour' (sancai) glaze. [Tang]

67 (left and centre) The aesthetic tastes of the Tang period preferred highly coloured, relaxed faces, full shapes, with loose flowing garments, and soft, elaborate hairstyles. This pair of courtiers, a man and a woman, fulfil this ideal of beauty perfectly. [Tang]

67 (above) Ladies and courtesans are often portrayed standing, their hair gathered at the nape of the neck or on the top of the head in a bun, while an elegant, enveloping garment flows softly down to their feet. [Tang]

This silver-gilt figure, donated in AD *871 by emperor Yizong of the Tang dynasty to the Famen Temple, was designed to contain a precious relic, possibly a finger of Buddha. A plaque inscribed with the emperor's prayer rests on the small tray in the shape of a lotus leaf.* [Tang]

was permitted to marry a Chinese imperial princess (641). Only the kingdom of Koguryŏ managed to escape Taizong's expansionist policy. The power and prestige of the empire reached new peaks, and Chinese culture exerted a strong influence over neighbouring states. The capital Chang'an, a great metropolis where tens of thousands of foreigners lived, had no equal.

The great territorial expansion was matched by equally impressive developments in trade and the economy. The land distribution and taxation systems of the Sui dynasty were maintained, with some modifications.

Craft activities and agriculture were boosted by the introduction of new techniques and tools. Communication routes were improved, and the transport of goods was made faster and safer. Underground warehouses with the capacity to store hundreds of tons of grain were built near the major routes.

Huge markets, which could accommodate not only Chinese traders but also the increasing numbers arriving from all over Asia, were set up at Chang'an and in the major cities along the Grand Canal, such as Luoyang and Hangzhou. It is estimated that at least 4,000 families from the West (mainly Arabs, Persians, Turks, Hindus, Uigurs, Sogdians and Tocharians) lived and worked in the Chang'an west market.

When Taizong died in 649 he was succeeded by his son Li Zhi, the emperor Gaozong (649–683), a fragile young man of weak character, with no aptitude for government. He continued his father's policies without introducing any particular innovations. In 655 one of his consorts, Wu Zhao – later Wu Zetian – was proclaimed empress. She had reached this powerful position by treacherously accusing empress Wang of crimes against her lord and having her banished and later murdered.

Wu Zhao is one of the most interesting and controversial women in Chinese history. Born into an influential family associated with emperor Gaozu, she had been one of Taizong's concubines. On his death she had to retire to a Buddhist monastery in accordance with custom. Gaozong, who had fallen in love with her, arranged for her to leave the monastery and made her his consort. Ambitious and fiercely determined, Wu Zhao orchestrated palace intrigues with great skill. She eliminated all her personal and political rivals in just a few years, and replaced them with people devoted to her. She dominated the court and the empire for over 50 years, until her death in 705.

Gaozong died in 684 and was succeeded by Li Zhe, emperor Zhongzong (684; 705–710), who was clearly influenced by his wife, empress Wei. He fell victim to his own mother, Wu Zhao, who had him deposed and replaced him with his younger brother Li Dan (Ruizong, 684–690; 710–712).

and ministers who had reached high office under Wu Zetian, and he did all he could to exclude the eunuchs and his wives' relatives from affairs of state. He chose his ministers on the basis of merit rather than family membership, and introduced an ingenious system of exchanging officials between the capital and the provinces in order to bring the peripheral regions under the direct control of the central government.

He had more humane laws drafted, and ordered them to be applied in an impartial manner. He promoted the formation of a new ruling class by

69 (below) During banquets, guests would enliven the atmosphere with drinking games. One of them involved fishing one of fifty silver plaques from a container like this candle-shaped one. The beginning of a saying by Confucius was incised on the plaque, and the rest had to be recited by heart. The inscription also specified what the contestant had to drink if the recital was incorrect. [Tang]

The overthrow of Zhongzong was not well received by the aristocracy or the populace. A revolt broke out in Yangzhou but was immediately and bloodily repressed. Twelve collateral branches of the imperial family were exterminated, as well as numerous dignitaries and officials considered disloyal. A reign of terror began, leading to a horrific series of purges and massacres in 697. In 690 Wu Zhao's monstrous ambition persuaded her to depose Ruizong too. For the first and only time in Chinese history a woman officially held imperial power; under the name of Wu Zetian (690–705) she founded a new dynasty, to which she gave the illustrious name of Zhou.

On Wu Zetian's death Zhongzong took back the throne. When he died in 710, probably poisoned by his wife, he was succeeded by his weak brother Ruizong, who abdicated after only two years in favour of his son Li Longji, emperor Xuanzong (712–756), the longest-reigning ruler of the Tang dynasty.

Xuanzong's first act on acceding to the throne, having grown up amid palace intrigues, was to get rid of the officials

69 (above) Both beautiful and practical, this openwork silver incense burner operates like a gyroscopic compass. A bowl inside the lower hemisphere is attached to two concentric rings with a universal joint which rotate around their own axes so that the bowl always maintains a horizontal position, thus preventing the incense from spilling. [Tang]

70 (below) In China the making of bronze mirrors dates back to the end of the second millennium BC. The surface of the mirror was shiny and reflective, while the back was decorated with geometric motifs and mythological scenes. Some examples were inscribed with short poems or auspicious mottoes.

The decoration of this mirror develops around a central perforated boss that allowed the mirror to be hung from a belt. Small mirrors, which were used mainly for cosmetic purposes, were sometimes also part of military equipment or used in magic, as they also had cosmological associations. [Tang]

improving the system of imperial examinations so that men of talent might emerge. A distinguished poet, painter and calligrapher, Xuanzong opened his court to intellectuals and artists, promoted the arts and welcomed new ideas. In 725 he founded the Imperial Academy, almost 1,000 years before such institutions were established in the West.

Xuanzong is one of the emperors most honoured by Chinese historians, who dubbed him Ming Huan (Enlightened Emperor), and attributed great merit to him, especially in the early part of his reign. Numerous poems and ballads tell of his love for the beautiful Yang Guifei, and their story became one of the favourite subjects of popular fiction.

Yang Guifei, who was born in Sichuan, was the wife of one of Xuanzong's sons.

in affairs of state, became chief minister and president of the Secretariat, at a time when the empire was facing a crisis resulting from threats along its borders.

The previous year, the Chinese army stationed in the western regions had suffered a crushing defeat at Talas by the Arabs, who had pushed further east and conquered territories in Central Asia, formerly Chinese protectorates. The dynasty finally lost military control of the settlements in the Tarim Basin and along the Silk Route, and trade supremacy on the caravan routes of Central Asia.

In the northeast, the Qidan defeated an army of 200,000 men commanded by An Lushan, a general of Sogdian origin who enjoyed imperial protection, having been adopted by Yang Guifei. In the southwest, the imperial militia had suffered a heavy

70 (right) and 71 In the middle of this bronze mirror, with decoration in silver and gold, is a seated animal with a thick mane. Around it are felines, phoenixes and birds among scrolls of leaves and branches. [Tang]

The emperor desired her for himself, and arranged for her to leave her husband and enter the palace in 745, disguised as a Daoist priestess. From the very start, she exerted an evil influence on the emperor and the court. Within a few years her family had acquired great power. In 752 her cousin Yang Guozhong, who had already been appointed military governor of Sichuan although he was inexperienced

defeat at the hands of troops from Nanzhao, an independent kingdom founded years earlier in Yunnan with the consent of China, with the aim of countering the growing power of Tibet.

The political and military crisis had repercussions on the precarious imperial finances, weakened by the excessive expenditure of an increasingly numerous and demanding nobility (Xuanzong had

59 children and 55 grandchildren by his fourth son and 58 by his sixth). In 755 An Lushan rebelled after being accused by Yang of treason, and proclaimed himself emperor. He founded the Great Yan lineage, which was never included in the ranks of the dynasties recognized by official histories.

Leading an army of 150,000 men he marched south, razed the city of Kaifeng, conquered Luoyang and reached the gates of Chang'an. Xuanzong, Yang Guifei, Yang Guozhong and a few officials fled by night towards Sichuan. When the party was stopped on the road by Tibetan troops, their escort mutinied. Holding the beautiful concubine and her inept cousin responsible for the disaster, they murdered Yang Guozhong and insisted that Yang Guifei should also be executed. A tearful Xuanzong had to order the chief eunuch to strangle her with a silk ribbon. In the meantime, the heir Li Yu had proclaimed himself emperor – Suzong (756–762). In a few months, Chang'an and Luoyang were under Tang rule again.

Imperial power was slowly weakened by the increasing independence of the military governorates. Suzong's 13 successors tried to restore a centralized organization, but their authority was undermined by the pernicious interference of the eunuchs and the lack of regular revenues; no emperor ever reigned for long, and some neglected state affairs and took refuge in religion. The Buddhist church gained increasing power, wealth and privileges, and exerted its influence at political level, making it a serious threat to the state.

In 845 emperor Wuzong (840–846), an unbalanced fanatic and a disciple of Daoist practices designed to achieve immortality, ordered the destruction of temples and monasteries, confiscated millions of acres of land, and expelled 200,000 priests and nuns who had enjoyed exemption from taxation. Over 4,600 monasteries and 40,000 sanctuaries were destroyed. Although the Buddhist faith suffered a serious blow, the persecution was insufficient to restore the emperor's prestige, and the decline of the dynasty proved unstoppable.

An Lushan's revolt had initiated a new phase, which was to change the fate of the empire. The adult population registered for tax stood at 53 million in 754, but had fallen to 17 million by 774. In 763 the Tibetan army, which had conquered many of the settlements in the Tarim Basin marched as far as Chang'an, which was occupied until 777. Tibetan presence in the area continued even after the city was retaken by the Chinese.

The last great defender of the unity of the empire was Xianzong (805–820) who, thanks to a series of administrative and economic reforms and some successful military campaigns, restored the social order and prestige of the empire. When he was murdered by the eunuchs in 820, a short period of relative stability followed, but the situation soon deteriorated again.

The last three emperors, Xizong (873–888), Zhaozong (888–904) and Zhaoxuan (904–907, also known as Aidi) were puppets in the hands of the eunuchs or military governors. In 875 Henan suffered a severe drought, and the population rebelled. In 879 the rebels reached Guangzhou (Canton), and slaughtered 120,000 of the 200,000 foreigners who lived there, mainly Arabs, Hindus, Persians, Chams, Khmers, Sinhalese and Javanese. In 880 they took Chang'an, forcing the emperor to take refuge in Sichuan.

In 904 Zhu Wen, a rebel general who had offered his services to the dynasty, got rid of the eunuchs by having them slaughtered en masse, murdered emperor Zhaozong and placed Zhaoxuan on the throne. In 907 he usurped the throne, bringing the Tang dynasty to an end. He proclaimed himself emperor of the Later Liang dynasty, and another period of political and social chaos began.

72 (opposite) This fully armed soldier carved from white stone is the attendant of an officer, so in addition to his own weapons (sword, sabre, bow and arrows) he also carries those of his superior officer. [Tang]

72–73 The nature of the decoration on this unusual octagonal porcelain rhyton, with the head and legs of a lion, suggests that is based on a model made of metal, perhaps silver. [Tang]

CHINESE CIVILIZATION THROUGH THE AGES

Prehistory

The early Bronze Age

The end of the Bronze Age

The first empire

The first representatives of Homo sapiens in China appeared roughly 40,000 years ago, preceded by remote ancestors like Yuanmou Man, whose fossilized remains date back to 1.7–1.6 million years ago, Lantian Man, who lived 700,000–650,000 years ago, and Peking Man, whose oldest settlements date to some 500,000–400,000 years ago. From the 10th/11th millennium BC, communities of hunter-gatherers and fishermen, which had so far been nomadic, began to engage in agriculture, animal-rearing and pottery making, and settled in the first permanent villages. Numerous centres of Neolithic culture sprang up in the huge Chinese territory, and discoveries were progressively shared between them as a result of a trading network. The main crops were varieties of millet in the north and rice in the south. Rice was first cultivated possibly as early as the 7th millennium BC. Numerous tombs contained grave goods, and jade articles demonstrating a high level of craftsmanship have been found in addition to stone artifacts. Metalworking, first of copper, gold and silver and later of bronze, began towards the end of the 3rd millennium BC. (Dates are approximate.)

Palaeolithic (1,700,000–8500 BC)
Neolithic (8500–1700 BC):
Xinglongwa, Xinle, Hongshan (8500–2000 BC);
Cishan-Peiligang, Yangshao, Dawenkou, Daxi, Longshan (6500–2000 BC);
Majiabang, Hemudu, Qingliangang, Liangzhu (5000–2200 BC);
Dapenkeng, Shixia (5000–2480 BC)

According to tradition, the first Chinese kingdom was founded by the Xia dynasty, which ruled from 2205 to 1751 BC. Seventeen kings held power, guaranteeing the continuity of a government which changed its capital nine times. Archaeological excavations have brought to light a city at Erlitou which was inhabited from 2010 to 1324 BC. The great palace that stood in the middle of the city perhaps confirms what was once considered to be only a legend. The exquisite grave goods from Erlitou demonstrate the presence of a stratified society in which political power coincided with religious authority, legitimized by the possession of cast bronze ritual vessels, the first to be found in China. The decline of the Xia dynasty corresponded to the rise of the Shang dynasty, a class of shaman kings that ruled over a confederation of clans whose organization reflected a complex system of kinship. Excavations have confirmed the historical existence of this dynasty and brought to light two capitals, at Erligang and Anyang. The great progress made in metallurgy during the Shang dynasty facilitated large-scale production of ritual bronze vessels, while the divinatory practices systematically performed by the court led to a major development in writing. Human sacrifice was practised.

*Xia dynasty
(23rd–18th century BC):
Erlitou (1700–1500 BC)
Shang Dynasty
(16th–11th century BC):
Erligang-Zhengzhou phase
(1500–1300 BC), Anyang phase
(1300-1050 BC)*

In 1045 BC the powerful troops of Wu, king of the Zhou, a population that lived in the lands to the west of the Shang kingdom, defeated the Shang armies in the epic battle of Muye, thus bringing to an end the dynasty that had controlled the Chinese central plain for over six centuries. Shamanic practices lost their importance under the Zhou rulers, while the system of kinship maintained a central role in the distribution of government office. During Zhou rule, which lasted for eight centuries, great progress was made in agriculture. In the 8th century the dynasty grew gradually weaker, and in 771 BC the barbarian Quanrong tribe expelled the Zhou from the capital Hao, forcing them to move to Luoyi, where they maintained religious authority, but lacked any political power, until 221 BC. The kingdom split into numerous kingdoms continually warring against one another. This situation benefited the outermost regions, whose borders were less threatened than the states of the Central Plain, with its older civilization. Seven states (Zhao, Wei, Han, Qin, Qi, Yan and Chu) fought for supremacy during the Warring States period. Despite the huge amount of resources expended, the demands of war in fact promoted internal reorganization of the kingdoms and technological progress, especially in the field of metallurgy, which in turn greatly benefited agriculture. Impressive defensive walls were built and major irrigation schemes undertaken. In 221 BC, thanks to the ruler Zheng, an outstanding strategist, the Qin defeated their adversaries and founded the empire.

*Western Zhou dynasty
(1045/1050–771 BC)
Eastern Zhou dynasty
(770–221 BC): Springs and
Autumns Period (770–475 BC),
Warring States Period
(475–221 BC)*

Qin Shihuangdi, the First August Emperor of the Qin dynasty, endeavoured to extend the laws and principles of government in force in the kingdom of Qin to the populations he conquered. He divided the territories of the empire into governorates and districts, and introduced an administrative structure which was conducive to central control and limited the privileges of the aristocracy. He unified systems of writing, money and measurement and the wheel-gauge, and promulgated a code which remained the basis of Chinese legislation for over 20 centuries. He initiated the construction of gigantic public works which would leave their mark on Chinese history, such as his tomb, protected by thousands of terracotta soldiers in full battle array, the completion of the Great Wall, which stretched for over 5,000 km (3,100 miles), and the construction of an extensive road and river network that allowed faster movement of men and goods. On his death in 210 BC, no successor emerged who was capable of dealing with the threat posed by neighbouring populations, internal revolts and the growing economic crisis associated with impoverishment of the peasants engaged in the construction of public works. In 206 BC a popular insurrection led by Liu Bang, of humble birth, and Xian Yu, from an aristocratic family, brought the Qin dynasty to an end. It had only lasted a short time, but long enough to pave the way for a strong, well-organized empire which was soon to experience economic and social expansion and wealth.

Qin dynasty (221–206 BC)

75 Their elaborate
hairstyles, elegant
garments with painted
and gilded floral
patterns, wide double
sleeves that fall softly
down the body and
lotus-shaped shoes
with upward curling
tips denote the
aristocratic lineage
of these elegant court
ladies, with their
straight backs and
haughty bearing.
[Tang]

76–81 Hunting
scenes and processions
of knights are
recurrent themes in
Han funeral
iconography. The line
of carriages indicate
the high rank of the
deceased, probably a
senior official. At one
side is a crow,
symbolizing the sun.
According to legend,
there was a time when
ten sun-crows flew in
the sky, and their heat
was about to destroy
the entire human race.
Hou Yi, armed with a
powerful bow, killed
nine of them, thus
saving the world from
certain destruction.
[Eastern Han]

82 The chignon was
the most fashionable
hairstyle among the
ladies of the Tang
aristocracy. Plaited
or plain, it was worn
raised, tilted forwards
or to one side, or on
the nape of the neck.
It was sometimes also
covered with an
elaborate headdress or
gilded coronet. [Tang]

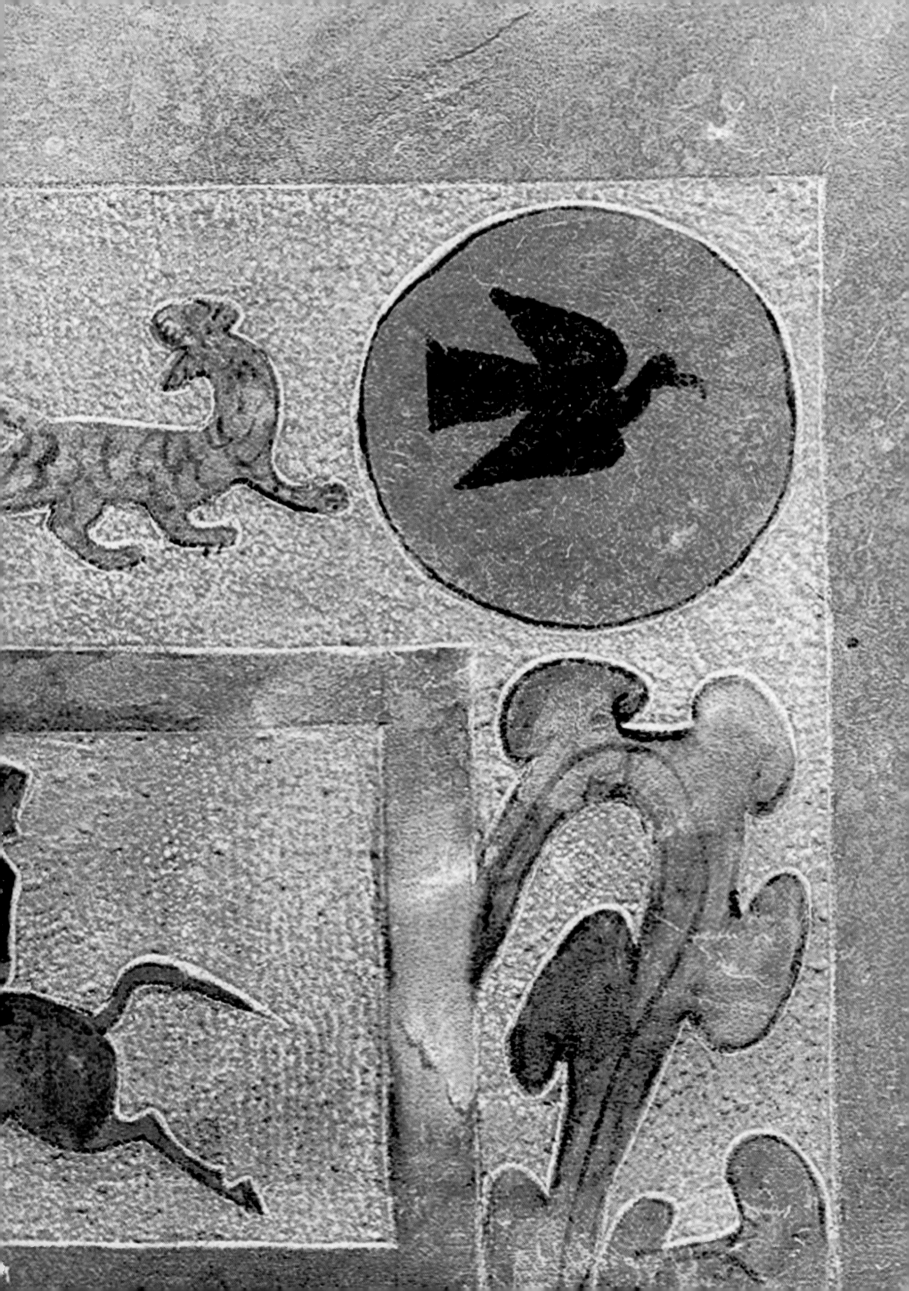

The splendour of the early empire

Liu Bang became the first emperor of the Han dynasty. He established his capital at Chang'an, and shared power with seven kings as a reward for their support. These privileges were abolished by his successors to reinforce central power. The greatest of the twelve emperors who ruled the empire in the early part of the dynasty, the Western Han, was Wudi. He ruled for 54 years, and during his reign the empire enjoyed immense prosperity. Major reforms and important civil engineering works created great affluence; the borders of the empire were extended in all directions, and Chinese influence reached Western regions along the Silk Route, which promoted trade and exchanges between different cultures. The arts and sciences flourished. During the second part of the dynasty, however, the gradual extension of large estates impoverished the peasant masses. Wang Mang rose in opposition, seized power in AD 9 and founded the short-lived Xin dynasty. He abolished land ownership and redistributed the land to the peasants. A few years later, in AD 25, the Han dynasty was restored by Liu Xiu, a member of the Han imperial family. He established the capital at Luoyang and reintroduced a policy in favour of the aristocracy. The new dynasty, known as the Eastern Han dynasty, attempted to restore the fortunes of the empire. Periods of stability alternated with periods of economic and social crisis. Child emperors held the throne from AD 89 to 220. The bloody power struggles that broke out between the palace eunuchs and the dowager empresses generated riots and military repression, and inexorably led to the disintegration of the empire.

***Western Han dynasty
(206 BC–AD 9)
Xin dynasty (AD 9–24)
Eastern Han dynasty
(AD 25–220)***

The period of division

The fall of the Han dynasty in AD 220 was followed by a long period of decline and the disintegration of imperial institutions, which had serious economic and social consequences. Three kingdoms (Wei, Shu Han and Wu) emerged, and were united for a short period in AD 280 by Sima Yuan, a powerful general who took control of Wei and founded the Western Jin dynasty. Continual warfare allowed penetration by the semi-nomadic peoples who lived along the western and northern borders of the empire, whose military leaders aimed to achieve political dominance. The Sixteen Kingdoms period, from AD 304 to 439, was marked by a situation of territorial fragmentation and the prevalence of military commanders from non-Chinese races, such as the Xiongnu and Xianbei. The increasing influx of populations from the steppes of northern China led to an unstoppable exodus of Chinese peoples to the southern regions, where various dynasties ruled without managing to consolidate their political and military power. The Buddhist religion, which had entered China from India during the Han period and was received with great enthusiasm, especially by people who had recently immigrated, became widely practised during this period.

***Three Kingdoms period
(AD 220–280): Wei dynasty
(AD 220–265); Shu Han dynasty
(AD 221–263); Wu dynasty
(AD 222–280)
Western Jin dynasty
(AD 265–316)
Eastern Jin dynasty
(AD 316–420)***

The northern and southern dynasties

By the 5th century AD, the process of integration between barbarian and Chinese peoples and between northern and southern regions was a fait accompli, aided partly by the rapid spread of the Buddhist religion, which had achieved great popularity. The first cave temples date from this period. The Tuoba, a population of Xianbei origin, settled in Shaanxi and founded the Northern Wei dynasty, which gradually extended its power to the whole of northern China, assimilating local customs. Land was redistributed to the peasants and the central administration strengthened. After AD 493, when the capital was transferred to Luoyang, the Tuoba population were actively encouraged to assimilate Chinese customs. Some of the aristocracy refused to support this policy and rebelled, bringing an end to a period of relative stability. In AD 535 there was a split between the Western Wei kingdom – where an attempt was made to restore Tuoba customs – and the Eastern Wei kingdom, which favoured integration. The Western Wei dynasty was succeeded by the Northern Zhou. The latter were overthrown by Yang Jian, a member of a powerful family of warriors from the north, who conquered the southern provinces in a successful military campaign and reunified the empire, founding the Sui dynasty.

***Northern dynasties
(AD 386–581): Northern Wei
(AD 386–534); Western Wei
(AD 535–557); Eastern Wei
(AD 534–550); Northern Zhou
(AD 557-581); Northern Qi
(AD 550–577)
Southern dynasties
(AD 420–589): Liu Song (AD
420–479); Southern Qi
(AD 479–501); Southern Liang
(AD 502–556);
Chen (AD 557–589)***

The renaissance and splendour of the second empire

The Sui dynasty promoted agricultural and tax reforms and undertook major irrigation schemes, thus beginning the reorganization of the empire. However, some unsuccessful military campaigns and the excessively luxurious court life brought about its fall. It was followed by the Tang dynasty, which gave the empire 21 rulers. They included Taizong, a man of great political ability, who favoured the unrestricted spread of Confucianism, Buddhism and Daoism. He perfected the administration, boosted trade and the economy and extended the borders of the empire, exerting great cultural influence over the neighbouring populations. Under his rule the empire was restored to its previous glories. The capital Chang'an became a magnificent city, with no fewer than 2 million inhabitants. On Taizong's death empress Wu Zhao deposed her own sons, and became the only woman ever to hold the Chinese throne, under the name Wu Zetian. Her successors included emperor Xuanzong, who reinforced the central power, promoted an efficient ruling class and encouraged culture and civil and religious tolerance. However, his enlightened policies did not prevent some military defeats, which limited China's influence in central Asia and along the Silk Route. Central power gradually weakened, to the advantage of the military governorates. A period of religious persecution took place, during which the great estates of the Buddhist monasteries were confiscated. Despite the happy interlude of Xuanzong's reign, the decline of the dynasty was inevitable, and rebellions and violence continually broke out. The last Tang emperor, Aidi, was deposed in AD 907.

***Sui dynasty (AD 581–618)
Tang dynasty (AD 618–907)***

CIVILIZATION AND CULTURE IN ANCIENT CHINA

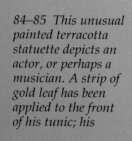

84–85 This unusual painted terracotta statuette depicts an actor, or perhaps a musician. A strip of gold leaf has been applied to the front of his tunic; his exaggerated headdress (yingwu) and thick false beard were the props sometimes used by musicians and actors to add an exotic touch to their performances. [Tang]

RELIGION

The Jesuits who visited 'the Middle Kingdom' to preach the Christian gospel conveyed to Westerners the image of a land inhabited by people who were not devoutly religious, but who were governed by wise philosophers. This was misleading, as it overlooked the strong religious feeling that had pervaded Chinese society since time immemorial. The earliest human settlements in China contain objects and images that are clearly linked with beliefs in deities and the world of spirits.

Burial practices indicate that a complex system of beliefs, ceremonies and rituals existed in the Neolithic. Tools and vessels containing food and drink were buried with the deceased to meet his or her needs in the next world. The grave goods in the richest tombs featured allusions to spirits and deities believed to inhabit a world parallel to that of the

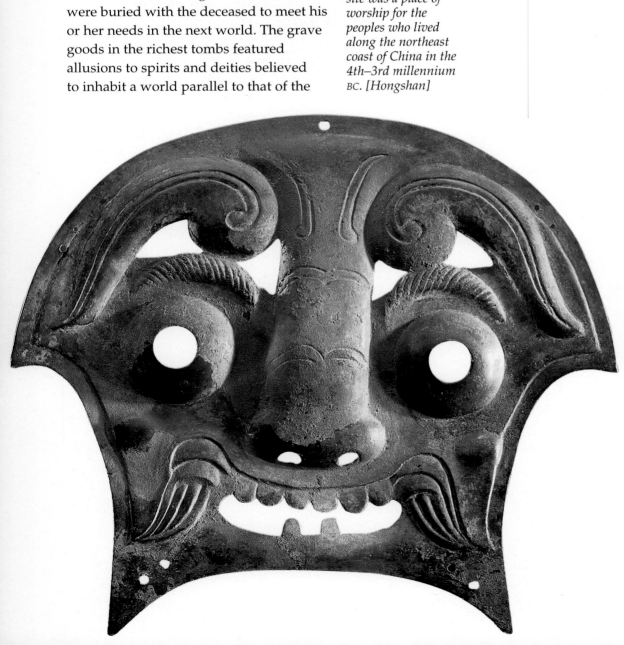

86 (above) This head of unfired clay with jade eyes may represent a goddess to whom an important temple in a religious complex at Niuheliang was dedicated. The site was a place of worship for the peoples who lived along the northeast coast of China in the 4th–3rd millennium BC. [Hongshan]

living. Numerous items of jewelry and objects of jade, often decorated with mysterious human and animal masks and probably intended to protect the deceased against evil spirits, were placed next to the body. Temples have been found at Dongshanzui and Niuheliang (Liaoning), containing evidence for a link between political power and shamanic rites.

From the Neolithic period, a system of kinship involving an extensive network of lineages guaranteed strong cohesion within the dominant clans. Society was animated by a constant rivalry to achieve supremacy and the need for material resources to maintain it. Political power and religious authority coincided perfectly, the former being subordinated to the shamanic powers deriving from the latter. The form of government of the Shang dynasty was emblematic in this respect, based as it was on the strict observance of rules sanctioned by the kinship system and on a close association between political prerogatives and ritual duties. Behind this lay the conviction that instructions for the conduct of human life would be received from another world inhabited by deities and the spirits of the ancestors. Those who had access to that world received the mandate to rule. The

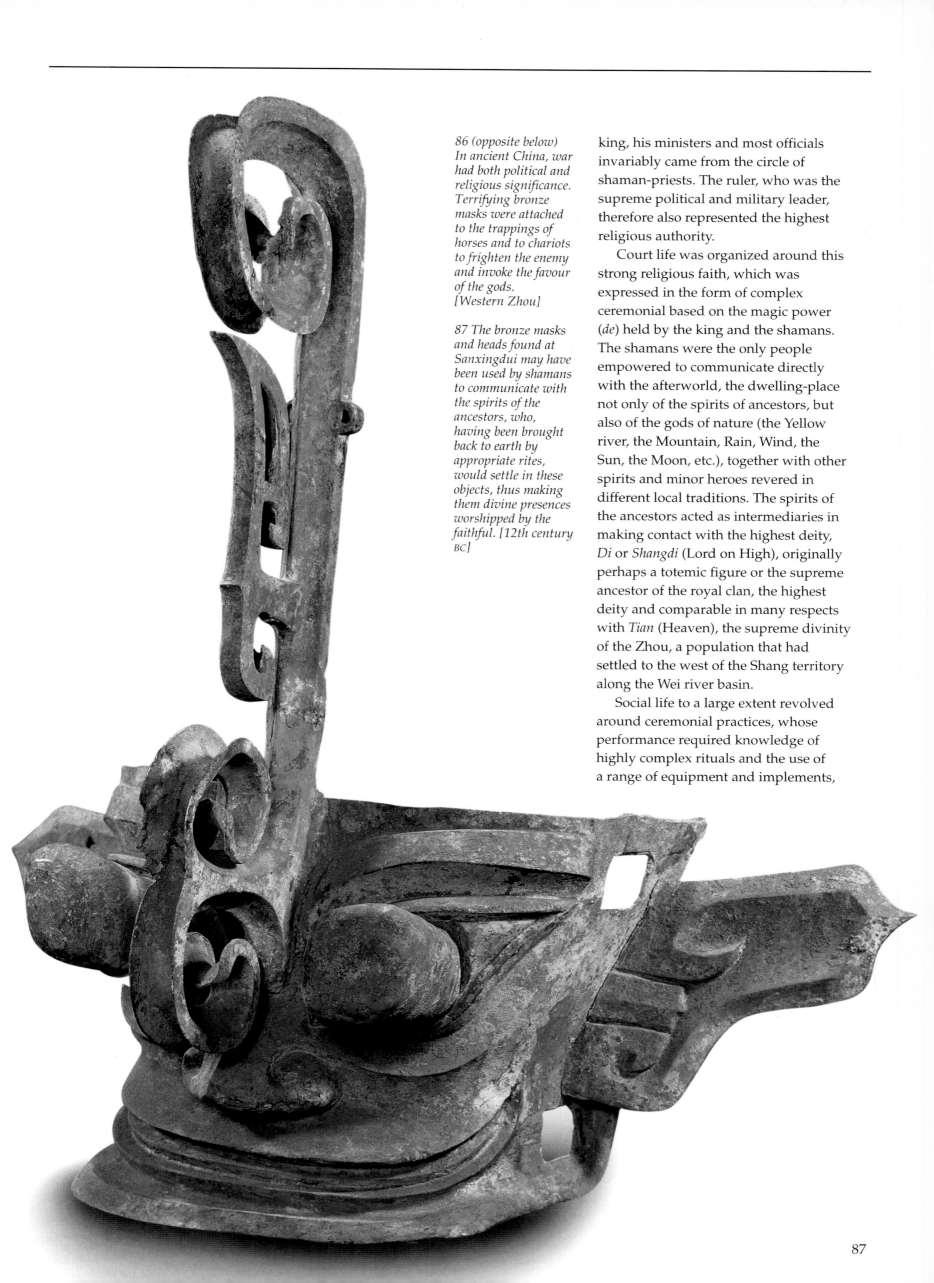

86 (opposite below)
86 (opposite below) In ancient China, war had both political and religious significance. Terrifying bronze masks were attached to the trappings of horses and to chariots to frighten the enemy and invoke the favour of the gods. [Western Zhou]

87 The bronze masks and heads found at Sanxingdui may have been used by shamans to communicate with the spirits of the ancestors, who, having been brought back to earth by appropriate rites, would settle in these objects, thus making them divine presences worshipped by the faithful. [12th century BC]

king, his ministers and most officials invariably came from the circle of shaman-priests. The ruler, who was the supreme political and military leader, therefore also represented the highest religious authority.

Court life was organized around this strong religious faith, which was expressed in the form of complex ceremonial based on the magic power (*de*) held by the king and the shamans. The shamans were the only people empowered to communicate directly with the afterworld, the dwelling-place not only of the spirits of ancestors, but also of the gods of nature (the Yellow river, the Mountain, Rain, Wind, the Sun, the Moon, etc.), together with other spirits and minor heroes revered in different local traditions. The spirits of the ancestors acted as intermediaries in making contact with the highest deity, *Di* or *Shangdi* (Lord on High), originally perhaps a totemic figure or the supreme ancestor of the royal clan, the highest deity and comparable in many respects with *Tian* (Heaven), the supreme divinity of the Zhou, a population that had settled to the west of the Shang territory along the Wei river basin.

Social life to a large extent revolved around ceremonial practices, whose performance required knowledge of highly complex rituals and the use of a range of equipment and implements,

88 (left) On this
bronze wine vessel a
shaman places his
head in the mouth of
a feline creature which
perhaps acted as an
intermediary,
allowing the shaman
to make the journey to
the afterlife, where he
could communicate
with the ancestors of
the royal clan and
other deities. [Shang]
88–89 This bronze
monster with silver
damascening may
represent the oldest
portrayal of the bixie,
the mythical winged
feline believed to
overcome evil.
[Eastern Zhou,
Warring States]

mostly made of jade and bronze.
The large-scale production of objects
manufactured with increasing skill from
these materials was therefore closely
linked with religious considerations.

In this respect, Chinese art of the
Neolithic and early Bronze Age periods
can be seen as the expression of the
relationship between the ruling class and
the divine sphere, while the practice of
shamanism – the prerogative of the ruler
and his clan – was a tool of government.
Divination was extremely important as it
was the means by which the shamans
communicated with the next world to
obtain advice on the decisions to be taken
in court affairs. The questions to be asked
of the deities were incised on animal
bones and the undershells of tortoises,
which were then exposed to great heat.
Interpretation of the cracks caused by the
heat determined the answers, which were
carefully transcribed on the bones. The
court scribes filed these documents in
archives, many of which have survived.
Other important elements of the rituals

were animal sacrifices, songs, dances, and offerings of food and drink in special vessels. Wine was drunk by the shamans during the ceremonies to aid them in achieving the state of trance required for divination. The animals portrayed on Shang and Zhou bronzes have been interpreted as the intermediaries used by the shamans to ascend to heaven and communicate with ancestors and deities.

When Wu, king of Zhou, overthrew the Shang dynasty, he claimed legitimacy for his deed because he held the favour of *Tian*, the deity worshipped by the Zhou,

whose will he would interpret and carry out. The Zhou believed that this supreme deity, who had been revered by them before the conquest of the Shang, resided in the celestial firmament (*tian*), with which he was identified. Some elements of Shang religion were accepted and absorbed by Zhou culture, including the worship of *Shangdi*, who was venerated by the Zhou in the same way as *Tian*.

The figure of *Shangdi* underwent a radical change, losing direct links with the royal family. A clear division was thus created between the divine sphere and the world of the ancestors. Equally, the *de* no longer represented the magic force that allowed communication with the other world, but became a sort of moral force

considered indispensable to implement the Way of Heaven (*Tian dao*).

Heaven, the source of cosmic order and the supreme entity, soon acquired the status of an impartial, omnipresent judge, capable of giving moral guidance to rulers and men alike. The king, known as *Tian zi* (Son of Heaven), became *Tian's* representative on earth. He ruled by virtue of the Mandate of Heaven (*Tian ming*), which could be revoked if his conduct proved unworthy. This cause could be used to legitimize the overthrow of a dynasty by force of arms (and was invoked for this purpose many times over the centuries); if the ruler was inept and corrupt, and devoid of *de*, Heaven, angered and disappointed, would manifest its annoyance, first by sending warning signals such as floods, famine and misfortunes, and then by revoking the Mandate of the sovereign and his family to reign, and giving it to the head of another clan who had proved to possess the necessary *de*.

The Mandate of Heaven was not an inalienable right; on the contrary, it was constantly subject to the judgment of Heaven, which thus maintained its control over the actions of rulers. Heaven and sovereign thus constituted a single

89 (right) The image of tigers with a man's head in their jaws forms the menacing motif on this bronze yue axe, and testifies to the power and authority of its owner. It was used as the royal insignia, and the central section is engraved with the name of queen Fu Hao. [Shang]

entity. The king's orders were therefore identified with the commands of Heaven, as the former fulfilled the latter's will; disobeying and rebelling against one inevitably meant contradicting the wishes of the other. The identification of Heaven with the figure of the sovereign permanently established the political authority of the new dynasty.

The institutional apparatus of the Shang period, based on a rigid political-religious structure, had undergone sweeping changes in the Zhou dynasty. The king now ruled over a kind of feudal organization; although the crucial importance of kinship and family cults was maintained, much of his authority was based on a set of ritual rules and the principle of hereditary succession – not only for political office but also in administrative and social appointments. In addition, the ceremonial forms of the Shang period were gradually modified.

Divination with animal bones and tortoise shells was largely abandoned, and increasing importance was attributed to the strict performance of rituals, the rules that governed them and the paraphernalia that made religious rites more solemn. In time, ritual regulations were extended to spheres other than the strictly ceremonial, until they became a code of political and social conduct.

The first phase of the dynasty was characterized by a period of peace and relative well-being, but this situation inexorably declined, until it became little more than a memory. In the Warring States period, the precarious status quo gradually deteriorated. Heaven showed no further sign of benevolence towards the king, and the inability of the rulers to guarantee social order jeopardized the image of a supreme entity that intervened in the destiny of man. Its will became incomprehensible and unpredictable, and

91 Followers of Daoism firmly believed in the existence of immortals. The earliest references to these mysterious supernatural beings date from the Eastern Zhou dynasty, but their popularity was greatest during the Han period. [Eastern Han]

91 (below) The Queen Mother of the West is shown here in a carriage flying above mountains among floating clouds and celestial flowers, driven by an Immortal and drawn by three great phoenixes. Other fantastic creatures, some winged and others carried by phoenixes, accompany her on her journey. [Western Wei]

a kind of religious scepticism pervaded society. Numerous philosophical movements developed, all of which aimed to counter the political, moral and ideological confusion with spiritual values that could form the basis of a new order. Confucianism and Daoism were to prove crucial to the development of a fresh religious sentiment.

At first, Confucianism and Daoism were more like philosophical doctrines than religious systems, representing two ways of viewing life and humanity's relationship with nature and the community. The Confucian school endeavoured to restore social and political harmony, proposing ethical values and models that were said to have formed the basis for the good government of the legendary pre-dynastic rulers and the first Zhou kings.

Inspired by an idealized golden age, Confucius and his disciples had little interest in the shamanic practices and religious beliefs prevalent during the Zhou period. Although they maintained an attitude of reverential respect for Heaven and all forms of ritual, the Confucians attributed the highest importance to kinship, family rites and sacrifices in honour of the ancestors. The family was considered the

92 *A powerful, disquieting demon is depicted on this terracotta tile, which probably decorated the wall of a pagoda.* [Tang]

93 (opposite above) *Chinese craftsmen displayed great imagination in the portrayal of the guardians who defended important tombs. This pair of winged monsters, with a particularly terrifying appearance, are a magnificent example of their creativity.* [Tang]

cornerstone of society. Instruction on the values of the past, culture and a commitment to improve oneself were considered the essential tools for the moral progress of the individual and the formation of a genuine social conscience, needed to create order and harmony.

The Daoist school has traditionally been divided into two currents of thought: philosophical and religious, though this distinction seems more theoretical than real, and is difficult to delineate. Daoists were more interested in the individual than in society. They viewed man as just one of the infinite number of beings in creation, and did not place him at the centre of the universe. They despised Confucian values, and

aspired to a simple existence devoid of ambition, in which they could live in contemplation and perfect harmony with nature, preferably having little to do with society. To perceive the profound meaning and participate in the true value of the Dao ('the way'), the original cosmic force, it was pointless to exert oneself or study in the illusion of improving oneself; what was needed was a mystical life which every individual would be capable of once liberated from the conditioning and constraints of the physical world.

Daoism was thus a doctrine of individual salvation, which aimed to lead its followers towards immortality, partly through techniques involving diet, ecstasy, respiratory and sexual health and

alchemy. While Confucians abhorred shamanic practices and attributed no particular importance to the world of the spirits and the beliefs connected with it, Daoists were interested in all traditions handed down by popular religions.

Archaeological discoveries made in the last few decades offer important and surprising evidence of the religious beliefs of the late Zhou dynasty and early imperial period. They testify to the devotion manifest in every walk of life, and the complexity of traditions.

Funerary art displays the conviction that there were a number of parallel worlds populated not only by evil demons, but also by deified mythological figures, auspicious animals and hybrid

creatures with strong apotropaic powers. The adoption of Confucianism as the official doctrine of the empire during the reign of Wudi of the Western Han dynasty hastened the decline in the importance of religious rituals. The evolved form of Confucianism was no longer viewed as the antithesis of Daoism, nor was it considered unusual for Confucian officials who were integrated into the civil service to cultivate ideas and attitudes of clear Daoist inspiration in private or after retiring from public life.

With the gradual degeneration of the economic and social situation, large sectors of the population felt the need for spiritual comfort. Thus numerous politico-religious communities were formed, sometimes associated with secret sects that fomented riots and revolts. Towards the end of the Eastern Han dynasty, the movements known as the Yellow Turbans, the Way of Great Peace and the Heavenly Masters (also known as the Five Pecks of Rice movement), all of Daoist inspiration, prophesied the return of a mythical golden age. During ceremonies, people publicly confessed

their sins, amid scenes of mystical exaltation, denouncing them as the cause of sickness and adversity.

A further development took place after the fall of the first empire, when discontent spread among intellectuals disillusioned with Confucianism which, though it had dominated society, had proved unable to prevent institutional, material and spiritual collapse. The alternative represented by the various movements within the Daoist school began to gain ground. Many decided to retreat from the world, rejecting all forms of social commitment and participation, to rediscover the pleasure of the contemplation of philosophy, music, poetry and painting as an end in itself. The School of Pure Debate (*Qingtan*) and the School of the Study of Mysteries (*Xuanxue*) were of this type. The occult arts, dietary, breathing, sexual and meditation techniques, and alchemistic practices aimed at discovering the elixir of immortality, all attracted new interest.

The development of Daoism and the profound ideological crisis that followed the collapse of the unity of the empire

94 This seated gilt-bronze bodhisattva is a magnificent example of the naturalistic style that flourished towards the end of the 8th century AD. The clinging garments feature particularly complex drapery, and numerous elegant jewels adorn every part of the body. [Tang]

encouraged the spread of a new religion, Buddhism, which had been introduced into China from India during the 1st century. At first, Buddhism was perceived as a doctrine similar to Daoism; to make converts, missionaries used Daoist terminology and tried to emphasize the similarities rather than the differences between the two doctrines.

Both the Mahāyāna (Great Vehicle) and the Hīnayāna (Small Vehicle) schools were soon popular with the élite of the north and south. The Mahāyāna school attracted the largest number of followers, especially after it developed into an indigenous variation of Buddhism influenced by Chinese cultural values. In addition to speculations of great complexity, doctrinal elements that were easily comprehended by the mass of the less educated and more pragmatic acolytes were developed. For example, nirvana, the state of eternal beatitude, was described as a celestial paradise which could be entered by uttering the name of Buddha Amitābha on one's deathbed.

Buddhism reached the height of its glory during the first two centuries of the Tang dynasty, when it spread all over the empire, inspiring considerable religious fervour among the population and obtaining the benevolence of the court. But in 843–845 emperor Wuzong, a mad fanatic obsessed by the search for the elixir of immortality, ordered the destruction of thousands of temples and monasteries of various religions, but primarily Buddhist, and confiscated much property and land. Over 200,000 monks and nuns were forced out of their orders, including thousands of Nestorians and Zoroastrians (these religions, along with Manicheism, Islam and perhaps Judaism had been introduced into China centuries earlier, and were mainly professed by the foreign communities).

Numerous schools of Buddhist inspiration flourished over the centuries. Among them were the Tantric school of the True Word (Zhenyan) and the schools known as Tiantai (Tiantiajiao), Pure Land (Qingtujiao), Three Stages (Sanjejiao) and Chan Meditation (Zen in Japanese), which undoubtedly represented the most original expression of Chinese Buddhism. Religious literature of Indian and Chinese origin underwent extensive

the Western Paradise; Mañjuśrī, the bodhisattva of wisdom; and the bodhisattva Avalokiteśvara (Guanyin), who embodied redeeming compassion.

The development of Buddhism influenced Daoism in organizational as well as purely doctrinal terms. In the 5th century, Master Kou Qianzhi (died 448) tried in vain to have Buddhism made the state religion. Later, the popularity of Buddhism and Daoism, together with the need to restate Confucian doctrine as the ideological basis for the restoration of imperial institutions, produced a new situation. A syncretist ideology emerged, combining elements of all three doctrines – Confucianism, Buddhism and Daoism.

95 (left) The Buddha Sākyamuni presents his teachings to Prabhūtaratna, the former Buddha: a gilt-bronze composition, dating from 518. In keeping with the style popular in Longmen in the 6th century, the characters are rather basic, with lean features, and are enveloped in ample clothing. They almost seem to disappear into the great flaming haloes above their heads. [Northern Wei]

95 (below left) This Sākyamuni Buddha, portrayed in a meditative position with hands together, bears an inscription which dates the statue to 338, making it the oldest known gilt-bronze Chinese sculpture to portray Buddha. [Northern Wei]

development. The acquisition of original Sanskrit texts from India and their translation into Chinese was a huge task, in which thousands of Indian and Chinese monks, pilgrims and acolytes participated from the 3rd century on.

The Buddhist pantheon comprised a wide variety of deities, Buddhas and bodhisattvas – people who have achieved enlightenment but choose to remain in the world to help others on the difficult path to sanctity instead of reaching eternal beatitude and sharing in nirvana.

Extensive evidence of popular worship is offered by the numerous depictions of deities in cave-temples scattered all over northern China, a wide variety of religious paintings and a wealth of sculptures. The most popular deities were Maitreya, the Buddha of the future, the expected saviour of humanity who would bring peace and justice and the favourite disciple of Sākyamuni, the historical figure of Buddha, often portrayed with his right hand raised, palm outwards, to indicate comfort and blessing, and his left hand lowered in the act of giving; Amitābha, the Buddha who presided over

LIFE AFTER DEATH: GRAVE GOODS FOR THE NEXT WORLD

96 The tradition of placing small jade ornaments on the body of the deceased dates from the Neolithic. From the Zhou period, the jades were arranged to create designs with magical or religious significance. The pieces shown here were sewn on the shroud covering the face of the deceased. [Western Zhou]

The wealth of grave goods found in China in the tombs of aristocrats and rulers is both evidence of the practice of paying homage to the deceased with honours worthy of their rank, and a reflection of the belief that life did not end with death. In the millennia that separated the Neolithic from the Tang dynasty, various religious and philosophical beliefs were held at different times. The complex iconographic repertoire of grave goods changed correspondingly, providing archaeologists with a great deal of information about beliefs relating to the afterlife in the various periods.

Grave goods and tombs discovered in the last few decades have revealed unexpected symbolic references and religious themes, many of which are not found in written texts. The literal and allegorical meanings of ancient Chinese funerary art are not always apparent to modern eyes, nor is it easy to trace the lines of development or define similarities and differences. However, a reliable overall picture can be outlined.

During the Neolithic period, tombs were merely pits dug in the ground. In some, tools and pottery vessels containing the food and drink needed by the deceased in the next world were placed next to the body. The remains of lacquered wooden coffins and numerous jade objects have been found in burials of the Liangzhu culture. Plaques, pearls and pendants were placed around the head of the deceased, *congs* – quadrangular blocks with a cylindrical hole running through them – on the chest, *bi* discs on the lower part of the body, and ceremonial axes on either side. The discovery of skeletons and jades showing clear traces of burning seems to indicate the practice of cremation or the existence of sacrificial rites. The bronze and jade objects found in the sacrificial pits of Sanxingdui (Sichuan), dating from the 12th century BC, had been deliberately smashed and burnt before being buried.

In the eastern cultures of the late Neolithic and during the pre-imperial

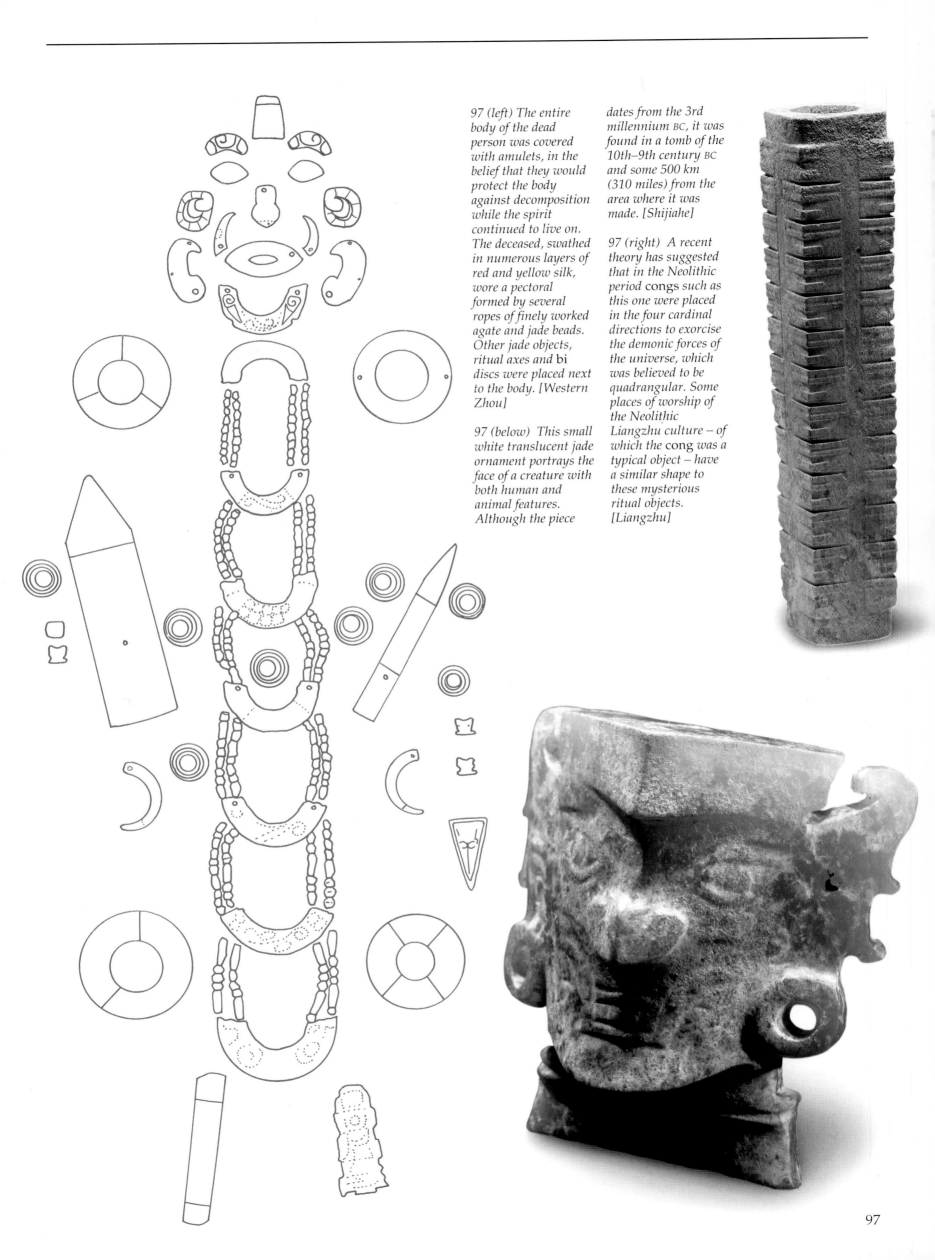

97 (left) The entire body of the dead person was covered with amulets, in the belief that they would protect the body against decomposition while the spirit continued to live on. The deceased, swathed in numerous layers of red and yellow silk, wore a pectoral formed by several ropes of finely worked agate and jade beads. Other jade objects, ritual axes and bi discs were placed next to the body. [Western Zhou]

97 (below) This small white translucent jade ornament portrays the face of a creature with both human and animal features. Although the piece dates from the 3rd millennium BC, it was found in a tomb of the 10th–9th century BC and some 500 km (310 miles) from the area where it was made. [Shijiahe]

97 (right) A recent theory has suggested that in the Neolithic period congs such as this one were placed in the four cardinal directions to exorcise the demonic forces of the universe, which was believed to be quadrangular. Some places of worship of the Neolithic Liangzhu culture – of which the cong was a typical object – have a similar shape to these mysterious ritual objects. [Liangzhu]

period, the royal tombs were large
enough to hold great quantities of objects
and numerous sacrificial victims. The
grave containing the coffin was
surrounded by a stepped platform or
tiered terrace (*ercengtai*) on which the
burial goods were placed. Some of the
Shang royal tombs were very large, with
a depth of over 20 m (66 ft) and an area of
over 2,500 sq. m (26,910 sq. ft). Many had
access ramps, with major ones aligned
north–south, and secondary ones
east–west. The body, in a inner coffin,
a wooden sarcophagus (*guan*), inside a
outer coffin which served as the funeral
chamber (*guo*), also made of wood, was
placed in the centre of the tomb.

All around lay the bodies of those
whose duty it would be to assist and
defend their lord in the afterlife: relatives,
servants and soldiers. There was also
another category of sacrificial victims –
slaves and prisoners of war, who were
equated with animal victims. They were
usually bound and decapitated, and were
sometimes buried in external pits placed
around the perimeter of the main tomb.

It seems that the belief that after death
the deceased could maintain the same
social position and enjoy the same
privileges as during life was widely held
from the Neolithic on. For this reason

their most valuable possessions were
buried with them. Grave goods could
amount to veritable treasure troves, such
as the 7,000 cowrie shells found in the
inner coffin of queen Fu Hao of the
Shang dynasty, together with 755 jade
objects; this was the largest jade hoard
ever found. Cowrie shells were not yet
used as currency, but gave their owner
great prestige since their use was
restricted to the ritual sphere.

From the Eastern Zhou period, it was
common practice to construct tombs of
the nobility to resemble magnificent
dwellings. The funeral chamber (*guo*)
was enlarged, and other chambers were
added, each with a different purpose and
all interconnected so that they would be
accessible to the occupants of the tomb-
dwelling. The practice of reproducing
homes and palaces on a small scale, and
sometimes adding pits to contain the
grave goods, developed to an even
greater extent in later centuries, when the
imperial mausoleums were built.

The most important tomb complexes
were covered with mounds of earth or
wooden constructions which probably
acted as ancestral temples, surrounded
by parks and protective walls. The
impressive tomb of Qin Shihuangdi, a
grandiose manifestation of his power or

*98–99 (above) Each
of these figures, with
a human body and
an animal head,
represents a sign of
the Chinese zodiac.
They are the horse,
the goat, the monkey,
the rooster, the dog,
the boar, the rat, the
ox, the tiger, the
rabbit, the dragon and
the snake. [Tang]*

*98–99 (below) The
many treasures found
in the tomb discovered
at Mawangdui in
1973 include this
delightful painted
wooden orchestra.
[Western Han]*

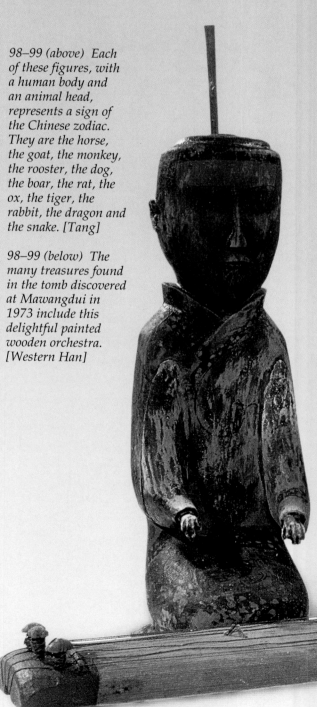

100 (above) The
magnificent pillow on
which the head of
prince Liu Sheng rests
is 44.1 cm (17 in)
long. Large, finely

incised jade plates are
set in the gilt-bronze
frame; a support of
ash wood was
inserted inside it.
[Western Han]

100–101 It is
estimated that it
would have taken at
least ten years for a
specialist craftsman
to make a suit of jade
such as this. Over 40
such funerary
garments have been

found so far in tombs
dating from the Han
period, the most
famous being the one
belonging to prince
Liu Sheng. Jade
amulets closed the
body's orifices.
[Western Han]

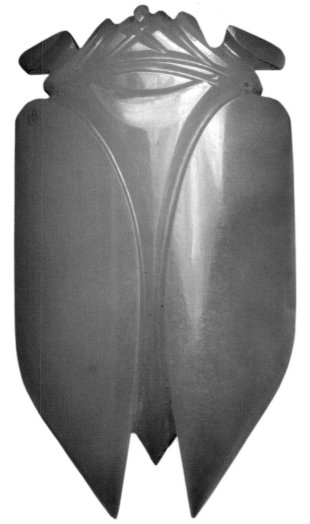

101 (below) Jade amulets placed in the mouth of the deceased often took the form of a cicada, which symbolized the continuance of life after death. [Western Han]

perhaps his megalomania, was designed to recreate the most favourable conditions for the afterlife of the First August Emperor. Stables with horses, bronze chariots to carry the emperor to the land of the Immortals and a huge terracotta army in fighting array were all elements in the ambitious project of reconstructing the empire in the tomb.

The significance attributed to bronze vessels and the rituals connected with them were now in decline. Grave goods no longer consisted solely of objects that indicated the social status of the deceased and the equipment needed to perform the ceremonial functions prescribed by his rank (*jiqi*, 'sacrificial vessels'). They now also included his personal effects (*shengqi*, 'articles of daily life'). There were two forms of human sacrifice, one performed specifically as a sacrificial offering (*rensheng*, 'human offerings') and one which involved immolating people devoted to the deceased, who would accompany and serve them in the afterlife (*renxun*, 'companions in eternity'). Both practices were gradually abandoned from the 5th century BC, and small statues made of wood, terracotta or stone, called *mingqi* ('spirit articles') or *guiqi* ('articles for the ghosts'), were placed in the tombs instead of human victims.

The gradual adoption of this practice led to the final disappearance of human sacrifice. The *mingqi* had great symbolic value; they included models of buildings, rural scenes, and the vessels and musical instruments essential for ceremonies and rituals, usually made of painted terracotta but sometimes of bronze. Terracotta was the material most commonly used in northern China, especially at Qin, while wood was preferred by the craftsmen of the central and southern regions, especially Chu. The *mingqi* of the Han and Tang dynasties are particularly attractive.

In the imperial period, funerary art reflected rapidly evolving religious beliefs. A dualist concept, which held that a person possessed a spiritual soul (*hun*) destined to return to Heaven after death and a bodily soul (*po*) destined to return to earth, was associated with the growing belief in the existence of special beings who could escape death – the Immortals. It was also believed that eternal life could be achieved by taking substances that had the power to prolong life indefinitely, or by preserving the body against decomposition, thus allowing the bodily soul to survive.

Various expedients were used in the hope of achieving this aim; sometimes the body was buried in a number of coffins

102 The numerous glazed terracotta models of granaries, farms and fortresses made for funerary use in the Eastern Han and Three Kingdoms periods are an invaluable source of information about the architecture of the time, especially since none of the actual buildings have survived.
[Eastern Han]

102–103 In addition to the practice of placing statuettes of servants and courtiers in the tomb to assist and entertain their lord after his death, it was customary to reproduce places and rooms familiar to the deceased in the form of models.
[Three Kingdoms]

inserted inside one another; sometimes it was immersed in a special fluid or placed in a suit of jade (or similar material) or glass; and special plugs, mostly made of jade, were inserted in the orifices. The sumptuous grave goods, consisting of thousands of objects, served to prove the social status and wealth of the deceased, and were intended to be presented to a demanding, meticulous being that lived in the underworld and was responsible for accepting or rejecting the bodily soul of the deceased.

The image of a heavenly world above the earthly world, which in turn was separated from a dark underworld, is wonderfully represented in the magnificent funerary banner of Lady Xin Zhui of Dai (died 168 BC) found at Mawangdui, near Changsha (Hunan), which was laid on the lid of her coffin,

103 (left) This small gold-inlaid bronze pavilion containing two singers and four musicians playing their instruments dates from the 5th century BC, and is the oldest architectural model found to date. [Eastern Zhou, Warring States]

the innermost of a set of four. The painting shows the entire universe, inhabited by mythological figures and sacred animals, and describes the stages on the deceased's journey to immortality. A complex symbolism indicates the stages on the voyage of the spiritual soul and the bodily soul. The various moments of the ascent, the world of darkness, the funeral ceremony and heaven are portrayed on parallel horizontal planes, surrounded by the sinuous upward movement of perfectly symmetrical entwined dragons. The sky, with the sun and moon, is inhabited by deities and sacred animals also in a perfectly balanced composition.

To protect the deceased from demons and evil influences and help the spiritual soul on its difficult journey, the paintings on tomb walls and the decorations on funerary objects and lacquered coffins increasingly featured apotropaic images and pictures of deities like Nü Wa, the goddess who created the human race and could transform herself up to 70 times a day, or Xiwangmu, the Queen Mother of the West. Models of soldiers in battle array, austere guards and fierce, threatening heavenly guardians protected the tombs and the bodies.

Some typical examples are the terracotta guardians of the Tang period, glazed in three colours (*sancai*), sometimes portrayed in the act of subjugating monstrous demons. These creatures, often shown in pairs, are associated with the *lokapāla*, the protectors of the kingdom of the Buddhas found in cave temples. They sometimes appeared with hybrid creatures with a human or animal face, a fierce expression, a strong, winged torso and hooves.

104 and 105 The famous painted silk banner from tomb 1, Mawangdui, which illustrates the journey to immortality of the wife of the Marquis of Dai, was found on her coffin. It portrays the underworld (lower part), the earthly world (centre) and the celestial world (upper part), using complex and sometimes obscure symbols.

The dead woman is shown standing in the centre; her relations, kneeling around her, call on her soul to return to its former abode. At the sides are two great dragons, which act as intermediaries for the ascent to the celestial regions. Above them opens the door to the heavens, guarded by its faithful keeper, the bat. [Western Han]

106 (left) The cosmetics used by the ladies of the court to enhance their soft, full features can clearly be seen on the cheeks of this elegant female tomb figure of painted terracotta. [Tang]

106 (below) Figurative art often reflects the sometimes amused interest taken by the Chinese in foreign customs and the Western populations which they increasingly came into contact with. This merchant is portrayed with marked, somewhat stern features, riding his camel. [Tang]

ARCHITECTURE

108 (left) A model of a house of several storeys, which measures 132 cm (52 in) high, gives a good impression of the structure of Han buildings. The walls are painted and pitched roofs are supported on a complex system of brackets. [Eastern Han]

Only a few traces of ancient Chinese architecture have survived because buildings were mostly constructed of perishable materials. For centuries, structures consisted of wooden load-bearing frames filled with wear-resistant materials, with the result that all buildings from the pre-imperial period have disappeared, as have nearly all those of the imperial period before the Tang dynasty. Not even the magnificent royal palaces, frequently described in literature, which praised their grandiosity and beauty and their luxurious furnishings, have survived. Apart from a few stone or brick pagodas, built in the 6th/7th century, all that remain are the traces of a few buildings constructed before the end of the Tang dynasty. The most important are the Buddhist temple of Nanchansi (782), the oldest wooden building now surviving in China, and Foguangsi temple (857), both in the Wutan mountains (Shanxi).

108 (opposite below) Ancient buildings and palaces have not survived as they were built with perishable materials such as wood and rammed earth. As a result,

painted ceramic models from the Han period are an important source of information about the history of Chinese architecture. [Eastern Han]

108–109 Reconstruction of the 4th century BC Zhongshan royal palace, based on the gold design impressed on a huge bronze tray found in a tomb.

109 (bottom) Great landowners often built pavilions and follies on their estates to spend their leisure time in, such as this lake pavilion represented in a

detailed pottery model. Inside are dancers, musicians and singers, while four archers scan the horizon from the balcony. [Eastern Han]

Our knowledge of the buildings of the pre-imperial period is thus limited and fragmentary, though there are various sources of evidence which help to reconstruct the appearance of houses and settlements. Occasional references in literary works provide descriptions of palaces, while some pottery vessels and other objects are decorated with depictions of buildings. The most elaborate tombs retain architectural elements and contain miniature bronze or pottery models of houses and palaces among the grave goods. Also, enclosure walls, terraces and stone bases for pillars and columns have been found on some archaeological sites, and hinges, metal trimmings for portals and beams, and ceramic tiles have been discovered in

excavations. The foundations of large residential complexes and palatial structures dating from different periods enable archaeologists to reconstruct the structure of towns and villages.

It is thus possible to visualize the great wood and straw building that stood in the middle of the Neolithic village of Banpo (Yangshao), the palaces that sometimes cover over 10,000 sq. m (107,640 sq. ft) at Erlitou (Xia), Panlongcheng, Xiaotun and Zhengzhou (Shang), and the ceremonial pavilions built over Shang and Zhou royal tombs, surrounded by huge parks and high walls. The grandiose tomb of king Cuo of Zhongshan at Pingshan (Hebei), dating from 310 BC, is depicted on a bronze tray found in the tomb.

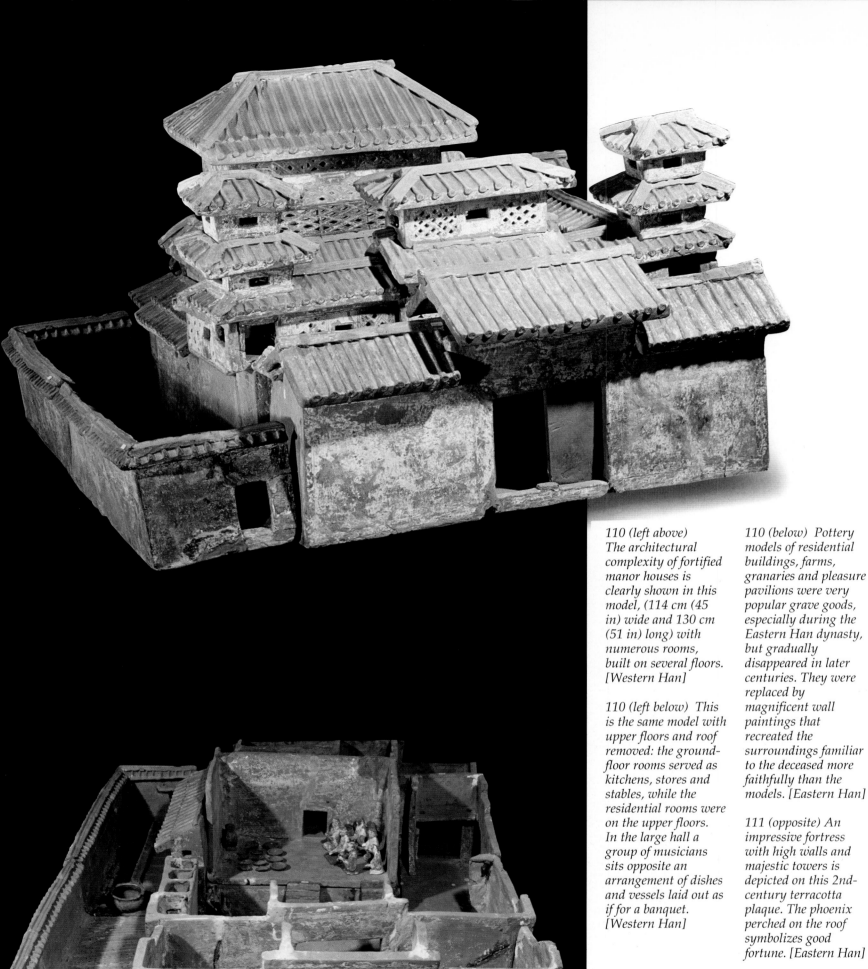

110 (left above) The architectural complexity of fortified manor houses is clearly shown in this model, (114 cm (45 in) wide and 130 cm (51 in) long) with numerous rooms, built on several floors. [Western Han]

110 (left below) This is the same model with upper floors and roof removed: the ground-floor rooms served as kitchens, stores and stables, while the residential rooms were on the upper floors. In the large hall a group of musicians sits opposite an arrangement of dishes and vessels laid out as if for a banquet. [Western Han]

110 (below) Pottery models of residential buildings, farms, granaries and pleasure pavilions were very popular grave goods, especially during the Eastern Han dynasty, but gradually disappeared in later centuries. They were replaced by magnificent wall paintings that recreated the surroundings familiar to the deceased more faithfully than the models. [Eastern Han]

111 (opposite) An impressive fortress with high walls and majestic towers is depicted on this 2nd-century terracotta plaque. The phoenix perched on the roof symbolizes good fortune. [Eastern Han]

At the Neolithic site of Banpo houses were built with sunken floors, while in the south they were built on stilts. From the 9th century BC thatched roofs, which covered several storeys and projected to allow rainwater to run off, were gradually replaced with flat or semicylindrical earthenware tiles. The wooden supporting structures were reinforced to carry the extra weight, and complex systems of brackets were used.

During the first empire there were major innovations in architecture, as reflected in buildings constructed in major cities. The houses of ordinary people remained modest, and still had thatched roofs, while the residences of the rich and the nobility were beginning to acquire the structure that was to remain unchanged in later centuries. Important buildings consisted of several elements and the wealthiest residential complexes were surrounded by courtyards, separated from one another by walls pierced by wide passageways. Majestic towers stood at the sides of the palace portals and on either side of the entrances to large estates. A great ceremonial hall, which formed part of the inner buildings, was oriented so that the main axis and the entrance aligned with the opening of the outer gate. Buildings of one or more storeys stood on either side of the hall. Pavilions and watch-towers up to four or five storeys high sometimes formed part of the complex. Buildings in cities were enclosed by walls, and were for both residential and government use.

The Han imperial palaces built at Chang'an and Luoyang were burnt down and destroyed before the end of the dynasty, but the remains of some Qin royal palaces built in Xianyang have been found, and the structure and appearance of one of them has been reconstructed.

In the imperial period, palaces consisted of various buildings erected on raised terraces of beaten earth or masonry, and were usually oriented on south–north axis, with the main façade facing south. The buildings were connected by raised, roofed corridors and passageways. Large wooden posts that acted as the load-bearing columns for the entire structure rested on stone bases positioned at regular intervals along the embankments. They supported finely decorated beams

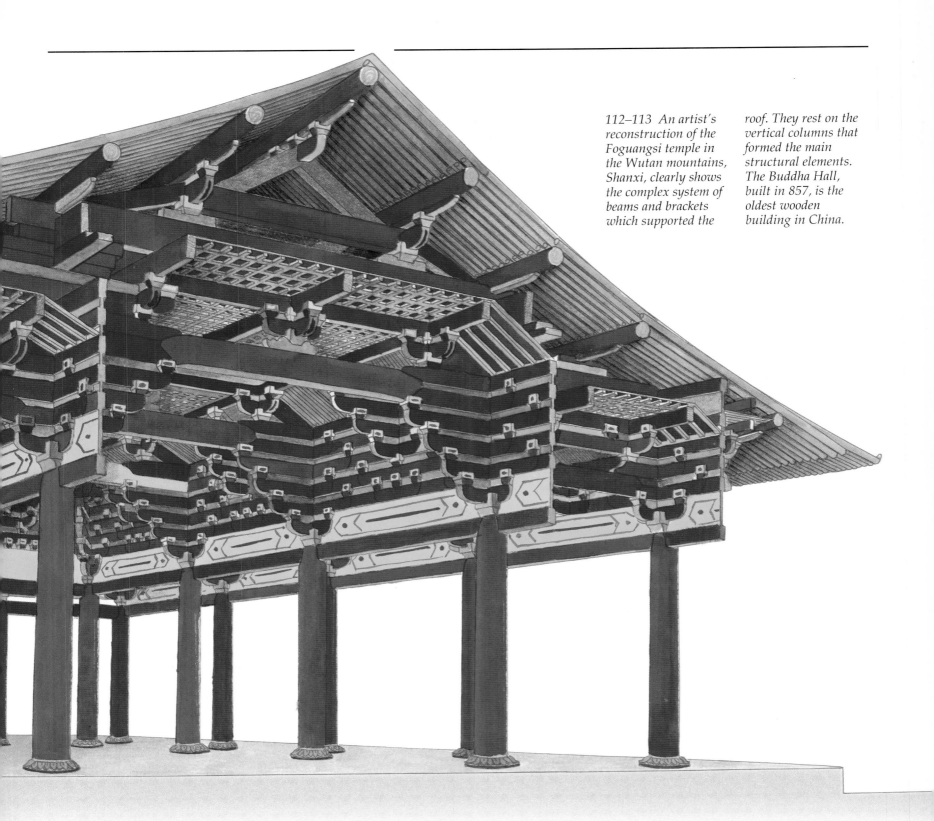

112–113 An artist's
reconstruction of the
Foguangsi temple in
the Wutan mountains,
Shanxi, clearly shows
the complex system of
beams and brackets
which supported the
roof. They rest on the
vertical columns that
formed the main
structural elements.
The Buddha Hall,
built in 857, is the
oldest wooden
building in China.

and a system of brackets for the roof. Tie-bars installed along the long axis of the building, from front to back, and mortise-and-tenon joints guaranteed the solidity and at the same time the elasticity of the whole structure.

Walls, which were not load-bearing but just partitions, were whitewashed, and usually painted with scenes of everyday life or mythological and geometric motifs similar to those used to decorate textiles and lacquerware. In the first empire the walls were sometimes made of hollow bricks, impressed or incised with geometric patterns or animal motifs. The columns themselves, painted in deep colours or lacquered, were sometimes draped with precious silk or taffeta in delicate colours. The floors were also plastered and painted or paved with well-crafted bricks.

The roofs, covered with ceramic tiles ending in a decorated drip moulding, rested on beams and pillars. Complicated systems of brackets (*dougong*), which became increasingly elaborate the more the beams projected out from the building, increased the span possible between the columns and improved the distribution of weight.

In the Tang dynasty, thanks to the introduction of ingenious architectural elements such as the *ang* (a long sloping bracket arm installed diagonally to the rest of the complex), the roof contour increasingly acquired the curved 'bird's wing' shape, which flourished in later Chinese and Far Eastern architecture.

112 (opposite, above left) The attractive decoration of this ceramic tile which would have adorned an eave beam demonstrates the care lavished on even the smallest details. [Qin]

112 (opposite, centre) Bronze hinges, door decorations and joints, the stone bases of columns, and ceramic tiles and water pipes are the only early architectural elements that have survived the ravages of time. [Western Zhou]

112 (opposite below left) This bronze joint plate is decorated with the 'coiled serpent' motif (pan she). The wooden beams were placed in the two open ends and secured with a wooden peg inserted in the central hole. [Qin]

112 (opposite below right) The relief decoration on this right-angled bronze joint for wooden beams is also a variation of the 'coiled serpent' motif. [Qin]

Historical accounts, works of literature and paintings describe and depict the lives of Chinese rulers and aristocrats, but very little is known of the customs of the ordinary people. Life at court and in the magnificent mansions of the nobility was strictly regulated by complex ritual codes, which not only established rules for the conduct of public and private ceremonies, but also prescribed correct behaviour within the family, laying down the appropriate conduct in all circumstances for each member of the huge clans.

Sumptuous furnishings provided an appropriate setting for this strict, solemn lifestyle. The palaces were great treasure-houses containing the products of exquisite workmanship created over the centuries by a multitude of craftsmen of exceptional talent and skill.

At the opposite social extreme, the humble dwellings of the vast majority of

114 (above left)
A pottery statuette of a peasant shows him with his spade and an iron-tipped wooden sword; this was used for everyday work in the fields but also served as a weapon in case of war, when huge numbers of peasants were conscripted. [Eastern Han]

114–115 (above)
In this painting the teachings of Buddha are symbolically represented by clouds swollen with beneficial rain, the source of life and prosperity for the peasants, who are shown both working and relaxing (Dunhuang, cave 23). [Tang]

114–115 (below) The ox-drawn cart was the most common vehicle for ordinary people, and was mainly used to transport agricultural products. As in all rural economies, the sale of part of the harvest and the animals reared, together with minor trades, contributed to the subsistence of the peasants. [Northern Dynasties]

115 (above) The monastic life included periods of intense agricultural activity. This painting, which depicts the various seasons of work in the fields, is one of a set of five frescoes that illustrate the Sutra of Maitreya (Dunhuang, cave 25). [Tang]

115 (below) From the Neolithic period, rice-growing was one of the most important agricultural activities in China. According to recent information, rice may first have been cultivated around the 7th millennium BC. This terracotta model from the Han period shows paddy fields irrigated by a stream. [Eastern Han]

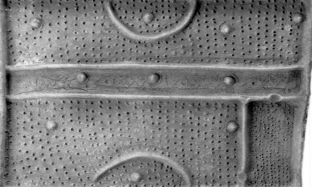

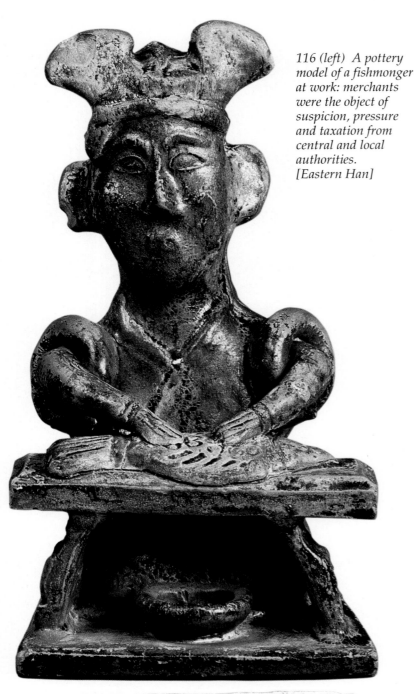

116 (left) A pottery model of a fishmonger at work: merchants were the object of suspicion, pressure and taxation from central and local authorities. [Eastern Han]

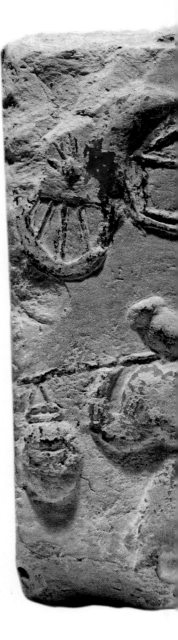

ordinary people huddled together on the edges of villages and towns, outside the area reserved for the huge residences of the nobility, large landowners and wealthy merchants.

Although our knowledge is still scanty in some respects, a general picture of the living conditions and occupations of the less wealthy classes can be obtained. For instance, in the last few decades archaeology has revealed more information about the evolution of trades and agriculture. Alongside the many innovations and inventions made by the Chinese over the centuries, traditional crafts such as jade working, with its highly sophisticated techniques handed down through the generations, persisted.

Chinese society evolved from the small farming communities of the Neolithic into true city-states, which grew and expanded until they formed kingdoms and principalities. Eventually, a huge empire was created; although its boundaries varied greatly over the centuries, its territory was always vast. Through time, the social gap between those who held political and religious power and the population they governed widened more and more. The difference between the wealth of the ruling classes and the poverty of the masses, decimated at intervals by famine and natural catastrophes, became immense, and it

remained so throughout the history of ancient China, until modern times. The homes of the majority of ordinary people were small, bare, sunken huts with thatched roofs, while the palaces and mansions of the aristocracy had immense roofs covered in magnificently decorated ceramic tiles.

The imperial cities grew to enormous size and a rigid social organization developed in parallel. One such city was Chang'an, one of the most densely populated cities in the ancient world, which was destroyed and rebuilt several times. During the Tang dynasty it was famous for its cosmopolitan nature and the magnificence of its buildings. With over a million people living within its walls (at least another million lived in the surrounding countryside), the city covered an area of over 80 sq. km (30 sq. miles). It was defended by impressive walls with watchtowers and 12 access gates, and was divided into 112 rectangular districts, each of which was surrounded by thick walls.

The roads intersected at right angles to form a perfectly rectangular grid. A huge

116 (opposite below) A scene of everyday life: a stallholder sells wine to a customer as a peasant goes by with his wheelbarrow, a Chinese invention. Taxes were levied on the sale of alcohol, guaranteeing large revenues for the imperial treasury. [Eastern Han]

116–117 (above) The stages in the making of alcohol are depicted on this painted ceramic tombstone. The dead person was presumably involved in making wine, and the relief was designed to facilitate the continuity of life after death. [Eastern Han]

117 (below) It is fairly unusual for models portraying settings or scenes from everyday life to be made of bronze, as is this statuette which portrays a peasant working at a grindstone. However, the presence of the tortoise, an auspicious animal, may suggest that the scene is mythological or has some symbolic significance, rather than being a direct representation of reality. [Han]

118–119 (above)
A scene from the
Saddharmapundarika
Sutra is depicted in
this fresco. The son of
a rich lord renounced
luxury in favour of a
period of poverty and
wandering. He later
agreed to work
incognito as a stable
boy in his father's
house. Only after 20
years' hard work did
he agree to become his
father's heir.
(Dunhuang, cave 85)
[Tang]

118 (left) Granaries, areas for rearing animals and living rooms on the upper floors are depicted in this terracotta farm. [Eastern Han]

main road led from the south gate to the imperial palace on the northern border of the city. For reasons of security, the gates to the city and to each district were closed at night, when it was strictly forbidden to walk the streets which were guarded by patrols of armed soldiers. Two huge government markets supplied all the goods needed by the population; the one in the eastern sector of the city was used by local merchants, and the one in the western sector by foreigners. According to contemporary sources, over 4,000 families from all over Asia lived in the city.

Much information about the everyday life of ordinary people comes from 'spirit articles' (*mingqi*) and grave figurines (*muyong*), large numbers of which have been found in the tombs of the rich. They include animal and human figures (peasants, servants, soldiers, acrobats, musicians) and models of arable and paddy fields, buildings for animals or trades (such as pigsties, kilns and grindstones), fish ponds, farmhouses and granaries, and tools of various kinds.

While the subjects painted on the walls of the tombs of the princes and dignitaries between the 5th and 10th centuries testify to the sophistication of court life –

depicting pastimes of the nobility with a wealth of detail – the pictorial repertoire of the preceding period (2nd century BC to 4th century AD) more often portrayed the activities of the common people, especially their work and leisure. There are some magnificent pictures of the tumblers, jugglers and acrobats who entertained people at local festivals. Scenes of work in the fields, a genuine expression of a more humble but certainly more immediate art, were often painted on the walls of rock temples.

119 Fish farming was very important to the economy of peasant families, as depicted in this model. A small boat, ducks and some aquatic plants can be seen on the left. [Eastern Han]

MUSIC AND ENTERTAINMENT

120 Dancers, ballad
singers and acrobats
were very popular in
China, both at the
imperial courts and
among ordinary
people. This group
shows a troupe during
a performance: the
actors are shown very
expressively gesturing
and miming. [Tang]

In ancient Chinese texts the word for 'music' (*yue*) was written with the character that could also mean 'joy', 'pleasure', 'entertainment'. Indeed Xunzi, one of the most brilliant minds of the 3rd century BC, said 'music is joy'. 'It is the movement of the heart', said the unknown author of a work on ancient Confucian philosophy which contains the chapter *Yueji*, on music.

Music held a very important place in Chinese tradition, whether it was the music of nature revered by the Daoists, based not on humanly created sounds but on the natural notes of the respiration of the earth and the cosmic breath that inspires everything, or the music of the

soul of which the Confucians spoke, a melody capable of modifying human character, helping them to control their emotions, cultivate the self, improve their moral strength, and enabling them to live in a harmonious relationship with others, nature and the whole universe.

As fullness of life consisted of respect for the symbolic order of the harmony of the cosmos, music was in some ways even more important than rituals and ceremonial. As the poet Ruan Ji, one of the Seven Sages of the Bamboo Grove (*zhulin qixian*, a group of Daoist intellectuals who met in a wood near Luoyang to play music and compose verses) said around the year 250, 'music

121 The Chinese were fascinated and amused by Central Asian culture, including music, which was very popular at court, especially during the Tang dynasty. The musicians and singer shown here riding a camel are of Middle Eastern origin. [Tang]

is the substance of the universe, the nature of beings; it is in the union with this substance, and the agreement with this nature, that harmony is achieved'.

According to tradition, at the basis of cosmic order is a sound – if mankind were in tune with it, harmony would prevail on earth. The wise kings of ancient times, having understood this truth, created music and melodies to promote harmony between people, respect for the ties of kinship and social obligations, and observance of the ceremonies and rules which lie at the basis of community life, so as to bind humanity and the universe in an indissoluble unity. Chinese musical scholarship sought to reproduce this primary sound; moral and social order, through music, was mysteriously bound up with the natural order of the stars, seasons, colours, life and death.

The Chinese system of musical notation comprises five pitches (*wusheng*) and twelve half-tones (*lülü*), based on the sounds made by the bamboo pipes (*lü*) which the legendary Yellow Emperor introduced at court to imitate the song of the phoenix. The *lülü* notation fixes the pitch of notes with reference to the basic sound of the first pipe, called the *huangzhong* (yellow bell). This note, from which the others derive, varied according to the period, and was established by decree from time to time.

Chinese traditional music is of very ancient origin. The first instruments (bone flutes, whistles and pottery ocarinas) date from the late Palaeolithic and early Neolithic. Under the pre-imperial dynasties, music played a very important part in court ceremonies, as demonstrated by finds of bronze bells and other instruments. Small Shang bells

122 (opposite below) The elaborate hairstyle, with symmetrical chignons, the long sleeves emphasizing the fluid gestures of the arms, and the soft garment that comes down to the feet, endow this dancer with grace and elegance. [Tang]

122–123 These white terracotta statuettes of female musicians show traces of a thin buff-coloured glaze and black, red and green pigments. Each woman is holding a different instrument: a four-stringed lute, a small lacquered drum and two kinds of flute. [Sui]

123 (right) Many painted and glazed ceramic statuettes portraying musicians, dancers and jugglers have been found in tombs dating to the imperial period, which give an insight into the fashions, customs and musical instruments of ancient China. [Tang]

found at Anyang are matched by the numerous large bells of the southern kingdoms. One of them, of the *nao* type (a bell with no clapper that was mounted mouth-upward and struck on the exterior), found with other similar bells in Ningxiang (Hunan), weighs 154 kg (340 lb). From the Zhou dynasty onwards, other types of bell became common, and a range of percussion, wind and stringed instruments made of various materials (bronze, stone, wood, bamboo, terracotta, leather, silk, lacquerware) were introduced.

The tomb of Marquis Yi (buried *c.* 433 BC), the ruler of the small southern kingdom of Zeng, contained no fewer

124–125 (above) The most impressive set of bronze bells yet discovered dates from the 5th century BC. It consists of 64 bells of different sizes arranged in decreasing order of size on a large wooden stand. Each bell is marked with its note, inscribed in gold characters. [Eastern Zhou, Warring States]

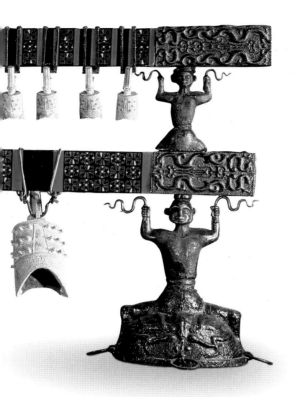

than 124 musical instruments. The most spectacular is an impressive set of bells arranged on three levels on a wooden stand consisting of two parts joined at right angles and supported by bronze human figures. A total of 64 bronze bells are arranged in decreasing order of size; all are richly decorated and bear inscriptions in gold indicating their tones. The same tomb also contained two huge *fu* bells (130 cm (51 in) high, and 110 cm (43 in) in diameter), stone chimes, clappers, drums, bamboo flutes, simple and more complex panpipes, mouth-organs and zithers.

An office of music (*yuefu*) was instituted during the rule of emperor Wudi of the Western Han dynasty. Its functions were to collect popular ballads and music and organize musical performances at court and military parades. When the office was abolished in 7 BC, 830 musicians, players, singers, acrobats and dancers worked for it. Even that is a small number compared with the 30,000 employees of the imperial organizations responsible for court

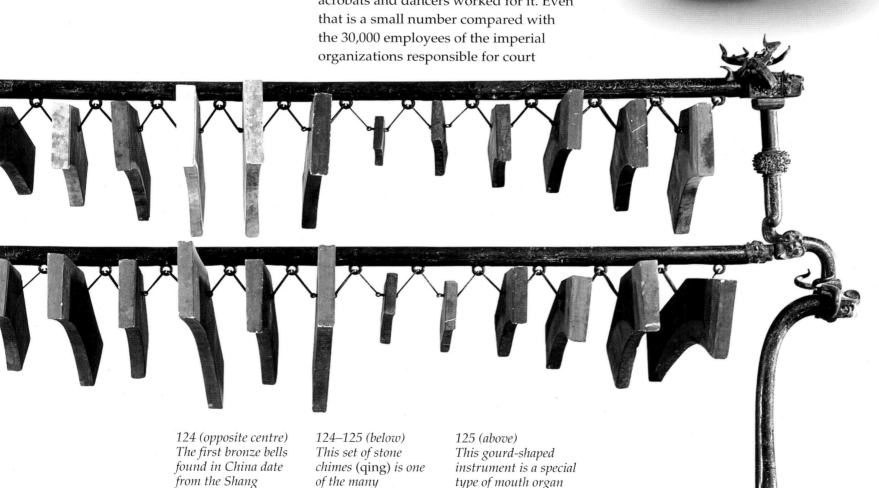

124 (opposite below left) This **bo** bell was used in southern regions and could be rung together with the bell shown next to it from the Western Zhou period onwards. [Western Zhou]

124 (opposite centre) The first bronze bells found in China date from the Shang dynasty. They had a purely ritual function, being used in religious ceremonies. The one shown here (yongzhong) is part of the set of 64 bells found in the tomb of Marquis Yi of Zeng [Eastern Zhou, Warring States]

124–125 (below) This set of stone chimes (qing) is one of the many instruments found in the tomb of Marquis Yi of Zeng. Each stone corresponds to a different note, and melodies of five, six and seven notes can be played. [Eastern Zhou, Warring States]

125 (above) This gourd-shaped instrument is a special type of mouth organ characteristic of Yunnan from ancient times. It is still very popular today, especially among the minority Yi, Wa, Nu, Lahu, Dai, Naxi and Penglong peoples. [Eastern Zhou, Springs and Autumns]

referee, were played on pitches surrounded by walls or sunk into the ground, with 12 goalposts each defended by a goalkeeper. The ball was heavy and did not bounce; this made the game very tiring and in fact it was used as military training. It was not until after the Tang period that the inflated leather ball was introduced and football became pure entertainment. New rules were introduced, and the number of goalposts was gradually reduced to one, placed in the middle of the pitch. It consisted of stakes driven into the ground; a net with an opening at the top was fixed between the stakes, and in order to score, the ball had to pass through the hole.

The game of polo was imported from Persia in the Tang period and its popularity is demonstrated by several murals and numerous burial figurines.

music and dances during the reign of Xuanzong of the Tang dynasty, when a special type of musical composition known as *yanyue* (convivial music) was very popular for court entertainments.

Performances and entertainments were not confined to the court. Scenes of dances and acrobatic performances performed in public are often portrayed on bricks and tombstones. Pottery models depict popular entertainments, such as street festivals and figures of dancers and acrobats. Folk festivals (*paixi*) included musical and acrobatic performances, dances, and displays by jugglers, fire-eaters and ballad singers.

Football was a popular pastime, played by the nobility and apparently even by emperors from the Han period onwards. The matches, supervised by a

126–127 Four musicians with large hats dance and play drums, rattles and long, curved horns with streamers. This relief is of a procession in honour of the deceased, who probably had received similar tributes during his lifetime. [Northern dynasties]

127 (centre) The relief on this tombstone depicts acrobats performing on moving carriages. While this may seem so difficult as to be impossible, similar exercises are depicted on other tombstones of the same period. [Eastern Han]

127 (bottom) Two jugglers dance and balance, holding plates in their outstretched arms, heedless of the snake which curls its tail round the foot of one and bites the leg of the other. A pin on the back allowed this object to be attached to a belt. [Western Han]

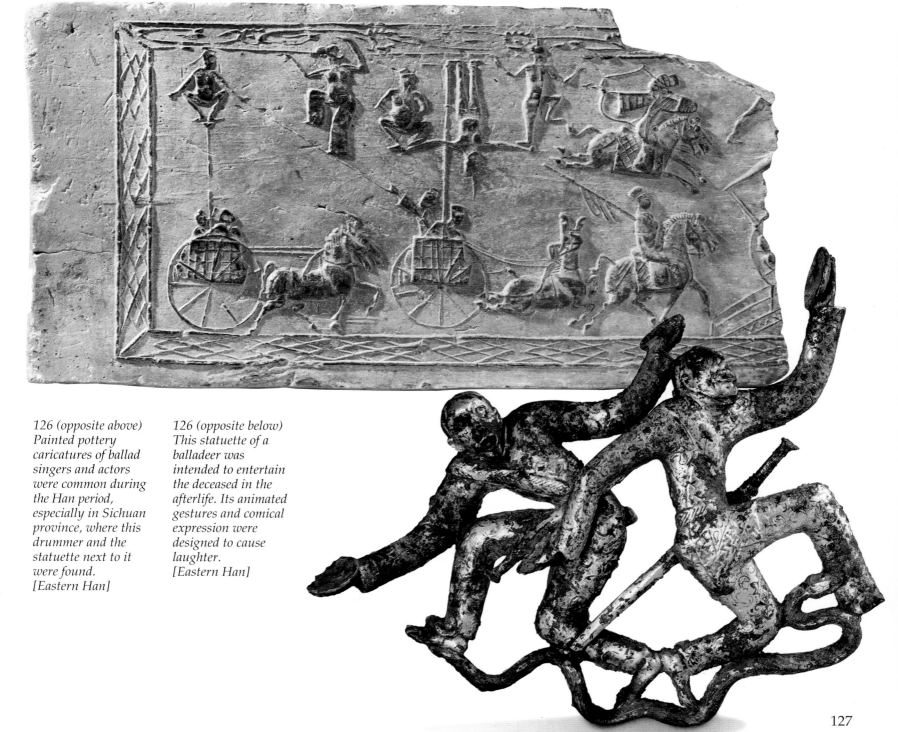

126 (opposite above) Painted pottery caricatures of ballad singers and actors were common during the Han period, especially in Sichuan province, where this drummer and the statuette next to it were found. [Eastern Han]

126 (opposite below) This statuette of a balladeer was intended to entertain the deceased in the afterlife. Its animated gestures and comical expression were designed to cause laughter. [Eastern Han]

127

During the Tang dynasty, riding was the prerogative of the nobility: an edict of 667 prohibited merchants and artisans from riding. At court, one of the most popular performances on special occasions and celebrations was the horse dance, when teams of trained horses, richly decorated with silk and jewels, entertained the audience with impressive exercises.

The aristocracy enjoyed a great variety of pastimes, some of which had been known since ancient times, such as archery, one of the six disciplines considered essential to the education of a gentleman (the others were music, rituals, calligraphy, chariot driving and mathematics). During contests, as in the case of many other games, the penalty for the loser was a specified drink. Betting was frequent, especially at cockfights, dog and horse races, and during games of skill, card games and games using dice with 6, 14, 18 or 22 sides.

Weiqi (*go* in Japanese), an ancient game of strategy, was held in high regard by intellectuals, ministers and soldiers. In the Tang dynasty it was so popular at court that the best players were rewarded with prestigious offices and honorary titles. Badminton, played with the feet

130 (above) The game of dice was popular even among the poorer sections of the population. The bronze players shown here seem to be involved in a lively game. [Western Han]

130 (right) and 131 (opposite above) The stone table shown opposite was used for the game of liubo (six sticks), with various tiles decorated with coiled snakes, masks of fantastic creatures, dragons and tigers; it dates to the Warring States Period. The routes for the pawns are indicated by straight or L-shaped bars. Later, when the game itself was no longer so popular, the patterns of the liubo board survived as decorative motifs on bronze mirrors called 'TLV mirrors' because of the characteristic bars in the shape of these letters and similar to liubo bars. This bronze mirror dates from the Western Han period.

and legs, was very popular with women and Buddhist monks. Other games fashionable at court, especially for women, included elephant chess (*xiangqi*), of ancient origin but perfected during the Tang dynasty, and the game of double six (*shuanglu*), which perhaps derived from another game, *liubo*, the game of the Immortals, also dating back a long time and especially popular during the late Zhou period and Han dynasty.

The equipment needed to play *liubo* consisted of a square board on which routes bounded by straight or L-shaped bars were pictured, 12 pawns in the shape of a cube, and six bamboo sticks or two 18-sided dice. Sets in good condition have been found in various parts of China. The board was usually made of stone, and the pawns could be made of ivory, bone, bronze, jade or rock crystal. The exact rules of the game are unknown, but it is believed to have developed from divinatory practices and cosmological concepts. The patterns of the board were used as ornamental motifs on bronze mirrors called 'TLV mirrors' (because some of the motifs take the shape of these letters), which survived the decline in popularity of the game towards the end of the Han dynasty.

Numerous paintings depict men and women engaged in such pastimes in a serene, apparently timeless atmosphere.

131 (left) Two liubo *(six sticks) players seem to discuss the game. In addition to the board, there were 12 pawns which had to be moved along fixed routes. Six bamboo sticks or two 18-sided dice were thrown to decide the moves. [Eastern Han]*

LUXURY

In every period of the long history of China, resources were distributed in such a way that a small élite owned a huge proportion of them, while the great mass of the populace lived in poverty, threatened by natural disasters such as frequent floods, or overburdened with forced labour. In this respect ancient Chinese civilization was no different from other civilizations of the past. Great wealth was concentrated in the hands of a few, leading to incredible displays of luxury.

Chronicles and literary works abound in descriptions of the privileges and pleasures reserved for the rich and the nobility. The luxury of the royal and imperial courts was well known in the ancient world, and still amazes archaeologists who come upon the rich remains of the past. Numerous finds made this century have confirmed accounts that once seemed exaggerated or the work of the imagination. Many of the tombs of the greatest kings and emperors have not yet been found. If ever they are discovered, treasures of inestimable value will come to light, as suggested by the rich grave goods that have been found in the tombs of princes, members of the imperial families and the nobility, powerful officials and military commanders.

132 (above) Lions and birds amid vine tendrils and bunches of grapes were a recurrent ornamental theme during the Tang period, as demonstrated by the detailed decoration on bronze mirrors, some of which were gilded. [Tang]

132 (opposite centre and below left) These silver discs are decorated with a complex gold design of two phoenixes, mirror images of one another, with long feathered tails. [Tang]

133 (left) These small bronze sculptures of leopards, with gold and silver inlay, served as weights for the corners of funerary covers or paintings on silk. [Western Han]

132–133 Sets of stands were used to support large vessels or trays. This magnificent example, one of four identical pieces, is in the shape of a tiger made of bronze with silver decorations. [Eastern Zhou, Warring States]

133 (below) Mirrors were square in shape as well as round. The decoration is still arranged around a central motif, sometimes in the shape of an animal, or a boss, as here. [Tang]

The luxury of the court and nobility was manifested in all aspects of life: clothes and jewelry, houses and furniture. The only Shang royal tomb found intact is that of Fu Hao, one of the secondary consorts of king Wu Ding. The grave goods it contained are clear evidence of the standard of living of the nobility of the period. Fine textiles and magnificent garments have also been found in tombs of the Zhou period and the early empire. There are delicate silk gauzes, finely embroidered with gold and silver with stitches so minute as to be almost invisible; brocades are decorated with motifs also seen on lacquerware and ceramics. Tigers and dragons face one another proudly, and graceful phoenixes hover in the air, and animals, leaves and flowers entwine in intricate patterns. Over 200 silk fabrics and garments were found among other precious articles in tomb no. 1 at Mawangdui, near Changsha (Hunan), belonging to the wife of Li Cang (a nobleman of Dai and prime minister of the king of Changsha), who died in 168 BC. The warp and weft of the fabric consists of some 35 x 100 threads

134 (above) Accessories for clothing were often highly imaginative, as demonstrated by this witty gilded and silver-plated bronze buckle in the form of a monkey, inlaid with turquoise. [Eastern Zhou, Warring States]

135 (left) This buckle is made of bronze inlaid with gold and silver and is in the shape of a fantastic creature with a dragon's head. [Eastern Zhou, Warring States]

135 (left) Very few iron buckles have retained their original splendour such as this one, with a slightly convex, rectangular shape ending in a dragon's head. [Eastern Zhou, Warring States]

135 (right) A sinuous dragon with a long tail looks out curiously between two trees on this bronze hilt with gold and silver inlaid decorations. [Eastern Zhou, Warring States]

per square centimetre, and as many as 46 x 100 in embroidered fabrics called *chengyun*. The looms employed for damask weaving used up to 120 heddles.

Liu Sheng, the prince of the small kingdom of Zhongshan, who died in 113 BC, and his wife, princess Dou Wan, were found in their precious suits of jade in two tombs at Mancheng (Hebei). Their grave goods consisted of thousands of objects and jewels made of gold, silver, jade, glass, bronze, lacquerware, silk and pottery, all reflecting their refined taste and delicate aesthetic sensitivity.

Sadly, the imperial palaces have not survived the ravages of nature and man. The few surviving ruins and the literary sources hint at their unrivalled magnificence, which made them legendary among neighbouring populations and the countries of Central Asia, which increasingly came into contact with the Chinese empire.

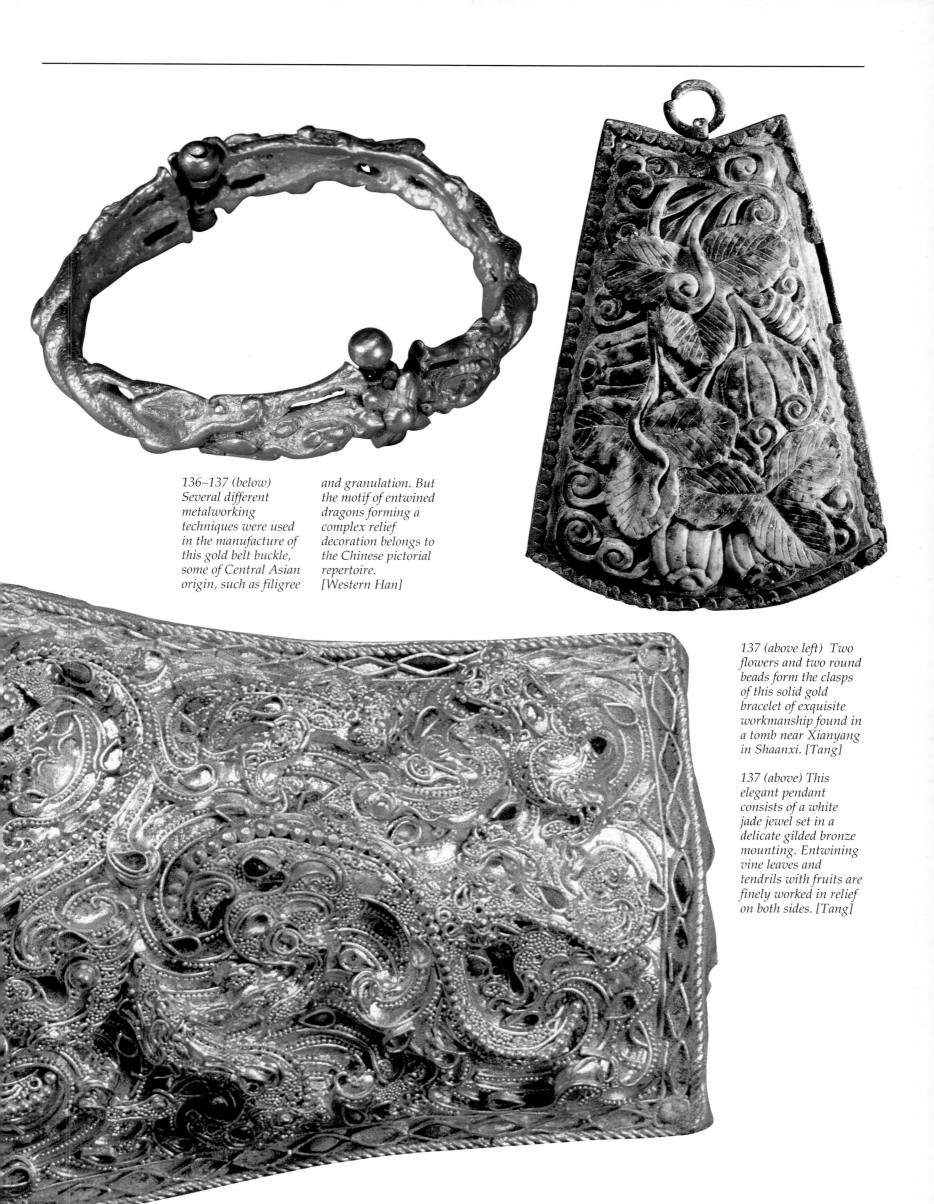

136–137 (below) Several different metalworking techniques were used in the manufacture of this gold belt buckle, some of Central Asian origin, such as filigree and granulation. But the motif of entwined dragons forming a complex relief decoration belongs to the Chinese pictorial repertoire. [Western Han]

137 (above left) Two flowers and two round beads form the clasps of this solid gold bracelet of exquisite workmanship found in a tomb near Xianyang in Shaanxi. [Tang]

137 (above) This elegant pendant consists of a white jade jewel set in a delicate gilded bronze mounting. Entwining vine leaves and tendrils with fruits are finely worked in relief on both sides. [Tang]

138 (left) Found in the Buddhist temple at Famen, this silver tea caddy has fine engraved decoration portraying scenes of life in the open air, and a variety of animals, birds and marine creatures.

138 (below) Tea was probably introduced from India or Southeast Asia during the Six Dynasties period and became popular in China in the Tang dynasty, more as a medicine than as a drink for everyday use. This silver grinder belonged to the imperial family and was used to grind the tea leaves into tiny pieces. [Tang]

Chronicles recount tales of banquets held in huge, richly furnished halls, attended by hundreds of guests, and performances in which large troupes of dancers, acrobats and jugglers performed to the sound of music. In the Tang period, dancing horses were famous. Richly caparisoned with silk and gold, with horns attached to their heads to represent unicorns and wings tied to their backs to imitate phoenixes, they advanced in rhythmic steps to the middle of the room. There they were served wine in gold cups which they had been trained to hold in their teeth. A magnificent gilded silver flask with a relief picture of a dancing horse holding a bowl of wine in this way was found in a Tang tomb excavated in the 1970s.

Acrobats, musicians, a battalion of guards wearing gold armour and 100 dancing horses accompanied by elephants were summoned to celebrate the birthday of Xuanzong (712–756), the 'Enlightened Emperor'. The royal family owned huge grounds and magnificent parks, such the one covering an area of over 155 sq. km (60 sq. miles) in which emperor Yangdi (604–617) used to ride in winter, among trees covered with silk flowers and leaves to give the appearance of summer.

139 (left) The decoration on the lid of this silver box consists of a densely interwoven pattern of gold reliefs portraying floral motifs, long-tailed birds and ducks. The lobed shape is typical of the goldsmith's art of the Tang dynasty. [Tang]

139 (right) Phoenixes with long feathered tails, birds, butterflies, lotus flowers and garlands interweave to form attractive geometric patterns, inlaid and in relief, on this large silver and gold container. [Tang]

140 (left) The gilded image of a dancing horse holding a bowl of wine in its teeth stands out in **repoussé** on the body of this silver bottle, shaped like the leather flasks used by the nomads of the steppes.

140–141 (above) This bronze buckle in the form of a tiger, inlaid with gold and silver, is of an unusual size – 24.5 cm (almost 10 in) long. [Eastern Zhou, Warring States]

141 (below) The naturalism of this recumbent ox demonstrates how carefully Chinese craftsmen observed life. Their artistry is displayed in the skilful contrast of the geometric inlaid silver decoration with the realism of the subject. [Eastern Zhou, Warring States]

140 (opposite below) The imagination and skill of Chinese craftsmen perhaps reached their peak in the manufacture of luxury items, such as this unusual pair of incense burners in the form of tortoises made of bronze, gold and silver inlaid with shell. [Western Han]

Follies such as the rotating pavilion built by architect Yuwen Kai, who lived during the Sui dynasty, must have been very impressive. According to contemporary sources, it could hold several hundred guests and turned smoothly thanks to a mechanism concealed in the foundations. Many considered it the work of a god, and barbarians who saw it were terrified, much to the emperor's amusement.

However, great displays of jewelry do not feature largely in paintings and statuettes that portrayed the ideal of womanhood. All the feminine graces are symbolized by the softness of the long-sleeved clothes, and even ladies of high status and wealth are depicted wearing no jewelry.

142–143 Some 1,400 years ago, in the kingdom of Sālva in India, 500 men rebelled against the oppression of King Prasenajit, but were defeated and slain. Their epic feats form the subject of this painting dating from 538/9, which can still be seen on a wall of cave 285, Dunhuang. [Western Wei]

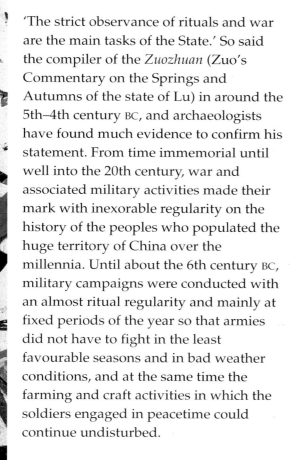

WAR

'The strict observance of rituals and war are the main tasks of the State.' So said the compiler of the *Zuozhuan* (Zuo's Commentary on the Springs and Autumns of the state of Lu) in around the 5th–4th century BC, and archaeologists have found much evidence to confirm his statement. From time immemorial until well into the 20th century, war and associated military activities made their mark with inexorable regularity on the history of the peoples who populated the huge territory of China over the millennia. Until about the 6th century BC, military campaigns were conducted with an almost ritual regularity and mainly at fixed periods of the year so that armies did not have to fight in the least favourable seasons and in bad weather conditions, and at the same time the farming and craft activities in which the soldiers engaged in peacetime could continue undisturbed.

Behaviour towards adversaries, both during battle and in the event of victory, was governed by a code of honour which every commander strove to observe. When the Zhou conquered the Shang capital Yin, they did not raze the city to the ground but allowed Wugeng, the heir apparent of the Shang dynasty, to rule under their strict supervision. Such principled acts of clemency were not uncommon.

The aphorism 'Who do you take me for, the Duke of Song?', which Mao Zedong is reputed to have quoted whenever important strategic decisions had to be taken, refers to this chivalrous attitude, taken to extremes by Duke Xiang of Song. In 638 BC, ignoring the insistent advice of his generals, the duke refused to launch a decisive attack against his enemies, who were temporarily in difficulty. Seeing that they had not yet deployed in perfect combat

142–143 (below) These pottery statuettes, dating from the 4th–5th century, portray warriors on horseback protected by heavy armour consisting of metal plates and pieces of leather sewn together. [Northern Wei]

143 (above) This bronze halberd of the ge type, dating from the Springs and Autumns period, has an inscription on both surfaces consisting four elegant gold characters in the so-called 'bird' script. [Eastern Zhou, Springs and Autumns]

144 (below) The diamond pattern on this bronze sword was created by a special technique using copper sulphide, which also protected the blade against rust. The gold inscription attributes the sword to King Gui Jian of Yue. [Eastern Zhou, Springs and Autumns]

144 (above) In an age when armed conflict was frequent and governed by a code of honour, great skill and expense were lavished on weapons. This bronze sword has a jade hilt and is decorated with inlays of gold, silver and turquoise. An inscription runs down both faces of the blade, which was cold-forged by hammering. [Eastern Zhou, Warring States]

formation after crossing a river, he refused to take advantage of the situation. As a result his troops suffered a heavy defeat, and he himself was wounded in the course of the battle.

From the 6th century BC and during the Warring States period, the rulers who fought to gain control of Chinese territory transformed the social and economic organization of their kingdoms to meet the requirements of war. The warrior nobility no longer prevailed in the composition of armies, whose strength lay mainly in the impressive infantry legions. The 'chivalrous' warfare of the past, conducted by sons of noble families expert in driving fast chariots, became no more than a faint memory.

Fighting troops, which numbered 30,000 men in the 7th–6th centuries BC,

were transformed into powerful armies at the service of unscrupulous commanders who decided which side to take in each situation. The war chariot, introduced during the Shang dynasty, remained an essential element even when huge cavalry forces became common in the 5th–3rd centuries BC. In the imperial period, armies were further strengthened and the emperor could move hundreds of thousands of trained, fully equipped men simultaneously along the borders.

Weapons gradually became more complex and sophisticated. In addition to the traditional lances, axes and halberds, weapons such as the bow and arrow, crossbow and sword came into widespread use. The Mozi, the basic text of Mohism, which dates from the 5th–4th century BC, describes offensive and

144 (opposite right)
An enormous number
of statues of various
sizes portraying
warriors have been
found in recent years.
They are invaluable in
tracing the history of
costumes and
studying the
development of
uniforms, armour and
weapons.
[Northern Wei]

145 (left) The Qin
army was supplied
with at least seven
different types of
armour. The heaviest
and simplest were
used by the troops,
while the lightest,
often trimmed with
silk ribbons, were
reserved for officers.
The complex topknots
ruled out the use of
helmets. [Qin]

145 (above) The
thousands of statues of
the terracotta army of
the First Emperor at
Xi'an are surprising for
their accurate portrayal

of the smallest details,
including shoes,
clothes, armour,
hairstyles and faces, all
with slightly different
features. [Qin]

defensive machinery mounted on chariots in minute detail, and explains the most effective ways of using it. Armour mainly consisted of rectangular leather pieces of various sizes joined together to form fairly flexible suits which allowed freedom of movement. Breastplates were often painted, and even lacquered. Towards the end of the Zhou period, iron plates joined by rivets or ties were also used. The statues of the terracotta army buried to defend the tomb of the First August Emperor of the Qin dynasty are depicted wearing a range of armour and headgear, reproduced in great detail.

With time, armour became increasingly functional, and was extended to protect the horses. In the Tang period, various types of breastplate were used; a contemporary text lists six metal and seven leather models. They were magnificently decorated and coloured, and sometimes had bright metal discs on the breast strap to reflect the light, so that the enemy would be

146 (below left) Two different types of helmet were worn: a one-piece bronze 'skullcap' which covered a greater or lesser area, like the one shown here, or one formed by plates of iron sewn together to form a helmet which came down to the neck, as seen in some examples dating to the Warring States period. [Shang]

146 (opposite above)
Originally fitted with
a wooden handle in
the hole in the centre,
this bronze axe is
decorated on both
sides with the image
of a creature with one
foot resting on the sun
and the other on a
crescent moon. It may
represent Taiyi, the
supreme deity whose
task was to combat
evil and prevent
military defeats.
[Eastern Zhou,
Warring States]

146–147 One of the
most common
weapons was the
halberd, used by
Chinese soldiers from
the earliest periods.
Bronze tips were
attached to the long
pole. [Eastern Han]

147 (above right)
The variety of the war
axes of the Shang
period is remarkable.
This is a yue axe, with
three circular holes in
the body of the blade.
Up to seven such holes
appear on other
examples. [Shang]

dazzled or frightened. Lighter cotton or
silk outfits, unsuitable for battle but very
elegant, were worn by the aristocratic
warriors for receptions at court.

During the Warring States period, the
theory of war as an art form was
developed. Treatises and works of great
interest were devoted to it. The best
known is the *Sunzi Bingfa* (The Art of War
according to Master Sun), a 5th-century
BC manual of politics and strategy, still
studied in the military academies of the
People's Republic of China, Taiwan and
other Far Eastern countries.

In 1972 some texts written on strips of
bamboo and dating from the 2nd century
BC were found at Yinjueshan (Shandong),
which included a different version of the
Sunzi Bingfa from the traditional one and
a version of the *Sun Bin Bingfa* (The Art
of War according to Sun Bin), a later text
whose existence had previously been
unknown. The discovery of these works
and others demonstrates the existence in
ancient China of various schools of
military strategy.

148 (above left) The bow had been known in China from ancient times and arrows were tipped with bronze during the Shang period. The crossbow was introduced later. [Qin]

148 (left) This archer on horseback, shown in the act of shooting an arrow, is the only surviving statuette made with the marbled clay technique, which produces a wood-grain effect. [Tang]

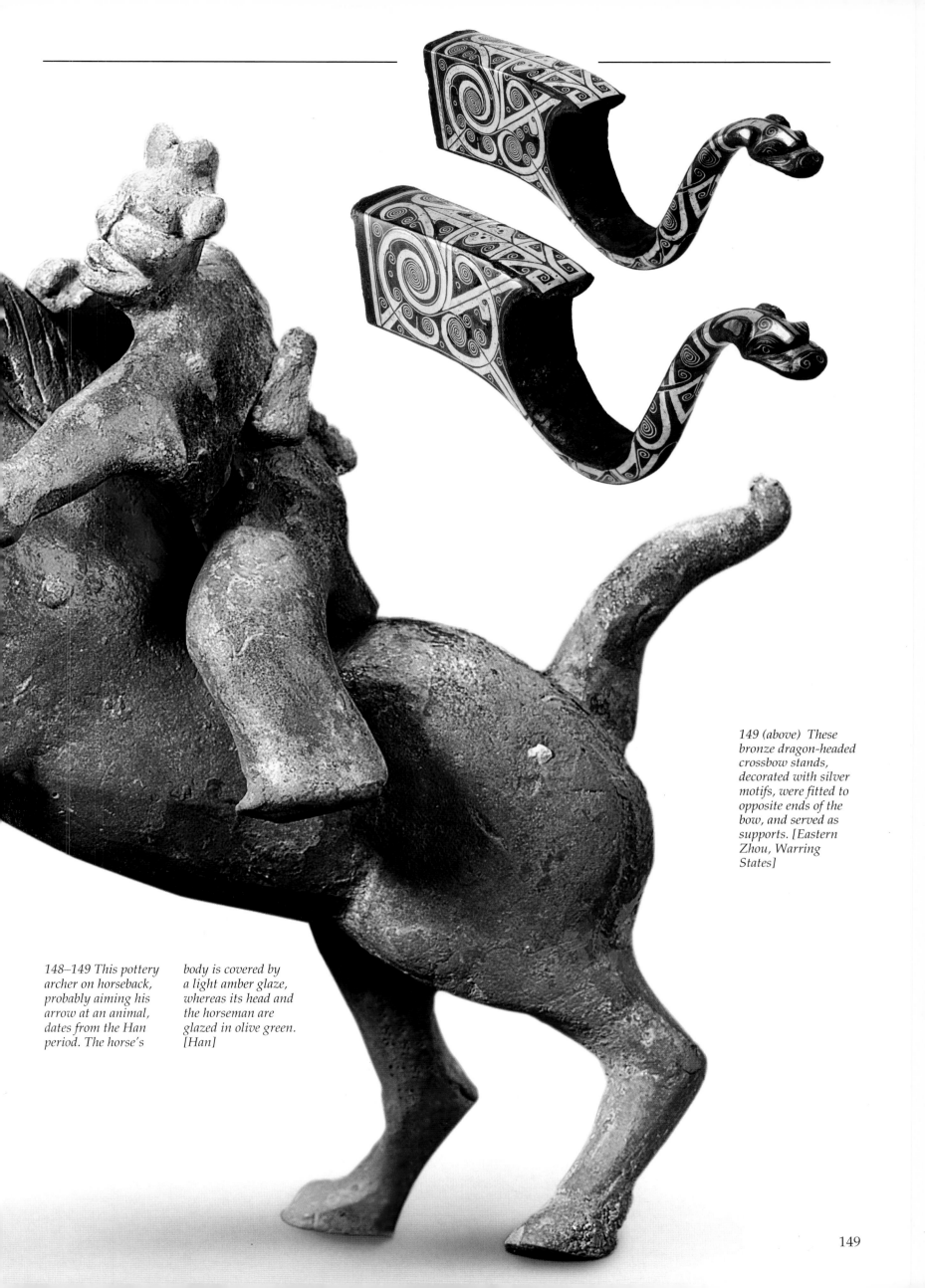

149 (above) These bronze dragon-headed crossbow stands, decorated with silver motifs, were fitted to opposite ends of the bow, and served as supports. [Eastern Zhou, Warring States]

148–149 This pottery archer on horseback, probably aiming his arrow at an animal, dates from the Han period. The horse's body is covered by a light amber glaze, whereas its head and the horseman are glazed in olive green. [Han]

CHINESE ART DOWN THE AGES

150–151 This magnificent bronze statuette of a 'flying horse', represents one of the tianma, *the powerful 'heavenly horses' imported from Central Asia from the 2nd century* BC *on the orders of the Han emperor Wudi. [Eastern Han]*

POTTERY AND PORCELAIN

The first pottery found in China dates from the 7th–6th millennium BC. Red or brown earthenware with a coarse, crumbly texture, shaped without the wheel and fired at low temperatures, has been found at numerous sites in Henan, Hebei, Shaanxi and Shanxi belonging to the Neolithic Cishan-Peiligang culture. Some vessels have impressed, corded and plaited decorations. In the same period, black pottery with thick, irregular walls was made along the east coast (Hemudu) using the coil technique. Corded decorations were impressed or incised directly into the clay; hand-painted decoration was very unusual. Incision was also the characteristic decorative technique for the pottery of the Neolithic cultures that developed

152 (above) The serpent motif appears in Chinese art very early on. Reptiles with more or less fantastic features are found in mythological tales, and are the origin of one of the most enigmatic creatures, the dragon.
[Taosi Longshan]

152 (below) Inside the rim of this bowl found at Shangsunjiazhai (Qinghai), is a frieze with two groups of dancers facing one another, holding hands. The same motif is found on bowls discovered nearby, at Zongri, on

sites dating from 3900 to 3500 BC. This suggests that the dating of the Majiayao culture in Gansu (3300–2050 BC) should be revised, or the existence of an independent culture in Zongri should be recognized.
[Majiayao, Zongri]

153 (opposite below left) Vessels of gui shape, with the characteristic tripod base were common in the Neolithic period, and were mainly used for boiling water. This magnificent example belongs to the Longshan culture of Shandong. [Longshan]

along the east coast, from the Hemudu to the Liangzhu and Longshan cultures, and remained predominant there after it became common in other cultures from the 5th millennium BC. The decorations on Shang and Zhou bronzes represent a development of this technique, but applied to the new material.

Pottery produced during the 5th and 4th millennia BC along the river valleys of northwest China and other centres of the Yangshao culture was made using the slow wheel, and was mostly ochre or red in colour. The walls of the vases and bowls were more regular, the texture finer, and painted decoration was the rule rather than the exception.

153 (above centre) Two terracotta female figurines, one of which is seen here, were found next to a stone structure identified as an altar of the Hongshan culture. Their presence suggests some form of fertility rites. [Hongshan]

153 (above) This grey clay jar surmounted by a small human head was found on a site of the Neolithic Songze culture in 1990. No parallels have been found for it elsewhere. [Songze].

Vigorous, strong brushstrokes characterize most of the products of this period. Regular, symmetrical geometric or floral patterns alternate with more finely drawn portrayals of animals or human faces. The marks and signs incised on some items of pottery represent the first attempts at writing.

The decorative repertoire was greatly extended during the subsequent cultures (Majiayao, Banshan and Machang) to include geometric patterns of thin wavy lines, densely packed in complex swirls or developing into open spirals, circles, and abstract portrayals of natural subjects, interpreted by some experts as flowers or birds. Anthropomorphic motifs are also found. Jars found in Gansu and Qinghai are particularly attractive; one example has a relief of a naked creature with human features and accentuated androgynous characteristics, and another has a human face whose body is merely sketched. These figures are animated by such an expressive tension that they seem to burst outwards from the vessel.

154 Fine black pottery vessels such as these stand out from other products of the Neolithic because of their surprising sophistication, elegant shapes and the high quality of the clay mixture used. This thin, strong pottery is known as 'eggshell'. The bei goblet, with its long openwork stem, perhaps the archetype of the bronze gu goblet which was popular during the Shang period, is one of the most attractive examples of eggshell pottery. [Longshan]

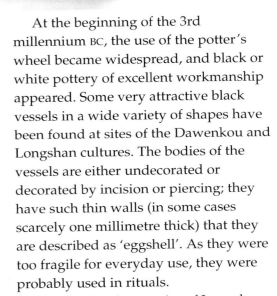

At the beginning of the 3rd
millennium BC, the use of the potter's
wheel became widespread, and black or
white pottery of excellent workmanship
appeared. Some very attractive black
vessels in a wide variety of shapes have
been found at sites of the Dawenkou and
Longshan cultures. The bodies of the
vessels are either undecorated or
decorated by incision or piercing; they
have such thin walls (in some cases
scarcely one millimetre thick) that they
are described as 'eggshell'. As they were
too fragile for everyday use, they were
probably used in rituals.

The fine black ceramics of Longshan
bear witness to the high technical level
achieved by the craftsmen of the
Neolithic. The best examples of white
pottery come from the area of the
Dawenkou culture, but some items of
outstanding quality have also been
found on sites of the Yangshao and
Majiayao cultures.

China clay was first used in this
period. Analyses of white pottery from
Shandong (Dawenkou culture) dating
from the end of the 2nd millennium BC
indicate that a temperature of around
1,200°C (2,190°F) was reached during
firing, far higher than the 800–1,000°C

(1472–1832°F) that had been achieved up to that time. Centuries later, these high temperatures made possible the development of a totally new technology, which produced the first true porcelain ware in the 6th century.

On the basis of the experience gained in controlling high temperatures and making white pottery, craftsmen began to coat the clay with a layer of opaque material to give it a coloured surface, using what is known as the slip technique. Pottery coated with a greenish-yellow or grey-brown glaze, called 'proto-porcelain', was produced from the 16th century BC, during the Erligang phase of the Shang dynasty. The basic mixture was a kaolin-rich clay with a small iron content.

These proto-porcelains, made using the coil technique and with corded or lattice decoration, were fired at a temperature of around 1,200°C (2,192°F) in two stages, one to fire the vessel and the other to fire the glaze. This latter process, perhaps first discovered by chance, initially involved exposing the pottery to wood ash in the kiln. The ash then liquefied in the high temperatures and combined with some constituents of the clay on the upper part of the pot, thus not always covering it evenly.

Glazed pottery was highly prized as early as the Bronze Age and the first empire. Its success, and the great prestige

156 (right) The design of this proto-porcelain vase, with its characteristic olive green colour, is very unusual as the shoulder is decorated with a geometric pattern of three horizontal bands of triangular holes. [Eastern Zhou, Warring States]

156 (left) This glazed pottery gui vessel, a magnificent example of proto-celadon, dates from the Eastern Zhou period. The relief pattern and the decorations applied to the body reveal its southern origin. [Eastern Zhou, Springs and Autumns period]

of bronzes, followed by lacquer, led to the gradual decline of terracotta, which was relegated to the production of vessels and objects for everyday use, decorations for funeral chambers and statuettes and other tomb models.

Towards the end of the Zhou dynasty and during the imperial period, the variety of grave goods was enriched by *mingqi*, figurines and models mostly made of terracotta or wood. They portrayed human figures of servants, soldiers, musicians, dancers, acrobats and animals, and replaced sacrificial victims. They were intended to serve the deceased and fulfil his or her needs in the afterlife. Models of buildings and rural scenes and portrayals of farming, hunting and trade were designed to create a familiar atmosphere, together with other objects from everyday life, miniature or lifesize, for the use of the deceased in the afterlife.

Towards the end of the Eastern Han dynasty, proto-porcelain, made mainly in southern regions, had reached an outstanding level of workmanship,

157 (above) This large glazed jar is a fine example of the beautiful ceramics in pleasing shapes that were created by highly skilled potters using good quality materials and a fairly restrained application of colour and decoration. [Western Jin]

157 (below) Certain motifs that at one time had ritual significance were later used purely decoratively, as on this pottery bowl, the shape of which is probably based on bronze vessels of the same period. [Eastern Zhou, Warring States]

158 and 159 These terracotta horses, one with a removable neck and the other (two views) made in a single piece, come from Sichuan. They are over 1 m (3 ft) tall; the first is portrayed standing still, and the second trotting. The erect head, pricked-up ears and open mouth as if neighing are characteristic features of the painted terracotta horses of the Han period. [Han]

160 (left) This kneeling man, perhaps a dancer or singer, is wearing a typical layered garment. The long sleeves that conceal the hands give him an elegant, appearance. [Han]

which was maintained throughout the subsequent period, reaching its peak during the Western Jin dynasty, when a different glazing technique was introduced. A liquid glaze (which became vitreous during firing) was applied directly to the surface of the object, which was evenly covered. Using this method, a single firing was possible, and the intensity and brightness of the colour could be precisely determined and regulated. Lead-based glazes produced white, amber, chestnut brown or olive green colours, while iron-based glazes produces greens, as seen in the magnificent celadons made from the Han period in the Shanxi, Henan, Hebei and Shandong areas. Fired at between 1,260°C (2,300°F) and 1,310°C (2,390°F), celadons had a bright, translucent glaze that adhered perfectly to the clay and evenly covered the entire vessel.

160 (left) These attractive boxes, designed to contain toiletry objects and cosmetics, were part of a lady's grave goods. Their shape recalls that of the gilded bronze zun *containers for alcoholic drinks which were common during the Han period. [Han]*

A type of whitish glazed stoneware, which made a characteristic ringing sound when struck and was very similar to true porcelain, appeared in the Sui dynasty. It was perfected in the Tang dynasty, and reached its greatest splendour during subsequent dynasties. The white pottery produced in the Xing kilns at Neiqiu and the Ding kilns at Quyang (Hebei), the porcelains with under-glaze painting from the Tongguan (Hunan) works and the celadons made in the Yue kilns near Yuyao (Zhejiang) became famous. Under-glaze painting was used to depict human figures, animals, and cloudy landscapes shrouded in fog, as well as compositions of plants, flowers and grasses, geometric patterns, verses and popular proverbs written in different styles of calligraphy.

Multicoloured glazes were popular in the Tang period. Some of the best-known objects are those decorated with a three-colour, lead-based glaze (*sancai*). Jars, plates, cups and dishes of various shapes have been found. Funerary figurines were made depicting imaginary or real characters, such as elegant ladies and serious dignitaries.

161 (left) The technique of allowing the glaze to trickle down the body of pottery vessels, leaving the lower part unglazed, was always popular in China, and also spread to Japan and other countries of East Asia [Han].

161 (above) In all periods, pottery imitations of bronze vase shapes were produced for reasons of cost. From the Eastern Zhou period, it became common practice to use copies in grave goods. This hu container was used for this purpose. [Western Han]

161

162 (right) An ancient legend tells how female tortoises mated with snakes due to lack of males of the species. The mating of the tortoise and the serpent, both of which issued from the bowels of the legendary Emperor of the North, symbolized harmony and happiness. [Northern Wei]

162–163 The ox and water buffalo played a very important part in the life of the Chinese. As well as being used for farm work and the transport of goods, they also pulled the carriages of aristocrats and officials. [Northern Qi]

163 (opposite above) The surface of this vase is covered with a pale white glaze. The shape of the vase and the decoration of medallions, flowers and lotus petals betray the influence of Persia and Sri Lanka, and reflect the cosmopolitan tastes of the Tang period. [Tang]

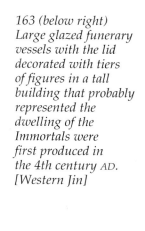

163 (below right) Large glazed funerary vessels with the lid decorated with tiers of figures in a tall building that probably represented the dwelling of the Immortals were first produced in the 4th century AD. [Western Jin]

Other subjects include soldiers, tomb guardians, foreigners and travelling wine vendors, and caravans of camels laden with merchandise and powerful horses with magnificent saddles, which are now famous all over the world.

Deep shades of blue, black, green and amber yellow were combined to create spectacular chromatic effects. Although apparently randomly produced by the flow of the materials, these in fact took great skill and are the result of a highly refined art which was fully conscious of the range of possibilities that could be achieved.

164 (above) Tang potters were masters in the production of pottery coated with 'three-colour' glaze (sancai), obtained by mixing clear glazes with metallic iron oxide (amber to brown ochre), copper oxide (leaf green) and cobalt oxide (blue). [Tang]

164 (right) The Tang potters also used lead silicates to achieve a wide range of deep coloured monochrome glazes which trickled irregularly down the body of the object, only partly coating it. The small bottle shown here was made with this technique. [Tang]

164–165 The decoration of this dish or tray for offerings was achieved using a particular technique: the central motif was incised in the wet clay so that the glaze was retained in the design, thus enriching the chromatic effects. [Tang]

165 (below left) Numerous spectacular possibilities are offered by the combination of different coloured glazes, often mixed apparently at random to create a natural, improvised effect. However, the random appearance is misleading – the sancai technique required great skill. [Tang]

165 (below) The imagination and skill of the Tang potters were unrivalled, as demonstrated by this magnificent jug in the shape of a bird of prey, in which the 'three-colour' glaze enhances the bird's shape. [Tang]

166 This glazed pottery amphora with its magnificent dragon's-head handles is inspired by shapes typical of Middle Eastern cultures, and probably derives from a metal model from Persia. [Sui/Tang]

167 (above) This magnificent olive green bottle was found in the secret crypt of the Buddhist monastery at Famen. The find, made in 1987, demonstrated the type to which mi porcelain (named by literary sources but not yet identified by archaeologists) corresponds. [Tang]

167 (right) This highly glazed jug so strongly reflects the influence of the Sassanid culture on Tang arts and crafts that it does not even look Chinese. [Tang]

168 (below) Tens of thousands of painted terracotta statuettes depicting servants, musicians, dancers, soldiers, noblewomen, polo-playing aristocrats and a wide variety of animals, especially Ferghana horses and camels, have been found at many different sites. [Tang]

168 (below) In the Tang period, the practice of placing huge numbers of pottery models in the tombs of aristocrats led to the issue of an imperial decree regulating the amount and size of items allowed for each tomb, depending on the rank and position of the deceased. [Tang]

169 (opposite) Chinese literature describes the proud Ferghana steeds that were the foundation of the strength of the imperial armies, as 'horses that sweat blood'. They must have played an important role in the rapid and unstoppable expansion of the empire. [Tang]

170 Ceramic figurines painted or glazed with the 'three-colour' (sancai) technique are found so frequently in Sui and Tang tombs that they are considered one of the distinctive features of the funerary art of these periods. [Tang]

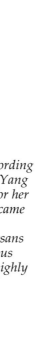

171 (left) A graceful simplicity of design, softness of hairstyle and elegance of clothes, characterize these glazed pottery female figurines, which are an exquisite expression of Tang art. [Tang]

170 (opposite left) There is a story that a sloe blossom fell from a branch on to the forehead of a princess sleeping in the shade of the tree, leaving a coloured mark. Her maids, believing that the girl had used artificial means to enhance her beauty, imitated her, and this was how the fashion for painting the face began. [Tang]

170 (opposite right) Court fashions of the Sui and Tang periods were very elegant, as demonstrated by this slender figurine, with exquisite robes, long, draping sleeves and elaborate hairstyle. [Tang]

171 (right) According to legend, when Yang Guifei, famous for her florid beauty, became the emperor's favourite, courtesans with full, generous figures became highly admired. [Tang]

172 (below) The camel was one of the favourite subjects of Tang craftsmen. The one seen here, 83.3 cm (33 in) tall, loaded with supplies and about to set off on a journey, seems to be showing its impatience. [Tang]

172 (right) The Celestial Kings were sometimes assisted in their role as guardians by terrible spirits (qitou or tugui) whose monstrous head, with both human and animal features, rested on a powerful winged body with strong hoofed feet. [Tang]

173 (opposite left) Looking very fierce in his armour and with a demonic appearance, this magnificent 'three-colour' Celestial King (lokapāla) imperiously stands on a recumbent ox in a composition well known in the Tang period. [Tang]

173 (opposite right) This fantastic and fierce guardian has particularly elaborate horns and wings. Traces of gilding are visible in places. [Tang]

174–175 According to court ritual, a kneeling position with hands held together in front of the body expressed humility and respect. This was the attitude which all those admitted to the emperor's presence had to adopt, including foreign diplomats. This red terracotta statuette, painted and decorated in gold, portrays a gentleman of the court. [Tang]

JADE

176 (below) This drawing reproduces the mask incised on a cong: *a man in ceremonial dress, probably a shaman, places his hands on the large round eyes of a fantastic, monstrous creature, which according to some experts may be the archetype of the* taotie *motif characteristic of Shang and Zhou bronzes. [Liangzhu]*

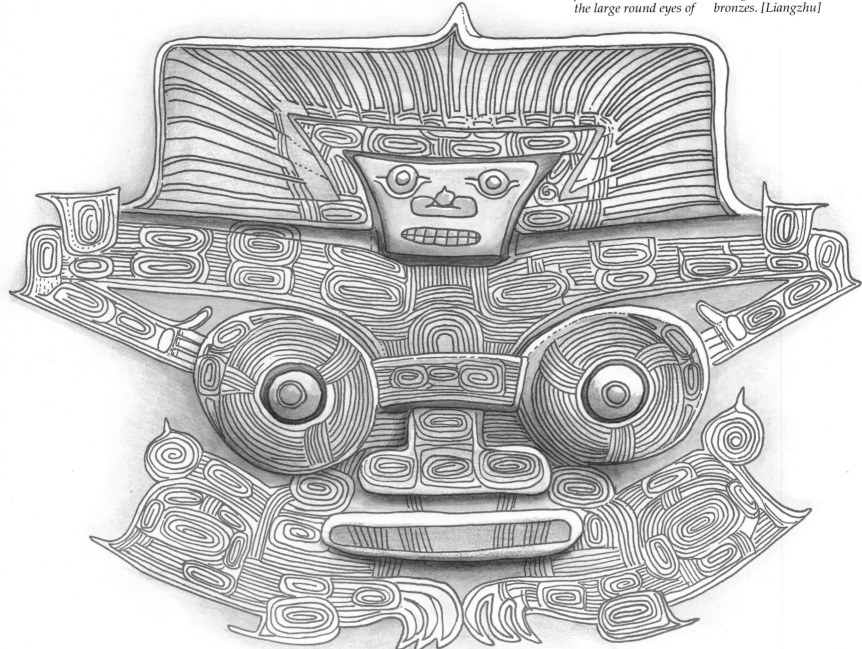

Jade was a material of great prestige in Chinese culture for thousands of years. This precious 'mountain essence' was highly prized as early as the late Neolithic period, when it became one of the symbols of religious and political power. Great magico-religious powers were attributed to it, and it was considered an intermediary between earthly and heavenly worlds.

The Chinese word *yu* (jade) refers to two minerals with a similar appearance but different chemical compositions, nephrite and jadeite (true jade), and sometimes to other varieties of stones which can be given a high polish (false

176 (opposite below)
This block of jade with
a rectangular shape
and large tubular hole
through the middle is
a cong, a mysterious
object, numerous
examples of which
have been found in
Neolithic graves.
The corners and sides
were often carved with
animal and human
masks. [Liangzhu]

177 (left) In China,
the earliest jade
swords are part of a
tradition which began
in the Neolithic with
stone and jade knives.
They were designed
for ceremonial or
funerary use, and
although their shape
varied from place to
place, there were
basically two main
types, ge and zhang.
The jade sword shown
here is a zhang type.
[12th century BC]

177 (right)
The strange creature
portrayed in this small
green-white jade of the
Hongshan culture, is
a pig-dragon, thought
by some to be the
precursor of the true
dragon. It has a coiled
body and the snout of
a pig, an animal often
sacrificed during
religious ceremonies
in the Neolithic.
[Hongshan]

177 (above) This dark
green jade pendant is
the oldest depiction of
a dragon yet found in
China. The smooth,
slender body with a
circular shape and the

long crest on the back
which seems to end
in a pair of small
wings give the
creature the
appearance of great
vitality. [Hongshan]

or pseudo-jade). The terms 'nephrite' and
'jadeite' used in the West derive from
the belief that these semiprecious stones
were a remedy for kidney disorders.
The Spaniards, who first imported them
to Europe from Central America, called
them *piedra de los riñones*, was Latinized
as *lapis nephriticus* (kidney stone), or
piedra de ijada (flank or loin stone).
Nephrite is a calcium, magnesium and
iron silicate, while jadeite is an inosilicate
of sodium and aluminium, combined
with varying amounts of other elements.

The colour of nephrite ranges from
white to brownish green. The Chinese
called the most highly prized variety,
which is white and translucent, 'mutton
fat'. Jadeite ranges in colour from
opalescent white to green, but depending
on its iron, chrome or manganese content
it can also take on other shades,
sometimes present together in the same
block of ore. Green, in its various shades,
is the most frequent colour. During the
late Neolithic and the early pre-imperial
period only nephrite was known and
mainly mined from local sources.

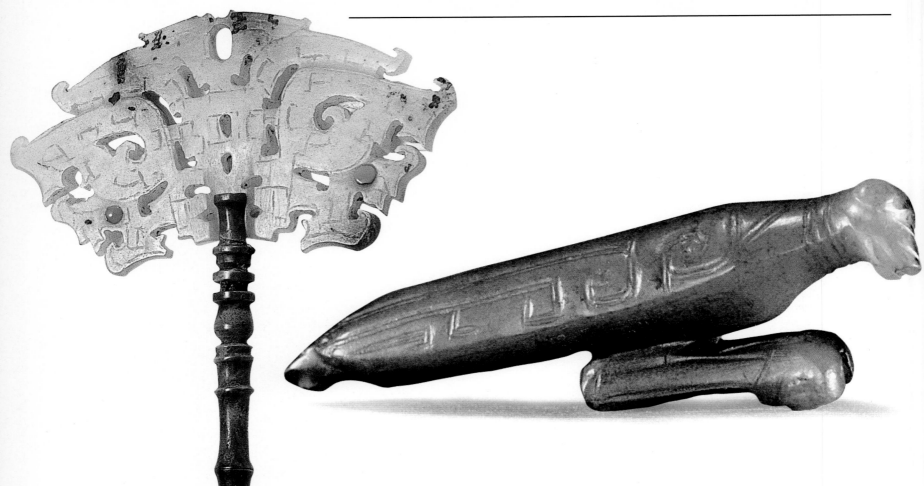

178 (right)
Many jade or bone
ornaments have been
found in tombs of the
Neolithic and the
Bronze Age. This
hairpin consists of a
long green jade stem
in the form of a
bamboo cane, with a
finely carved white
jade plaque decorated
with turquoises. The
grave goods of queen
Fu Hao of the Shang
dynasty contained
527 such ornaments.
[Longshan]

178 (above right)
This brownish-yellow
mantis-shaped jade
pendant was part of
the magnificent grave
goods of queen Fu
Hao, whose tomb was
discovered in Anyang
in 1976. Among the
755 jades found, there
are numerous
figurines portraying
humans and animals.
[Shang]

Jade is one of the most difficult stones to work and carve. On the 10-point Mohs scale which measures the hardness of materials, nephrite is 6.5, while jadeite is 6.75. Even steel is insufficient to cut and carve jade, but the Chinese craftsmen of the Neolithic became surprisingly skilful in using abrasive sands with greater hardness than jade; they certainly used quartzite (7–7.5) and perhaps garnets (7.5). Some researchers have recently suggested that they also used diamond-tipped tools (10). The sharks' teeth found in some Neolithic tombs of the Longshan culture may also have been used for this purpose. Drills, awls and saws made of wood, bamboo, stone, leather straps and gut were used in conjunction with the abrasives on the block of jade. Metal tools were used later, but still only in connection with the abrasive paste.

The oldest jades have been found at sites of the south Qingliangang culture, the direct descendant of the Hemudu tradition. Jade working reached its greatest artistic heights in the period between 3600 and 2000 BC in the east coast area stretching from Liaoning to Fujian, in the Hongshan, Liangzhu and Longshan cultures of Shandong. Recent excavations in Dongshanzui and Niuheliang (Liaoning), both sites of the

Hongshan culture, have revealed two large religious complexes containing stone structures and ceremonial altars. Marvellous jade objects have been found in some tombs belonging to the same culture, including rings, cloud-shaped objects and the first representation of a dragon, one of the mythological creatures most often reproduced by the craftsmen and artists of later centuries. The dragon found at Janping (Liaoning)

178 (opposite below right) Many small, finely executed jade carvings dating from the Neolithic and the Shang dynasty have been found, like this bird of prey just a few centimetres tall. They were hung from the clothes as a symbol of distinction and rank. [Shang]

179 Sixteen individual jade plaques form this rare mask portraying a human face with a flattened nose, wide nostrils and almond eyes – typically Asiatic features. The back of each plaque is pierced by a hole which enabled the pieces to be tied together. [Western Zhou]

is highly stylized, with a very coiled body and a head resembling that of a pig (the most important sacrificial animal).

Jade carving reached a high level of skill in the Liangzhu culture, with the objects produced acquiring greater and greater symbolic value. Tombs contain perfectly polished axes with blades showing no trace of wear, and large numbers of *bi* discs – thin, smooth circles of varying sizes with a hole in the centre. *Congs* (the name given to them later) are other objects of unknown function. They are rectangular blocks pierced by a perfectly cylindrical hole running through the middle. Strange human and animal masks (identified by some as the sun deity) are carved on their corners.

Some 3,200 jades were found in the complex of 11 tombs excavated near Fanshan (Zhejiang); one tomb alone contained 511 jades. The impressive number of finds (90 per cent of grave goods consist of jade objects) demonstrates the existence of a highly stratified and organized society ruled by an élite which held political and religious power. This élite also controlled massive human and material resources which could be used to create objects that served as symbols of rank, authority and wealth, and were inalienable even after a person's death.

With the passing of the centuries, jade was also used for other purposes. Over half of the 755 jades found in the tomb of queen Fu Hao of the Shang dynasty, the largest jade hoard discovered to date, had purely a decorative function. The practice of covering the deceased with face masks and long pectorals consisting of numerous elements was introduced during the Western Zhou period. The

180 (above left) The lid of this elegant, semi-transparent pale green jade cup, known as a Hotian cup, is surmounted by an elegant knob in the shape of an open persimmon flower. The cup is finely carved with cloud and grain motifs. [Western Han]

180 (below) This translucent jade rhyton, with veining in shades ranging from pale green to brown, belonged to Zhao Mo (137–122 BC), the second ruler of the southern kingdom of Nanyue. Cut from a single block, it was carved and decorated using various techniques: intaglio work, high and low relief and incision. [Western Han]

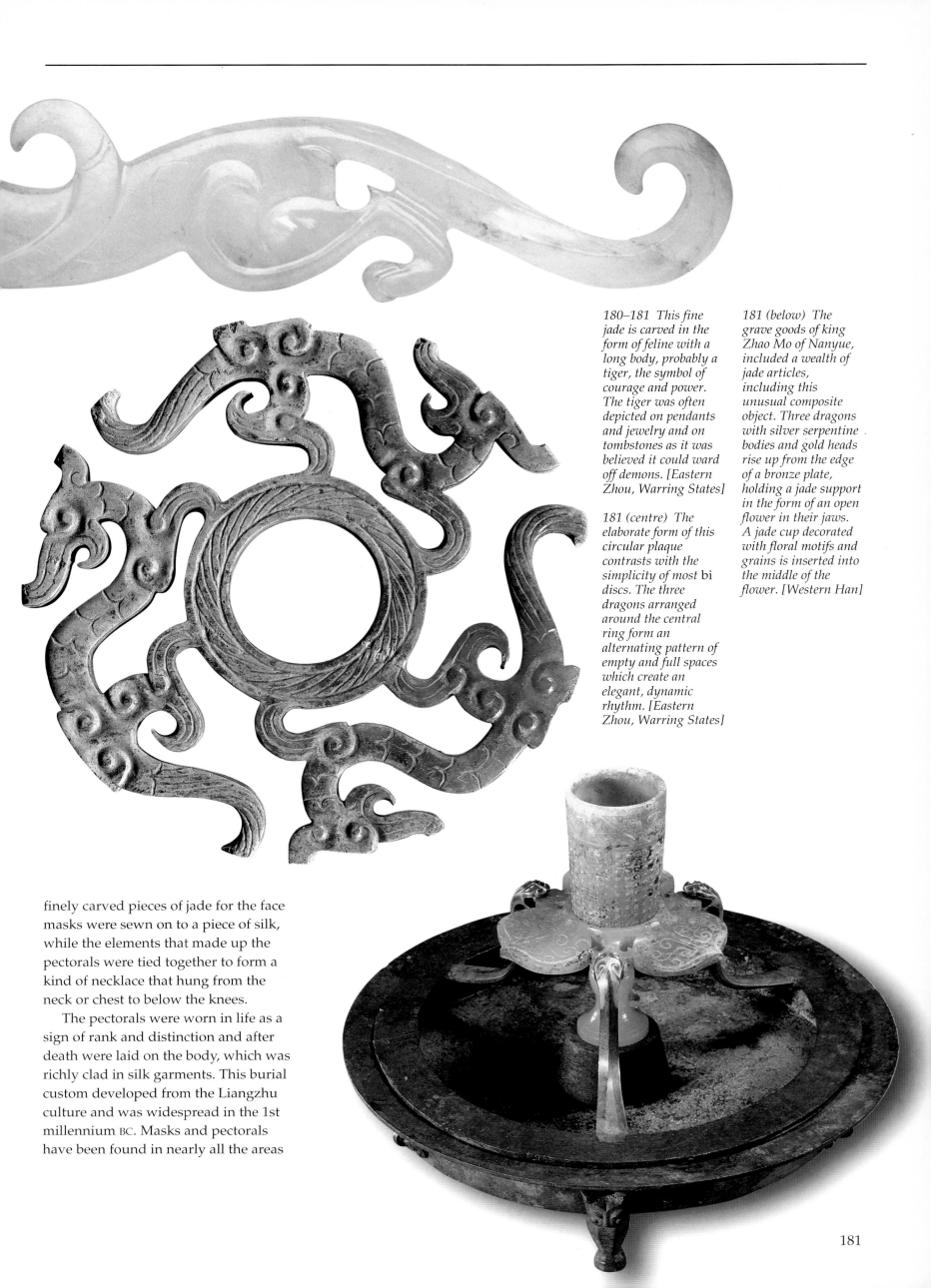

180–181 This fine jade is carved in the form of feline with a long body, probably a tiger, the symbol of courage and power. The tiger was often depicted on pendants and jewelry and on tombstones as it was believed it could ward off demons. [Eastern Zhou, Warring States]

181 (centre) The elaborate form of this circular plaque contrasts with the simplicity of most bi discs. The three dragons arranged around the central ring form an alternating pattern of empty and full spaces which create an elegant, dynamic rhythm. [Eastern Zhou, Warring States]

181 (below) The grave goods of king Zhao Mo of Nanyue, included a wealth of jade articles, including this unusual composite object. Three dragons with silver serpentine bodies and gold heads rise up from the edge of a bronze plate, holding a jade support in the form of an open flower in their jaws. A jade cup decorated with floral motifs and grains is inserted into the middle of the flower. [Western Han]

finely carved pieces of jade for the face masks were sewn on to a piece of silk, while the elements that made up the pectorals were tied together to form a kind of necklace that hung from the neck or chest to below the knees.

The pectorals were worn in life as a sign of rank and distinction and after death were laid on the body, which was richly clad in silk garments. This burial custom developed from the Liangzhu culture and was widespread in the 1st millennium BC. Masks and pectorals have been found in nearly all the areas

182–183 (right)
This unusual object,
formed of two joined
bi *discs, was placed*
at the feet of the jade
burial suit of king
Zhao Mo of Nanyue.
Although it may have
been linked in some
way with the bi disc
placed on the head of
the deceased, its
function is still
unknown. No similar
objects have been
found in any other
tomb containing jade
suits. [Western Han]

ruled by the Zhou dynasty, and also in
Han dynasty tombs. The masks had
religious rather than decorative
functions, as did the small jade amulets
which, particularly in the Han period,
were inserted into the bodily orifices
to protect the corpse and allow the spirit
to continue living.

In the Han period, magical properties
were attributed to jade, and entire suits
were made of it. The burial garments of
Liu Sheng, prince of Zhongshan, and
princess Dou Wan, found at Mancheng
(Hebei), are world famous; they
consisted of 2,498 and 2,160 jade pieces
of various sizes and thicknesses, sewn

182 (above) The
practice of adding an
openwork ornament,
usually depicting a
pair of dragons, to
jade discs, became
widespread during
the Han period.
[Western Han]

together with gold thread. Similar objects made from other materials, such as semiprecious stones and glass, have been found in many parts of the empire.

From the Han period onwards, jade was increasingly used to make luxurious ornamental articles. The manufacturing techniques and decorative patterns used evolved over the centuries and the craftsmen expressed their art with increasing skill and realism. The Chinese have maintained their reverential love for this noble stone over the centuries, reserving a special place for it in the long history of their civilization.

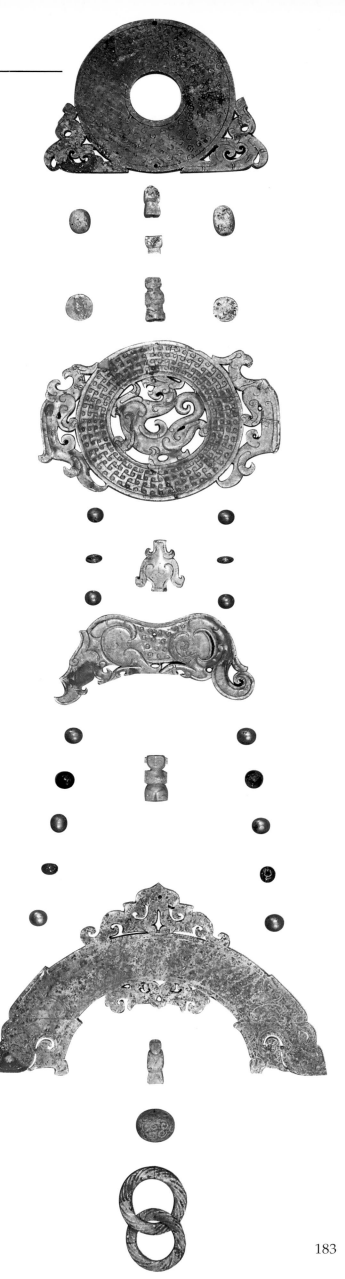

183 Complex jade and precious pearl pectorals, such as this one belonging to king Zhao Mo of Nanyue, were worn during life and placed on the body in death. Their length and weight forced noblemen to walk at a stately pace which emphasized their rank and authoritative appearance. [Western Han]

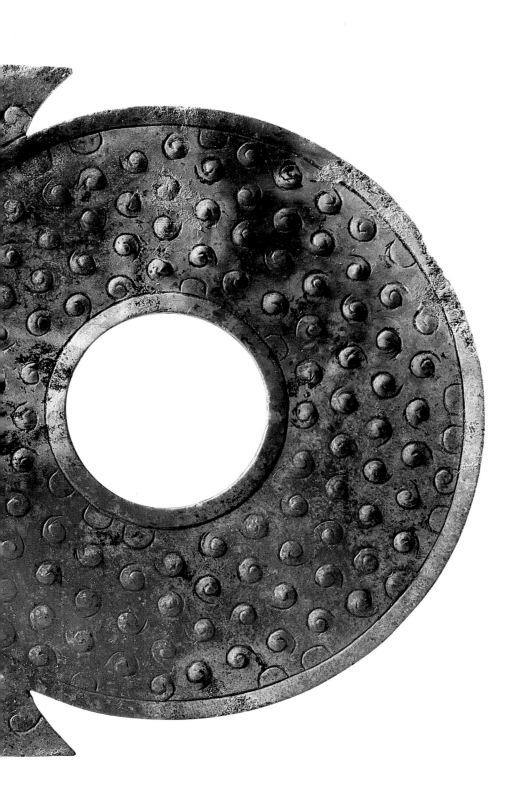

183

BRONZES

Perhaps the most important form of artistic expression in ancient China was the production of ritual bronze vessels. Nothing is more indicative of the splendour and elegance achieved by Chinese civilization than a Shang or Zhou vessel. Archaeologists think that bronze-working began later in China than in southwest Asia, which has led some researchers to suggest that metallurgy was not discovered by the Chinese themselves, but was introduced from elsewhere. As the use of copper and copper alloys did not begin simultaneously all over the world, it is possible that certain innovations were passed from one civilization to another, even over great distances. Another plausible hypothesis is that some fundamental inventions in human history

184 (right) The bronzes of the Shang dynasty are often richly decorated with depictions of animals, birds and dragons' heads in full relief, heavy ribbing that emphasizes the corners, dense geometric patterns and fantastic masks. This hu *vessel was a container for alcohol drunk during rituals.* [Shang]

184 (left) In the Shang dynasty, jue *vessels were used in complex ceremonies which involved the drinking of wine. The tombs of the nobility contained dozens of such vessels, which indicated the rank and prestige of the deceased. Forty were found in the tomb of queen Fu Hao.* [Shang]

184 (left) This jue *vessel, with its long spout and tripod legs, is one of the oldest examples of cast bronze known. Its shape derives from pottery models common in the Neolithic. The workmanship of the bronzes of this period, with little or no decoration, is still basic.* [Erlitou]

were made independently in different places at different times. Although the Bronze Age appeared a little later in China than in other Euroasiatic regions, recent archaeological findings strengthen the theory of indigenous development.

Metallurgy began in China during the Neolithic period. According to some archaeologists, the oldest surviving metal object is a mysterious semicircular object made of yellow copper, found in Jiangzhai in the district of Lintong (Shaanxi) in 1973, which dates from 4700 BC (Yangshao culture). The function of a small brass cylinder discovered on the same site the following year is also unknown. The first bronze article found to date is a small dagger discovered in 1975 at Lin, in the district of Dongxiang (Gansu), on a site dating from 3000 BC (Majiayao culture). Not all researchers agree with these dates; however, there is no doubt about the finds from numerous sites of the Qijia and Huoshaogou cultures in Gansu. Over 60 objects from the Qijia culture (mainly of copper) and over 200 from the Huoshaogou culture (mostly bronze), including mirrors, jewelry, weapons, tools and utensils of various kinds, have been discovered so far. Some crucibles used to smelt ore and other small ornamental copper objects found on sites of the Longshan culture date from the end of the 2nd millennium BC. But it was only from the time of the Xia dynasty, and especially during the Shang culture, that China acquired the technical knowledge to make bronze.

The simple metal objects made in the Neolithic period have been found in various regions, some of them hundreds of miles apart. The rarity of these finds means that only a fragmented picture of the development of metalworking techniques can be obtained. However, until new discoveries are made, at least some points can be made about specific features of Chinese metallurgy.

185 This fang zun container demonstrates the outstanding technical level achieved by the craftsman working on the periphery of the Shang kingdom. The southern artist who made it, though inspired by a style typical of Shang production, showed great originality in the choice of the complex decorative motif. [Shang]

For centuries, bronze objects (mainly vessels, but also weapons, musical instruments and small ornaments) were almost solely used for worship and as offerings in religious ceremonies, not for utilitarian purposes. Other materials continued to be used for everyday items and agricultural tools.

Also, it is interesting to note that from the manufacture of the very first vessels, Chinese craftsmen used a casting technique based on piece-moulds rather than the hammering process commonly used in Southwest Asia. This technique, which was unique in the ancient world, was probably a result of the abundance of metal ore (casting requires a larger amount of metal ore) and the ability to construct large kilns that could achieve high temperatures. The skill and experience acquired in firing the elegant pottery of the Neolithic was used to make earthenware moulds able to withstand the high temperatures needed

to cast metals. Pottery lost its prestige and was relegated to domestic use.

The various casting and decorative techniques based on the use of piece-moulds were used in China for over a thousand years, at least until the 5th century BC, when the lost-wax method was introduced, although it never entirely supplanted earlier techniques. It seems clear, therefore, that the lost-wax technique was unknown in China before this time, a hypothesis which seems to support the theory that metallurgy had a local origin.

Finally, the huge quantity of objects made during the pre-imperial period and the lack, with a few exceptions, of statuary of the human figure prior to the advent of Buddhism should be noted.

In the Erlitou phase of the Xia culture, dynasty bronze acquired the ritual functions and associations which it retained in subsequent centuries. In

186 (above) Human portrayals are rare in the decoration of Shang and Zhou bronzes and so the faces depicted on the sides of this fang ding *food container make it exceptional and demonstrate the originality of the craftsmen working in the southern regions.* [Shang]

186 (left) Taotie masks combined with the leiwen *spiral motif and a densely interwoven pattern of birds and dragons cover the entire surface of this vessel.* [Shang]

addition to simple tools like awls, augers, fish-hooks, *yue* axes, dagger-axes (*ge*), arrowheads and musical instruments, the first ritual bronze vessels for food and wine offerings appear. The few that have come to light include vessels for liquids of the *jue*, *jia* and *he* types, and food containers called *ding* and *li*. These vessels, which undoubtedly derived from pottery prototypes, are still rather coarse, and almost entirely undecorated.

The complex technique of casting with piece-moulds suggests a long prior development, still unknown to archaeology. Chemical analysis of one of the vessels indicates that the alloy consists of very precise percentages of copper and tin (92 per cent copper and 7 per cent tin), which demonstrates the makers' experience of mining, refining and processing ore.

Significant progress was made with the change from the Xia to the Shang dynasty, although the dependence on terracotta models remains evident. The thousands of bronze vessels dating from the first Shang period, identifiable with the Erligang site, are more elaborate than the early examples found at Erlitou, having a wealth of decoration with zoomorphic figures and stylized masks of imaginary animals.

Such abundance demonstrates the wealth of the élite that held religious and political power, and its preference for bronze as a sacred symbol. The types of containers became more varied, with a

187 (above) Taotie masks and running spiral motifs cover the surface of this large lei *vase for wine. [Shang]*

187 (left) Gui *vases, with the characteristic decoration of diamond patterns, rarely used in Shang rituals, were one of the most common containers used by the Zhou before they gained imperial power. [Western Zhou]*

range of 20 shapes that was the beginning of a complex repertoire. Many were containers for liquids, including *hu* vessels, goblets (*gu*) and water bowls (*pan*). Those used for food include *gui* vessels, for offerings of cereals, and *yan*, used for steaming. The rectangular vessel on four feet (*fang ding*), one of the most characteristic forms, developed from the circular tripod (*ding*).

In 1974, two large *fang ding* of excellent workmanship, which probably belonged to the royal court, were found near Zhengzhou. The casting traces on their surface indicate the stages of the process. First the handles were cast by casting in a double mould, then the flat-bottomed body and finally the legs, using two outer moulds and an inner mould.

189 (opposite above) Some scholars have suggested that this impressive bronze mask represents Can Cong, first king of the Shu, described in ancient legend as having large ears and protruding eyes. The kingdom of Shu flourished towards the end of the 2nd millennium BC. [12th century BC]

188 (above and right) Fifty-four bronze heads of varying sizes (from 13 to 50 cm (5 to 20 in) tall) were discovered in two sacrificial pits found at Sanxingdui in 1986. Archaeologists *have classed them into four types, based on the hairstyle and headgear. They are believed to have been part of complete statues although no trace of the bodies was found. Two of the* *bronze heads found at Sanxingdui are partly covered with gold leaf. They probably portray ancestors of the royal clan or divinities – or both, as was the case with the Shang. [12th century BC]*

Mastery of this sophisticated technique led to the production of an amazing variety of objects of great elegance and surprising size. A clay model of the vessel to be cast was made first. Then a layer of clay was applied to the model and divided into sections, the number of which depended on the type of vessel and the decoration. Mortise-and-tenon joints were applied along the edges of the sections to ensure the perfect reassembly of the individual parts. The thickness of the inner model was then reduced so as to form a gap between the inner and outer sections, and the entire model was reassembled. The thickness of the gap determined the thickness of the vessel. Small metal spacers were placed between the inner model and the outer sections to prevent contact or variations in the space between the two walls, and would be incorporated in the casting.

The decoration was not applied to the finished vessel, but was an integral part of the casting, as the craftsman incised the decorative patterns on the concave wall of the sections. Fragments of clay moulds, some with simple and others with complex decoration, have been found at Erlitou, and similar finds have been made at Erligang, but in larger numbers and better preserved.

Later, the reverse process was introduced: the decoration was carved on the inner model first, and then impressed on the outer mould during the preparation of the sections, allowing relief designs to be achieved. These techniques are unique to Chinese metallurgy. It was not until after the 6th century BC, with the introduction of inlaying, that decoration could be applied to the vessel after casting.

Not all vessels could be achieved by a single casting. The more complex shapes and decorations required some components to be pre-cast separately (one example is the *fang ding* described

189 (right) This bronze statue of a standing human figure found at Sanxingdui is the only known large-scale sculpture dating from the Bronze Age. The identity of the person is unknown; he may be a deity, a ruler, a shaman or a clan chieftain. In fact, these suggestions are not mutually exclusive: his crown in the shape of a lotus-flower symbolizes the sun, the emblem of both holiness and royalty. [12th century BC]

zoomorphic *gong* (or *guang*) and *zun* vessels introduced in the Anyang period.

In the Erligang period vessels for food and drink had relatively thin walls; most of them still had a flat bottom, while the tripods were supported by conical legs. The fairly simple decorations already included cloud motifs and spiral patterns, symbolizing lightning. The first depictions of animals and mythological creatures also appeared; among them were the *kui* dragon, and a fantastic creature with great staring eyes that became the most typical and yet most mysterious motif found on Shang vessels. It was called *taotie* in the Song dynasty (960–1279), and traditionally took the form of a head seen frontally, with great protruding eyes and a body split into mirror images at the sides, with claws and feet parallel to the body and the tail curling upwards. Seen from another perspective, the *taotie* masks appear to consist of two fantastic animals, probably *kui* dragons, facing one another in profile,

above). Elaborate applied additions, such as some types of handle and relief decorations, were cast at the second stage directly on to the body of the vessel, the surface of which was prepared with holes or projecting tenons that would guarantee a perfect union. The opposite process was also used; the attachment was made first, and the metal for the body of the vessel was then cast. In most cases, joints were made by casting, rarely by welding or riveting.

Shape and decoration were thus closely linked, and depended on the technique used. A decorative pattern consisting of symmetrical compartments typical of most Shang vessels arose from the need to conceal the flaws created along the vertical joints of the mould sections at the time of casting. Although such symmetrical decoration was preferred, the Shang founders were also able to produce vessels with asymmetrical friezes not organized in sections, such as the magnificent

190 (above) Three large-eyed *taotie* masks form the decoration on the body of this *liding* tripod vessel. [Shang]

190 (right) and 191 (opposite below) These two *you* vessels were cast by a craftsmen called Bo Ge who lived at the beginning of the Zhou dynasty, as revealed by the six-character inscription on the lids. The decoration of both is particularly complex and takes the form of both low relief and applied animal heads. [Western Zhou]

so that only one protruding eye of each, emanating a strong hypnotic power, is visible. Some scholars believe that the motif derives from the masks with large eyes found on jades of the Liangzhu Neolithic culture, but this theory is not universally accepted.

Around 1300 BC the capital moved to Yin, present-day Anyang. The sites found at Anyang and in the neighbouring areas demonstrate the existence of a highly advanced social and religious organization, documented by a large number of finds of all kinds, the huge foundations of buildings and the opulent royal tombs, which have no equal among those of the preceding period.

During this period, bronze work reached outstanding technical and

191 (right) A dragon with staring eyes and large horns curls its tail around the lid of this magnificent lei *container for wine, dating from the 11th–10th century* BC. *[Western Zhou]*

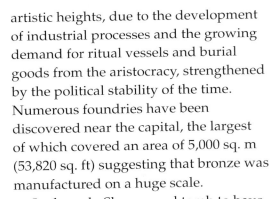

artistic heights, due to the development of industrial processes and the growing demand for ritual vessels and burial goods from the aristocracy, strengthened by the political stability of the time. Numerous foundries have been discovered near the capital, the largest of which covered an area of 5,000 sq. m (53,820 sq. ft) suggesting that bronze was manufactured on a huge scale.

In the only Shang royal tomb to have survived intact for over 3,000 years, that of Fu Hao, one of the numerous consorts of king Wu Ding (?–1189 BC), there were 466 bronzes among the 1,800 burial objects found: 195 ritual vessels and 271 weapons, bells, finely decorated mirrors and various tools, weighing a total of 1,600 kg (3,527 lb). The majority of the vessels were containers for wine (93 *gu* goblets and *jue* tripods), but there was also a pair of impressive *fang ding* (80 cm (32 in) high and 120 kg (265lb) in weight) and some pieces with unusual shapes (a pair of rectangular vessels for wine called *fang yi*, and a *yan*, a trilobed vessel in the shape of a steamer).

191

192 Another example of the artistry and ingenuity of Chinese bronzeworkers, this unusual lamp takes the form a servant grasping two snakes. The man's head is silver, and his eyes are two black stones. His bronze robe retains traces of cloud and scroll motifs in black and red lacquer. [Eastern Zhou, Warring States]

192 (right) The shape and decoration of this elegant food container (fang hu) reflect new trends that emerged towards the middle of the Zhou dynasty, when bronze vessels had lost their former symbolic and ritual significance. [Eastern Zhou, Warring States]

Typical characteristics of many Shang vessels from the Anyang phase are their massive, sometimes imposing appearance and a wealth of decoration. The largest vessel yet found is the Xi Mu Wu, a monumental *fang ding* (133 cm (52 in) high and 875 kg (1,930 lb) in weight), similar to those found in the tomb of Fu Hao. It is estimated that it took some 3,000 craftsmen to make it using at least 700 crucibles simultaneously; the molten metal must have been cast in the clay moulds quickly enough to prevent the metal from solidifying before the complex operation had been completed.

Shang bronzes were of excellent workmanship: the walls of the vessels were thicker, and the shapes were substantially modified, giving rise to new types. Decoration became more complex and elaborate and tended to

cover the whole surface of the vessels; *leiwen* (or *huiwen*) geometrical motifs began to appear, with different forms of spirals, clouds, diamonds, triangles, and patterns of leaves and flowers.

An increasingly wide variety of animals was also depicted, such as tigers, oxen, snakes, fish, birds, tortoises, cicadas, silkworms and fantastic monsters including the *kui* dragon, the long dragon and the phoenix. A pre-eminent position, however, was occupied by the *taotie* motif. The long dragon, centered on a single great eye, as if the animal had been painted in profile, was also common. The faces often had staring eyes and exaggeratedly open mouths, as if about to erupt into terrifying roars and sometimes they were cast in full relief, as if forcing their way out of the body of the vessel. In rare cases, human faces were portrayed. Some bronzes of the late Shang period were incised with short inscriptions, indicating the owner's clan or the name of ancestor in whose honour

192–193 Ritual wine vessels in the shape of an animal, like this magnificent inlaid bronze rhinoceros decorated with cloud patterns, were fairly common during the Warring States period. [Eastern Zhou, Warring States]

193 (below) Vessels and incense burners made in the shape of powerful animals, often decorated with magnificent gold and silver inlay work, demonstrate the great versatility of the bronze workers of the Warring States period and early empire. [Eastern Zhou, Warring States]

the vessel had been made. The practice of stating on the vessel the occasion for which it was made was introduced towards the end of the dynasty.

According to some experts, the zoomorphic images that recur so frequently on bronzes of the Shang period were deliberately designed as decorative elements of great visual impact, intended to strike fear and awe in the onlookers because of their menacing, terrifying appearance. Others, in view of the close link between art, religion and politics, attribute a largely propitiatory significance to these images. The animals and mythological beings portrayed were believed to be powerful allies, used by the shaman-priests to communicate with the gods and the spirits of the ancestors of the royal clan who lived in the next world. Contact with the celestial world took place through complex rites, during which the shamans sang and danced to the sound of drums and bronze bells, sacrificed animals and consumed food and drink until they reached a state of trance, in which they ascended, riding real or fantastic animals, to another sphere, to communicate with the deities and spirits.

The animals depicted on bronze vessels therefore represented the means by which the shamans reached the celestial sphere, and enabled them to cross the barrier between the human and spirit worlds. It was thus the role of these animals, rather than their terrifying appearance, that inspired awe and respect in the onlookers.

194–195 Dragons and phoenixes, mythical creatures that are found in Chinese imagery from the earliest times, entwine to form this unusual bronze table base with gold and silver inlay. The dragon and the phoenix were thought to symbolize prosperity and good fortune. [Eastern Zhou, Warring States]

Recent finds from southern regions and dating to the 13th to 11th centuries BC, reveal the existence of advanced bronze cultures that developed independent and wholly original features in areas not subject to direct Shang influence. A magnificent set of grave goods, consisting of over 450 bronze items (50 vessels, 4 bells and various weapons and tools), and a large amount of pottery (356 items) jades (150), and other items, was found in a tomb dating from the 13th century BC, discovered in 1989 at Dayangzhou in the district of Xin'gan, in Jiangxi.

Over 900 objects made of gold, bronze, jade, stone and pottery, which unusually had been smashed and burned before burial, were found in 1986 in two sacrificial pits dating from the 12th century BC at Sanxingdui near Guanghan (Sichuan). They demonstrate the

195 (right) This strange animal, made in bronze using the lost-wax technique, formed one part of a stand for a musical instrument, perhaps a drum. The expressive features and long curling tongue are typical of the figurative art of the southern kingdom of Chu. [Eastern Zhou, Springs and Autumns]

existence of a highly developed civilization which no written texts refer to and which we therefore know very little about. In addition to ritual vessels, the decoration of which recalls the style typical of Hunan, there were also some very large bronze sculptures in the form of trees, one of which measures 4 m (13 ft) high, and 20 fantastic masks with prominent ears, huge eyes with protruding pupils and a strange curling nose. There were also dozens of large

196 (below left)
A solid gold horseman, perhaps a portrayal of the deceased, rises above a circle of oxen on the lid of this container, typical of the Dian culture. [Western Han]

human heads, some of which were covered with gold leaf, and a very unusual figure, perhaps a shaman, standing on a tall pedestal, reaching a total height of 262 cm (8 ft 6 in).

These are rare examples of bronze sculptures of the human figure of this size dating from the pre-imperial period. Literary sources describe colossal statues cast around 1,000 years later by Qin Shihuangdi on the occasion of the unification of the empire, and by other emperors of the Han dynasty, but none has ever been found. Many centuries separate the enigmatic sculptures of Sanxingdui from these reported statues of the early imperial period, and it was an even longer time before the bronze statues of Buddhist inspiration were made, from the 4th century AD onwards.

The number of foundries multiplied in the Western Zhou period as a result of the introduction of the one-piece mould technique, which allowed the large-scale production of vessels. Bronzes were therefore produced in far greater quantities than in earlier times. In the first phase of the dynasty, there was stylistic continuity with the past, and deference for Shang tradition was given priority over the use of elements specific to the Zhou culture. In time, however, there were changes: vessels that were

196–197 Statuettes
of animals, especially
cattle and felines, are
typical of the
southern Dian
culture, which
flourished between the
4th and 1st centuries

BC in the area of Lake
Dianchi (Yunnan).
This intriguing table
or stand for sacrificial
offerings possesses
great expressive force.
[Eastern Zhou,
Warring States]

once strictly ritual gradually acquired
new functions and were increasingly
used for commemorative purposes.
Important political events, appointments
or donations received from the king,
formed the occasion for commissioning
the casting of vessels on which these
events were recorded so that they could
be presented to the ancestors and handed
down to posterity.

New ceremonial practices, influenced
by a form of moralism unknown to the
Shang, led to a drastic reduction in the
ritual use of alcohol, with the result that
once-common vessels and goblets
became increasingly rare in grave goods,
and gradually disappeared. On the other

hand, the number of cooking vessels,
especially the *ding* type, increased, as did
those for food storage, especially the *gui*,
which saw numerous modifications and
variations in form, size and decoration.
New forms of other well-known vessels
also appeared, such as the *jue* with four
wide legs in the shape of knife blades,
and there were variations of the *ding*, *zun*,
you and *zhi* types, some of which now
appeared in animal shapes. *Yu* jugs, *pan*
basins and *xian* vessels were made in
varied forms and food containers called
fu, *xu* and *yi* were introduced. *Bo* and *ling*
bells continued to be made, but the *nao*
type was replaced by the *yong*, which was
suspended from a hook with the opening

facing downwards – before this bells had
been fixed to a special stand with the
opening facing upwards.

Taotie masks were common in the first
phase of the dynasty but gradually went
out of fashion, giving way to new
ornamental motifs, such as birds, often
with large crests and long tails. Elephants
appeared with more and more frequency.
The animals were shown in a more
natural way, and appeared livelier and
almost playful. The ornamental elements
became more harmonious and geometric,
and the traditional repertoire was
enriched by concentric rings, herringbone
and tile patterns, and wavy lines, often
resembling fluttering ribbons.

197

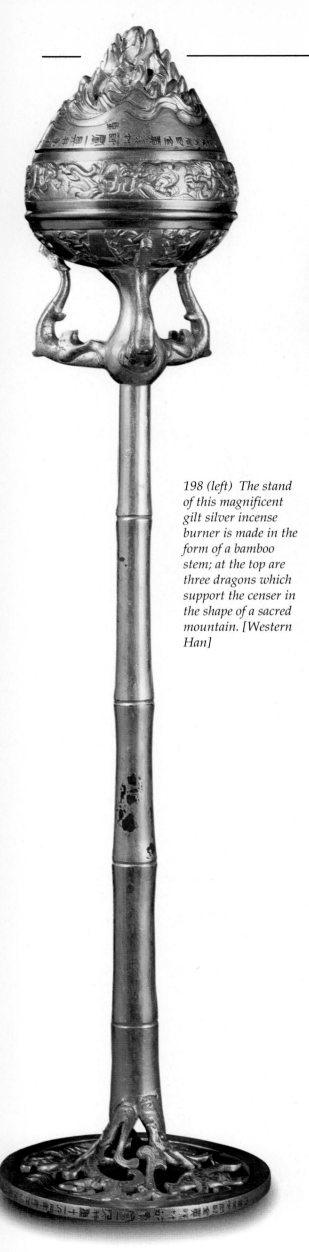

198 (left) The stand of this magnificent gilt silver incense burner is made in the form of a bamboo stem; at the top are three dragons which support the censer in the shape of a sacred mountain. [Western Han]

Inscriptions increased both in number and length, forming documentation of incomparable historical value, similar to the inscriptions on bone and tortoise shells of the Shang era. It is estimated that over 3,000 bronzes bearing inscriptions date from this period. The longest, on the *ding* of the Duke of Mao, has 497 characters, while the *bo* bell of the Marquis of Chi is inscribed with 492 characters. Some inscriptions have great literary value, such as the 110 characters of rhymed prose engraved on a *pan* basin, narrating the feats of Xuan, king of Zhou against the barbarian Xianyuan people.

Bronzes began to lose their ritual significance during the first phase of the Eastern Zhou dynasty, but their value as symbols of political prestige remained unchanged. The number of bronze vessels and tools used in everyday life by aristocratic families increased and new types of bells were introduced. Alloys were created which were more fluid at high temperatures, and new processes were introduced, such as the lost-wax casting technique, which could be used to produce an entire object, or in association with the traditional and still preferred piece-mould technique.

The discovery of malleable cast iron dates from this period. Swords made of natural carbon steel with a carbon content of 0.5–0.6 per cent have been found near Changsha (Henan). Welding, riveting and other techniques were also improved. Craftsmen now were able to inlay vessels, goblets, mirrors, bowls and ornamental items with elegant copper

198 (above) and 199 (opposite above left) Two of a set of weights in the form of leopards made of gilt inlaid with silver and eyes of garnet that were part of the magnificent grave goods of princess Dou Wan, wife of prince Liu Sheng of Zhongshan, who died between 113 and 104 BC. The Han aristocracy collected precious objects including antique pieces. These collections accompanied them to the afterlife. [Western Han]

199 (right) This magnificent **hu** ritual vessel for wine, made of finely inlaid bronze, was found with another similar one in the tomb of prince Liu Sheng. Its surface is entirely covered with an inscription in gold characters in the 'bird' script, which originated in the southern kingdom of Yue. [Western Han]

198 (opposite below) The clothes and facial features of this kneeling servant supporting an oil lamp indicate that he belonged to a non-Chinese race, probably the Xiongnu. Traces of malachite, cuprite and azurite have been found on the surface of the object. [Western Han]

199 (right) Four dragons hovering against a background of cloud motifs form the highly stylized decoration covering the surface of this bronze vessel. It comes from Mancheng, the site where Liu Sheng and Dou Wan were buried. [Western Han]

designs. A far greater and more elaborate range of decorative effects could thus be obtained.

The main motifs were patterns of scrolls, four-lobed swirls, friezes of leaves, coils, entwining birds, dragons and serpents. Entwined patterns gradually became one of the most common motifs, often consisting of more or less naturalistic creatures whose bodies were interwoven in a repetitive pattern, forming a kind of dense, seemingly endless web in which it was hard to discern the individual figures. Openwork decoration also began to develop during this period.

The second phase of the dynasty, the Warring States period, was characterized by large-scale production of a wide variety of iron and cast iron tools for agricultural use such as mattocks, picks and scythes, and other tools such as axes, chisels and metal parts for carts. Changes in society had widespread repercussions in religion too. Bronze vessels were now only used for secular purposes, and had been reduced to mere symbols of wealth and power.

Casting and metalworking techniques developed further and the decorative repertoire increased thanks to the introduction of new processes, for instance incising, chasing, gilding and inlaying, now not only with copper but also with silver and gold. Depictions of real and imaginary animals multiplied; these were often stylized, and lacked the mysterious, terrifying appearance of the images of the past. As the strong religious implications of bronze weakened, the first scenes from everyday life, characterized by simple yet vivid designs, appeared on vessels. Copper, silver, gold, malachite and turquoise inlays produced multicoloured objects, which have some of the richness and elegance of textiles such as brocade.

The kingdom of Jin is regarded as the birthplace of the Zhou artistic tradition and bronze production here reached unprecedented levels of perfection. The long forgotten motif of the *taotie* mask was reintroduced, often in combination with crossed dragons. Influences from local artistic traditions increased, especially those which had developed in the central and southern regions between the Han and Huai rivers. The southern kingdom of Chu also exerted a strong influence on neighbouring principalities because of the high quality of its artistic production.

In 221 BC the Zhou dynasty came to an end, and the imperial era inaugurated by Qin Shihuangdi, the First August

200 (centre) A mirror full of cosmological symbolism: around the edge are animals that symbolized the cardinal directions and the seasons – the Tortoise of the North, with the Snake coiled around it (winter), the Dragon of the East

(spring), the Phoenix of the south (summer) and the Tiger of the West (autumn). In the centre are Xiwangmu, Queen Mother of the West, the sacred Mountains of the Immortals and the hare, symbol of the moon. The hare

crushes the moon with a mortar and pestle under a cassia tree growing from the mouth of the toad. Chang E was turned into a toad after he had stolen the elixir of immortality and then found refuge on the moon. [Tang]

200 (bottom) The slow progress and curious, mild expression of the tortoise are brilliantly captured in this incense burner made of bronze with gold and silver inlays. [Han]

Emperor of the Qin dynasty, began. In the Han dynasty, the production of luxury objects for everyday life, such as all types of containers, lamps, mirrors and perfume and incense burners flourished.

Bronze-working certainly did not cease later, but the level of workmanship inexorably deteriorated. The production of bronze objects became increasingly rare and expensive as copper was now needed for minting coins. The emperor Wendi (179–157 BC) actually prohibited the use of bronze for making vessels and items of everyday use, while iron tools and weapons now replaced bronze. Hardening techniques had increased the

201 (left) In the Tang period the dragon was the symbol of the emperor and was very important to followers of Daoism. It was also associated with the mythical world of the Immortals and so was frequently represented in bronze. [Tang]

201 (below) Bronze was the most suitable material for making religious statues, which were cast using the lost-wax technique. Gilding was often used, as in the case of this seated Buddha. [Tang]

strength of swords and daggers, which could be made much sharper, with the result that bronze blades became obsolete.

The Bronze Age had now come to an end, and centuries were to pass before the use of this metal was revived. And once again it was for religious reasons – to create wonderful religious images, altar decorations and receptacles for Buddhist worship.

The art of bronze-making flourished anew with the magnificent *shengshou* mirrors (featuring deities and animals) which portrayed mythological characters like Xiwangmu, Queen Mother of the West, or Dongwanggong, King Father of the East, made in the Three Kingdoms period and the Eastern Jin dynasty. Silvery white mirrors, richly decorated with mythological motifs or grapes, flowers, birds, dragons and other real or imaginary creatures, were manufactured during the Tang dynasty.

Bronze objects, designed as the focal point of magical and ritual celebrations, remained the emblem of ancient Chinese tradition because of their monumental size, impressive shapes and detailed decorations, in which an extensive mythological repertoire was transmitted and perpetuated for centuries.

GOLD AND SILVER

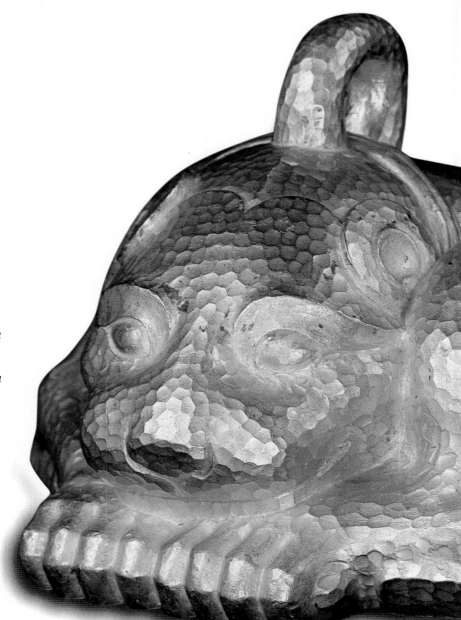

The first gold and silver objects found in China date back to the 2nd millennium BC. The oldest items made of precious metal ever found were discovered in tombs of the Qijia and Huoshaogou cultures. In China gold is found in seams and alluvial deposits, and in the earliest periods, most gold used came from the latter. Silver is only found in lodes, however, and therefore needs to be mined. As a result, it was far rarer than gold during the Bronze Age. It only began to gain in importance towards the end of the Zhou dynasty, and especially from the Han dynasty onwards.

Gold and silver never acquired the same prestige in China as in the West; more value was attributed to jade and bronze articles. Gold was mainly used to

202 (below) This gilded silver casket is part of a treasure found in the ancient Buddhist monastery of Famen, dating from the Tang period. The treasure was found when the brick pagoda which had been built over it in 1609 collapsed. The casket is one of eight, wrapped in silk and placed one inside another, found in a sandalwood trunk carved with images of Buddha and his disciples. [Tang]

make jewelry. Objects of Shang date have been found in Gaocheng (Hebei) and Shilou (Shanxi), in the form of beaten gold earrings and hairpins. An 85 per cent pure cast gold hairpin weighing 108.7 g (almost 4 oz) was found in Pinggu (Henan). Gold leaf less than a millimetre thick found in Shang tombs demonstrates that Chinese goldsmiths handled this highly malleable metal with surprising skill at an early date.

Numerous gold and gilded bronze buckles and clasps with gold and silver inlays date back to the Eastern Zhou dynasty. The technique of inlaying gold

and silver on bronze was frequently employed during this period. In addition to jewelry, the production of other luxury objects began. The magnificent gold basin belonging to Marquis Yi of Zeng, found in Leigudun (Hubei), is dated to the second half of the 5th century BC. It was cast in separate parts which were joined together, is 98 per cent pure and weighs 2,156 g (76 oz); the matching ladle weighs 56.45 g (2 oz).

Gold was used to mint coins in the kingdom of Chu at the end of the Eastern Zhou dynasty. In the early empire, gold and silver were used to make a variety of objects. The solid gold leopard, weighing 9 kg (20 lb), found at Nanyaozhuang (Jiangsu) in 1982, is particularly fine. Central Asian art exerted an influence in this period, and Chinese goldsmiths learned new techniques such as filigree work and granulation.

202–203 (above) In ancient China, objects made of solid gold were quite rare, apart from seals. Gold was used mainly in combination with other metals, such as bronze or silver, and for finer decorative effects such as openwork, granulation and filigree. This leopard, weighing 9 kg (20 lb), is therefore very unusual. [Western Han]

202–203 (left) This large gold vessel with lid and ladle, found with a gold cup under the coffin of Marquis Yi of Zeng, was probably a tureen for food. Possibly used during his life, the Marquis was buried with it for his use also in the afterlife. [Eastern Zhou, Warring States]

203 (above) The delicate decorations of birds and vines covering this small gilt-silver box in the form of a melon were created using the repoussé technique [Tang].

204 (left) This magnificent gold jug is densely decorated with motifs typical of the Tang repertoire: lotus flowers and ducks among curling tendrils, with lotus petals in relief below. A small tortoise on the handle holds a chain attached to the lid, in the shape of a lotus bud. [Tang]

204 (below) Persian influence on Tang art is evident in this octagonal gold cup. The relief dancers have Middle Eastern features, although the instruments some of them are holding and playing are Chinese. [Tang]

205 (right) Ducks swimming or perched on pomegranate or lotus flowers form the decorative motif of this magnificent silver and gold bowl, the tribute paid by a local official to the Tang court, which in turn donated it to the Famen monastery. [Tang]

The craftsmanship achieved by Chinese metalworkers in gold and silver reached its height during the Tang period. And electrum, an alloy of gold and silver which is also found naturally, was also now used. The Tang imperial nobility and the wealthy aristocracy were great patrons of the craftsmen involved in gold manufacture, strongly influenced by the Central Asian metallurgical tradition which was very popular at court. A hybrid style therefore developed, which is well represented by some jugs and goblets in which traditional Chinese decorative motifs blend harmoniously with stylistic elements typical of Central Asia, Sassanid Persia and India. Numerous techniques were used to produce works of great elegance; in addition to casting, objects were made using engraving, embossing, repoussé work, relief and incising.

In 1983, 956 silver objects were found on a single site in Dingmaoqiao (Jiangsu). In the same year, a treasure was discovered at Fufeng (Shaanxi) among the foundations of the pagoda of the Buddhist temple of Famen. It had fortunately remained hidden and intact for centuries, and contained reliquaries and votive offerings, including four finger bones venerated as belonging to Buddha, and no fewer than 121 gold and silver objects used in worship, mainly donated by the emperors Yizong (859–873) and Xizong (873–888).

206 This intricate gold dagger handle dating from the 4th century BC was made by the lost-wax technique which had been introduced into China a century earlier. It is the best example of the 'picturesque' Henan style applied to gold manufacture. The perfect balance of the pattern of densely interwoven dragons is impressive. [Eastern Zhou, Warring States]

207–210 The art of the steppes, and especially that of the peoples who lived in southern Siberia and Mongolia, had great influence on Han art. Rectangular plaques depicting wild beasts, often a hybrid of a bear and a wolf, sinking their fangs into horses and other animals, are typical of the Xiongnu culture. [Western Han]

211 Imported objects, especially ones made of metal or glass, were fashionable in the Northern Dynasties period. This silver-gilt jug, found in a tomb dating from 569, may be Sassanid or Bactrian, as suggested by the acanthus leaves and the classical style of the mythological characters of Greek inspiration depicted on the body. [Northern Qi]

was removed and replaced with a lighter supporting structure. More layers of lacquer were applied to the object thus obtained, often a statue, which could then be painted or gilded. Some magnificent Buddhist statues were made by this process from the second half of the 6th century.

Mineral or vegetable pigments were mixed in to change the basic colour. Red and black were the dominant colours, but brown and yellow were also used. Chestnut, green, blue, white, gold, silver and new shades of red and yellow were obtained later. The objects were painted with *lakes* – a reddish pigment from lac – or oil from the paulownia tree, or incised with a thin burin. In the *pingtuo* process, gold and silver leaf were applied to the lacquered base and covered with a number of transparent coats. Another decorative process which became popular in Japan was to spray gold powder on to the lacquered base. Some items were inlaid with metals, precious stones, glass and rock crystal. The intaglio technique, developed in the Tang period, became very common later, from the Yuan period (1279–1368) onwards. One of the earliest examples of this

214 Wooden carvings of animals, sometimes with long horns, were popular in southern regions in the 4th century BC. These two birds, probably cranes, with immensely long necks, are made from lacquered and painted wood. They probably functioned as a support for a musical instrument. [Eastern Zhou, Warring States]

215 (above) This small chest was designed to contain the garments of Marquis Yi of Zeng, which have have not survived. The chest was found open and floating on the water that filled the tomb. [Eastern Zhou, Warring States]

215 (below) Two images are depicted on the sides of this unusual duck-shaped black lacquerware box. On one side is a warrior dancing to the sound of a drum and on the other, seen here, is a shaman striking large bronze bells hanging from a support in the form of facing animals. [Eastern Zhou, Warring States]

216 (below) Spiral clouds and long festooned scrolls decorate this magnificent lacquer vessel, a container for wine. Chinese archaeologists are now highly expert in recovering lacquer objects, which are frequently found in the grave goods of the early empire. [Western Han]

216 (right) This large round lacquered wood tray from Mawangdui is decorated with alternate red and black bands, with typical deep red spiral/cloud patterns forming the motif. [Western Han]

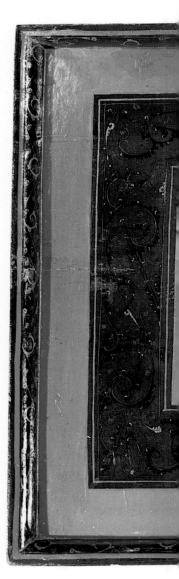

process is a suit of leather armour covered with pieces of lacquer carved in intaglio, from Miran in east Turkestan.

The great variety of techniques and materials used enabled skilled craftsmen to produce highly prestigious and original items. Over 200 lacquerware objects were found in an excellent state of preservation in the tomb of Marquis Yi of Zeng at Leigudun (Hubei) and hundreds of lacquerware items came from Mawangdui near Changsha (Hunan). Motifs include entwined stylized dragons and birds set against spiral patterns, clouds and waves to create a kind of dense brocade effect, and slender arabesques that complete and surround the ornamental patterns, recalling the complicated decorations of bronze vessels. There are also depictions of animals, imaginary creatures and hybrid beings. The shiny, hard nature of lacquer enhances the bright, vivid colours used, making the figures stand out sharply against the uniform background. In many cases the densely packed images demonstrate the exceptional skill of the craftsmen in depicting the smallest details.

217 (right) A set of eight cups with side handles was packed in a box (he), forming a service that could be used for food or drinks. The box and cups are made of lacquered wood and are richly decorated. [Western Han]

217 Also found at Mawangdui, this rectangular tray, with similar decoration to the round tray opposite, is thought to have been a table for eating meals off while seated on cushions on the floor, a custom still found in some Asian countries. [Western Han]

218 (above)
In Chinese, yu (fish) is phonetically related to yu (abundance); yu also indicated the male genitals, while fish and water represented sexual harmony. Wealth and fertility are therefore symbolized by the fish swimming around leaves, a symbol of longevity.
[Western Han]

218 (opposite below) This box is made by the pingtuo *technique, which was rare in the Han period. The lacquered object was decorated with thin layers of gold and silver leaf, then covered with a transparent coat. [Western Han]*

219 (right) Large stylized clouds and spiral motifs blend in the decoration of this impressive fang hu *vessel made of lacquered wood, found at Mawangdui. [Western Han]*

219 (left) This flat bottle for cereal wine, the largest found to date, is decorated with motifs typical of lacquerware made in central China in the second half of the 3rd century BC. Sinuous spiral-cloud lines blend perfectly with the agile bodies of the leopards, some winged, creating very elegant rhythms. [Western Han]

220–221 A detail of the coffin of the Marchioness of Dai, found at Mawangdui: fantastic figures and mythological beings with strange features chase one another amid swirling clouds on a black background. The task of these creatures was to ward off demons and evil spirits, to protect the deceased on their journey to the next world. [Western Han]

PAINTING

Thousands of graffiti bear witness to magical and religious beliefs in China during the Palaeolithic and Neolithic periods. The earliest painting on pottery took the form of fluid, decorative patterns or stylized representations of people and animals. Painting on pottery declined in the Bronze Age and since other materials used, such as wood and silk, are perishable, evidence for painting in the 1st millennium BC is scarce. The delicate lacquerware found in the tombs of the Eastern Zhou and Western Han dynasties is particularly attractive, however. The painted or carved coffins in which princes and kings were laid to rest are of very fine craftsmanship, such as those made of lacquered wood found at Leigudun (Hubei) in the tomb of Marquis Yi of Zeng (died 433 BC), painted with animals and hybrid creatures in various colours on a vermilion background. Other examples are the magnificent coffin with a black background found in tomb no. 1 at Mawangdui (Hunan) dating from 168 BC,

or the black limestone coffin found in a Tang tomb at Qianxian (Shaanxi), which takes the form of a house with carved doors and windows, surmounted by a lid that imitates a tiled roof. Its walls are decorated with delicate carved female figures performing simple, spontaneous actions – contemplating a flower or offering food to a bird (AD 706).

Some paintings on silk have also been found at Mawangdui, the most famous, of which, of outstanding artistic merit, is the banner found in the tomb of the wife of the Marquis of Dai. It is painted with a complex depiction of the journey of the deceased to the afterworld, described in the chapter on funerary art.

On the basis of the few archaeological finds of architectural fragments, it seems that the most important buildings were frescoed from the Eastern Zhou period on. Literary sources speak of imperial palaces richly decorated with depictions of deities or scenes based on stories of Confucian inspiration.

221 (below) Fantastic creatures, some armed with halberds, guard the internal coffin (nei guan) of Marquis Yi of Zeng. The rest of the surface is covered with complex geometrical and zoomorphic patterns, forming a magnificent decoration, which probably had great symbolic significance. [Eastern Zhou, Warring States]

222–223 Riding on horseback was a popular pastime for the Tang nobility, for hunting and pleasure. Camels, with loaded baskets on their backs, also appear in this scene. [Tang]

222 (right) This detail of a painting from the tomb of Li Xian at Qianling shows two courtesans in the gardens of the imperial palace. One is watching a hoopoe in flight. [Tang]

222 (left) A young servant girl, delicately painted, is just a small detail from the magnificent murals in the tomb of Li Xian, son of the emperor Gaozong. According to the official histories, the princes Li Xian (Zhanghuai) and Li Zhongrun (Yide), were killed, along with their sister Yongtai, by the powerful and ruthless Wu Zetian. [Tang]

Han dynasty tombs contained paintings on impressed bricks, stone slabs or plaster. They feature a huge repertoire of decorative themes; in some tombs religious and cosmological subjects prevailed, while in others there were scenes of everyday or public life and portraits of officials, as if to maintain a continuity between the human world and the afterlife. The figures, shown in profile and delineated with sharp contours, are usually painted in red and ochre. Tombs containing a wealth of wall paintings have been found at Holingor (Horinger) in Inner Mongolia (2nd century BC), at Yinan in Shandong (late 1st century) and at Taiyuan in Shaanxi (570). The wall paintings of the imperial tombs of the Tang dynasty, painted by, or under the supervision of, court artists, are particularly beautiful. The best preserved examples were found in the tombs of princes Li Xian (Zhanghuai 654–684), Li Zhongrun (Yide 682–701) and Li Xianhuai (Yongtai 684–701), at Qianling. They feature hunting scenes, polo matches, processions of guests and ladies-in-waiting with their retinues.

The spread of Buddhism in China led to the introduction of iconographic motifs and pictorial styles of Indian derivation. The thousands of religious paintings in temples built in the period of great religious fervour that began in the 4th/5th century are completely lost, whereas the treasures of the Mogao caves near Dunhuang, an important religious centre on the edge of the Gobi desert, have been preserved, including numerous wall paintings dating from the period between 366 and 1337. In the 492 surviving cave temples, a total area in excess of 45,000 sq. m (484,390 sq. ft) was plastered and painted with Buddhist art in pure Chinese style, although some elements were borrowed from foreign inspiration. For instance, the use of dense shadowing and the portrayal of characters with typically Indian features, are most evident in the earliest paintings,

while the undulating drapery and the arrangement of the decorative motifs and elements of the landscape show continuity with indigenous traditions.

From the 4th century, intellectuals and poets began to take an interest in painting, which had previously been considered to have the status merely of a craft, subject to the wishes of wealthy clients. Art criticism developed as a literary genre, and the leading painters became famous and founded schools. Despite regional differences, Chinese painting developed with considerable continuity of subject and style, so that it appeared uniform and to some extent monotonous to the Western eye. Orientals, however, tended to take the same view of European art.

223 (below) A group of guards of honour, wearing elegant dress uniforms, are pictured on the wall of the main corridor of the tomb of Li Xian. They probably formed the prince's personal bodyguard, deployed here to defend him in his new abode. [Tang]

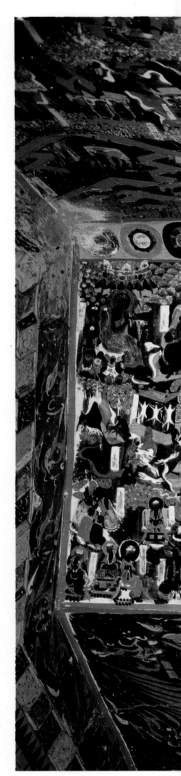

224 left Krishna Vāsudeva is shown here as an old man with a long white beard and a thin torso, his body covered with a few rags. The image   *contrasts sharply with traditional iconography, which shows him as young and vigorous (Dunhuang, cave no. 285). [Western Wei]*

Chinese painting, with its fluid, sinuous lines, was executed with a special brush which required great mastery to control the thickness and intensity of the strokes. The paintings often developed like a narrative, in which figures alternated with empty spaces. Painting on horizontal scrolls was introduced in this period and the composition was designed in sections, to be viewed as the painting was gradually unrolled, rather like reading a book.

One of the most outstanding artists was Gu Kaizhi (c. 345–406), who became as famous for his eccentricity as his art. His painting focused mainly on portrayals of the human figure; a few survive, although only in the form of copies made at later periods. The most famous is 'Admonitions of the Court Instructress', in which the female figures are skilfully delineated with fine brushstrokes. Other famous artists of the period of the Northern and Southern dynasties were Lu Tanwei, who was active during the reign of Mindgi (465–472), and Zhang Sengyou (fl. 500–550), an official in the service of the Liang dynasty. The works of both artists have been lost. However, Zhang Sengyou is known to have frescoed the walls of Buddhist and Daoist temples.

One of the most famous painters of the Tang dynasty is Yan Liben (died 673), a minister of emperor Taizong. A distinguished portrait painter whose work was very popular at court, he painted two famous works, including the 'Thirteen Emperors' and a series of scholars of the Northern Qi dynasty, now in the Museum of Fine Arts, Boston. His linear style, characterized by a full definition of the characters, is considered typical of the first Tang period. Li Sixun (651–716), regarded as the founder of the

224–225 Scenes from the famous Jakata *of Prince Sudāna. The colours are deep, rich blues and greens, and the paintings cover the surface entirely with dense details. (Dunhuang, cave no. 419). [Sui]*

225 (left) This fresco tells the story of a young man who was fatally wounded by his king by accident during a hunting party, and expressed his concern for his parents, both blind. Moved by the young man's filial love, the king took the two old people under his protection. In the end the young man's life was saved by divine clemency (Dunhuang, cave no. 302). [Sui]

Northern School, together with his son Li Zhaodao (*c*. 670–730) introduced a style of coloured landscape painting characterized by the use of deep colours like azurite blue and malachite green.

Wang Wei (699–759), a distinguished poet and landscape artist, used a monochrome pen and ink style and was the forerunner of the school of literati painters. Other great artists were Han Gan (*c*. 715–781), who specialized in painting horses, Zhang Xuan (fl. *c*. 713–742) and his most famous disciple Zhou Fang (*c*. 730–*c*. 800), Wu Daozi (fl. *c*. 710–760), known for his landscapes painted with vigorous thick and thin brushstrokes in the Buddhist and Daoist temples he visited during his frequent travels. Nearly all the works of these artists have been lost; but copies of some of them, reproduced in later centuries by scholar-painters fascinated by their famous predecessors, survive.

226–227 (below)
A scroll entitled
Ladies Wearing
Flowers in their
Hair, *usually*
attributed to Zhou
Fang: the painting
shows magnificently
dressed women in
rather languid poses.
[Tang]

227 (left) *Some*
scholars draw
parallels between the
features and posture
of the bodhisattvas
depicted in ink and
paint on silk from
Dunhuang, dating
from the Tang period,
two of which are
shown here, and the
ladies-in-waiting in
the works of Zhang
Xuan and Zhou Fang.
[Tang]

226–227 (top) *The*
scroll entitled Thirteen
Emperors, *a section of*
which is shown here,
portrays famous
emperors and their
retinues in separate
scenes. The linear,
flowing pictorial style
reflects the figurative
ideal popular in the
7th century. Tradition
attributes the
painting to Yan
Liben, the most
famous court artist at
the beginning of the
Tang period. [Tang]

227

STONE SCULPTURE

The art of three-dimensional sculpture (low or full relief) developed in China from the earliest periods, using various techniques and materials. Unlike Western statuary, in which there were separate traditions of religious and secular art, Chinese sculpture always remained closely linked to religious themes. Small items made of jade, rock crystal, marble or stone found in numerous Neolithic and later sites, and metal (mainly bronze) objects used in sacrificial ceremonies, large numbers of which were placed in the tombs of the nobility, were linked with an arcane ritual symbolism, which is still partly unknown. In the imperial period, the entrances to the most important tombs were guarded by statues of apotropaic animals with feline features, seated on either side of the 'spirit roads' (*shendao*). Impressive winged lions (*bixie*) with square jaws and massive, vigorous bodies warded off evil and suggested the idea of flight to the wonderful realm of the Immortals. Later, depictions of other more or less imaginary animals, like the *qilin* (unicorn) and the *tianlu* (similar to a deer) appeared. In the Tang period, the spirit roads became a royal prerogative, and were decorated with richly carved stone obelisks and statues portraying animals such as winged celestial horses or humans such as armed guards.

In the same period, tombs of the nobility were decorated with stone and sandstone slabs carved in relief; stamped pottery bricks were sometimes associated with stone elements in friezes. The techniques used display marked regional variations.

Buddhist sculpture developed rapidly from the 4th century, and constituted one of the main crafts of the empire. Thousands of stone-masons, potters, metalworkers and painters were

228 (right) A new style, influenced by the transformation of Buddhist iconography which had taken place in India during the Gupta period, was introduced into Chinese sculpture in the mid-6th century AD. The white marble stela shown here, carved on all four sides, dates from this period. [Northern Qi]

228–229 In the imperial age, the search for immortality permeated funerary art and led to the use of stone for tombs and the statues erected to guard them. Sculptures of animals and fantastic creatures, such as this menacing winged feline, lined the 'spirit road' that led up to tombs. [Eastern Han]

commissioned by noblemen and kings to decorate the numerous Buddhist temples and monasteries with paintings and sculptures. Dunhuang (Gansu), a huge complex consisting of 492 surviving caves, was consecrated in the 4th century. In 460 work began on the cave temples of Yungang (Shanxi), where a seated Buddha 14 m (46 ft) tall (cave 20) and a standing Buddha 15 m (49 ft) tall (cave 18) can still be seen.

Chinese Buddhist iconography initially derived from Indian art, combined with strong Central Asian influences, but from the 5th and 6th centuries new styles emerged, influenced both by Indian art of the Gupta period (300–600) and indigenous traditions.

The cave temples of Xiangtangshan, on the Henan-Hebei border, date from the late 6th century, while the cave temples of Longmen (Henan) were created over several centuries. Over the years,

229 (above) Streamlined, yet highly expressive, this stone horse head demonstrates the great sophistication of Chinese sculpture in the Han period. [Han]

229 (right) This statue of an officer stood on the 'spirit road' leading to the imperial tombs of Qianling, where Gaozong was buried in 684 and Wu Zetian in 706. This avenue is 2.5 km (1.5 miles) long, and is lined with obelisks, towers, stelae and impressive stone statues depicting real or imaginary animals and humans. [Tang]

hundreds of niches were cut into the Longmen caves, and 97,300 statues, many of which are sublimely beautiful, were placed in them. At the end of the 6th century the figures became fuller and the bodies, swathed in drapery, seemed to be bursting with vitality. Important innovations were introduced in the Sui dynasty, when Buddhist sculpture acquired a more natural, sensual style, perfectly balanced between the traditions of the past and the innovative schools that were to influence the style of the Tang period. Under the Sui emperor Wendi, at least 100,000 new statues were created and over a million existing works restored.

In the early Tang period, Buddhism, which enjoyed imperial favour and the fervent devotion of the people, spread rapidly throughout the empire. The statues of this period represent the height of Buddhist art, with harmonious, rounded figures, in accordance with the

230 (opposite above) A marble head of a bodhisattva, with an expression of infinite compassion and his complete, infinite willingness to intercede for his fellow-man. [Tang]

230 (opposite below left) Numerous statues are carved with one hand raised with the palm upwards indicating the absence of fear, and the other facing downwards in a gesture of offering. [Eastern Wei]

230 (opposite below right) The face of this bodhisattva, with its soft, full lines, expresses the detachment and serenity of one who, despite having achieved enlightenment, has decided to remain on earth to bring salvation to all men. [Tang]

231 (left) This sandstone head portrays a lohan. The task of these custodians of the doctrines preached by Sākyamuni was to disseminate the teachings of Buddha faithfully so that they were handed down, complete and unchanged, from generation to generation. It was believed that they were able to fulfil their mission because of magic powers, thanks to which they lived for ever. [Tang]

231 (below) The position of the hands (mudra) and legs and feet (āsana) in portrayals of Buddha had important symbolic meanings. [Tang]

taste of the age; faces were gentle and serene, their checks full, their lips fleshy, and the chin and neck grooved to suggest an opulence of flesh. The folds of the drapery fell naturally, hinting at a delicate sensuality.

In China there was a custom of erecting stone stelae with rectangular bases and arched summits. The surface, divided into horizontal sections, was decorated in low relief. On religious stelae one or more niches was carved in such a position as to highlight the small figures of Buddha and bodhisattvas in high relief. From the Han period onwards, stelae with engraved inscriptions were erected to commemorate the dead and celebrate important events.

Perhaps one of the more surprising aspects of Chinese civilization is that no ruler seems to have had the ambition of building a city that would survive down the ages. The pride of the various dynasties seems instead to have been committed solely to the monumental dwellings of the dead and the stories and images engraved in bronze and stone.

ARCHAEOLOGICAL ITINERARIES

**IN SEARCH OF A LOST WORLD:
A TOUR OF
ARCHAEOLOGICAL SITES**

**TESTIMONIES
TO A PROFESSED FAITH:
BUDDHIST CAVE TEMPLES**

232–233
*Scenes from the daily
life of the nomadic
populations who lived
on the western
borders of the Chinese
empire decorate
numerous caves at
Dunhuang. Groups of
huntsmen are shown
riding swift steeds in
pursuit of a herd of
gazelle or about to
attack a large tiger
(Dunhuang, cave no.
249). [Western Wei]*

A Dunhuang (Mogao)
B Sanxingdui
C Maijishan
D Xi'an
E Banpo
F Lintong
G Yungang
H Yangshao
I Longmen
J Luoyang
K Erlitou
L Zhengzhou
M Anyang
N Pingshan
O Mancheng
P Niuheliang
Q Leigudun
R Mawangdui
S Xin'gan

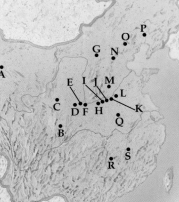

IN SEARCH OF A LOST WORLD: A TOUR OF ARCHAEOLOGICAL SITES

It is no easy task to draw up a list of archaeological sites in China for the visitor. One reason for this is the use of perishable materials for construction, which explains the lack of remains of monumental architectural works; in fact, it is the exception rather than the rule for the palaces and temples of ancient times, however imposing and majestic they once were, to have survived the ravages of time and the devastations of man which occurred in every period of Chinese history.

Moreover, it was only at a relatively late date that tombs were built for the dead in imitation on a smaller scale of the magnificent houses they had lived in during their life. Such tombs, consisting of a number of richly decorated chambers, illustrate developments in art and architecture that otherwise would not have survived. And the imperial tombs of the Han and Tang dynasties are either still unopened or were robbed and totally destroyed long ago. However, the large number of tombs discovered and the magnificent grave goods they contained bear witness to a civilization that was the equal of other great cultures of the past. Some tombs, stripped of their

treasures which are now displayed in collections and museums all over the world, may seem to have little to offer to the visitor, but in fact they do reward the interest of scholars of ancient China.

Archaeological sites dating from the earliest times do not always present any particularly spectacular elements, even in the case of major settlements like the Neolithic village of Banpo, one of the largest centres of the Yangshao culture, situated not far from the town of Xi'an (Shaanxi) and inhabited from *c.* 4800 to 3600 BC. This site, discovered in 1953, was completely excavated between 1954 and 1957. It consists of a residential area surrounded by a protective ditch some 300 m (984 ft) long and 2 m (6½ ft) deep, beyond which are a pottery-making area and a cemetery. Archaeologists have identified the remains of 45 sunken square and circular huts, all with south-facing entrances, 200 pits used for food storage, 6 kilns, thousands of artifacts, mainly for everyday use, and 258 graves, 81 of which contained the remains of children buried in clay urns under or near the homes. Much of the excavated area became a museum in 1958.

In 1920, Swedish geologist J. G. Andersson excavated the first Yangshao Neolithic site near the village of Mianchi (Henan), and a few years later the remains of *Sinanthropus pekinensis* (Peking Man) were found at Zhoukoudian, 42 km (26 miles) southwest of Beijing. The attention of the international scientific community was again focused on China in 1899 with the discovery of over 40,000 manuscripts,

mainly philosophical and religious texts but also some of a literary and administrative nature, written between the 5th and 10th centuries AD. This important archive had been walled up in a cave in the rock temples at Dunhuang (cave 17).

The town that once stood on what is now the Yinxu (the Wastes of Yin) archaeological site some 5 km (3 miles) from Anyang (Henan), on the banks of the Huan river and covering over 24 sq. km (9¼ sq. miles), was of crucial political importance, as it was the last capital of the Shang dynasty. The discovery and excavation of this area represented one of the most exciting episodes in research in China, and coincided with the origin of modern archaeology in the country. Chinese archaeologists had been led to Anyang in 1898 by the brilliant intuition that the so-called 'dragon bones' (*longgu*) of traditional Chinese medicine, had in ancient times been used as oracle bones (*jiagu*) by shamans to summon up the spirits in the afterworld.

Systematic excavations around the city of Anyang were the first major project conducted by the Chinese archaeological research institution, founded in 1926. The remains of the last Shang capital, identified in an area close to the village of Xiaotun and along the banks of the Huan river in Sanjiazhuang, were examined in detail. The raised beaten earth foundations (*hangtu*) of the numerous palatial and residential structures (over 50 of which were of immense size), probably dating from different phases, allowed researchers to establish the urban plan of the town.

The archaeologists also found the remains of impressive noblemen's residences, ritual structures (religious and ancestral), storehouses, and the homes of the numerous artisans who worked in the foundries, mainly casting bronze vessels and weapons, and in the workshops making pottery and carving ivory, bone, jade and other semiprecious stones. The largest foundry identified so far covered an area of some 10,000 sq. m (107,643 sq. ft). The foundations of the buildings were substantial and the most impressive building measured 14.5 x 85 m (47½ x 279 ft).

Magnificent royal tombs were found outside the town, near Hougang and along the Huan river at Xibeigang, near the villages of Houjiazhuang and Wuguancun. A total of 13 large royal tombs were found at Xibeigang (11 in 1934–35, one in 1950 and one in 1984); they had a cross-shaped plan and were equipped with access ramps leading to the pit in which the great wooden coffin (*guan*) containing the body was laid. The coffin, enclosed in a wooden burial chamber (*guo*), rested over a small pit (*yaokeng*), which in some cases contained the skeletons of sacrificial victims, either animals, mainly dogs, or sometimes people. Over 1,400 minor graves next to the royal tombs were evidence of the extent of human sacrifices.

Illicit excavations have taken place in the area of the Shang royal cemetery from early times. The most impressive tomb, M1001, measuring 66 m (216 ft) north–south and 44 m (144 ft) east–west, is thought to have belonged to the powerful king Wu Ding (*c*. 1189 BC). The only royal tomb still intact at the time of its discovery is in another area, less than 200 m (656 ft) from Xiaotun: this is no. 5, the tomb in which queen Fu Hao, one of Wu Ding's many wives, was buried. The tomb, excavated in 1976, was smaller than the those found at Xibeigang, and the wealth and magnificence of the grave goods it contained gives some idea of the immense treasures that must have been robbed from the royal tombs. Over 1,800 artifacts were recovered from Fu Hao's tomb, including 466 bronzes (195 ritual vessels), 755 jades, 564 bone items, 110 objects made of marble, turquoise and other semiprecious stones, around 30 made of pottery, mother-of-pearl and ivory, and around 7,000 cowrie shells.

235 Three layers can be identified in sacrificial pit no. 2 at Sanxingdui. In the first were some 60 elephant tusks, while, bronze statues, ritual vessels and masks were found in the second, and coins and objects made of jade and stone made up the third. [12th century BC]

The archaeological sites of Erlitou and Zhengzhou (Henan), Panlongcheng (Hubei), Ningxiang (Hunan) and Sanxingdui (Sichuan) have contributed much to our knowledge of the cultures of ancient China in the 2nd millennium BC. The Erlitou site, discovered in 1959 at Yanshi near Luoyang, on the river Luo, is the most important centre of Xia culture known to date. Of all the earth structures found, the largest terracing covers an area of over 10,000 sq. m (107, 642 sq. ft). Four different layers have been found at the site, which was inhabited from 2010 to 1324 BC. The third, 1700 to 1500 BC, dates to the Xia phase, and in the opinion of some experts is the site of the last capital of the first dynasty, as recorded in the traditional historical sources.

The site found near Zhengzhou in 1952–53 is believed to have been the second Shang capital, which reached the height of its glory around 1500 BC (Erligang phase), when the entire city was enclosed by a strong rammed earth wall almost 7 km (over 4 miles) long, built on foundations up to 20 m (66 ft) deep. Outside the wall are the remains of the huts, workshops, foundries and storehouses of small villages, mainly inhabited by artisans who made pottery and bronze, bone and lacquerware objects. The foundations of impressive palatial structures designed for residential use or religious purposes can be discerned inside the wall.

The site at Panlongcheng in Huangpi, near Wuhan, is smaller. It too was surrounded by rammed earth walls, built with the same technique as used at Zhengzhou, but much shorter (260 x 290 m; 853 x 951 ft). The town, and some of the tombs situated outside the walls, date from the first Erligang period, while the neighbouring constructions are considered to be contemporary with the Zhengzhou settlement.

Sites excavated at Ningxiang and Sanxingdui represent independent cultures which flourished outside Shang influence. The finds of Sanxingdui, in particular, have revealed the existence of a great civilization totally overlooked in the written sources.

Numerous discoveries dating to the early 1st millennium BC have yielded an enormous quantity of artifacts and much information. Thousands of tombs and various stores containing ritual bronze vessels have been found, together with the foundations of huge palaces and residential and religious complexes. Archaeologists' research at first mainly concentrated on Shaanxi, believed to be the area where the Zhou originated, but later extended to the whole area of Zhou influence which spread from Gansu to Liaoning and Shandong.

The settlements of greatest interest lie in the area around Xi'an and Chang'an, especially along the banks of the Feng river, the site of the two Zhou capitals, Feng and Hao (Zhouyuan). This is a huge area that runs from the counties of Wishan and Fufeng to the border of the present-day Baoji county, where the remains of the small kingdom of Yu have been found. Many important sites have also been discovered outside Shaanxi. A city of the Jin kingdom, founded according to tradition by a brother of king Cheng (1035–1006 BC), was located not far from Houma (Shanxi). The capital of the kingdom of Yan, governed by descendants of a brother of king Wu (1049/1045–1043 BC), was situated at Liulihe, near Fangshan (Hebei). Tombs of the nobles of the Wei kingdom have been found at Xincun (Henan), and remains of the Lu and Qi kingdoms have been discovered at Lu, near Qufu, and at Qi, not far from Zibo (Shandong).

The Zhou Plain (Zhouyuan) is a very interesting area. Its settlements, where the ancestral altars of a rich, powerful aristocracy were located, were the centre of major ceremonial activities. In addition to hundreds of tombs containing magnificent grave goods, large numbers of oracle bones dating from the predynastic period (before the 11th century BC) have been found, together with a dozen hoards of ritual bronze vessels, many bearing inscriptions that recount the history of their owners.

At Zhuangbai, near Fufeng, 103 ritual vessels which belonged to the Wei family for at least five generations (74 of them with inscriptions), have been found. The remains of residential and ceremonial complexes with roofs covered with ceramic tiles have been discovered at Fengchu, Shaochen and other sites.

Although the typical vertical structure of burial pits was maintained throughout the Eastern Zhou period, major changes were introduced in various local traditions, which had a significant influence on later developments. The custom of dividing the burial chamber containing the coffin into different parts was introduced towards the end of the Western Zhou period. From the Eastern Zhou dynasty, there was a tendency to place the coffin not on the floor of the pit but in a kind of niche cut into one of the walls. These niches were later enlarged to make room for grave goods, and eventually became mortuary chambers.

The practice of building tomb complexes consisting of a number of rooms (shi), with a main chamber and one or more interconnected secondary chambers, each of which had its own function, began as early as the Eastern Zhou dynasty, and became increasingly common in the imperial age. More durable materials were also now frequently used, such as stone pillars, beams and slabs; and hollow clay bricks, often with incised or impressed decorations, were used to cover the walls instead of the traditional wooden boards. The practice of plastering and then painting surfaces also spread.

By the Western Han dynasty the traditional vertical pit had given way to burial complexes which consisted of as many as nine chambers (as in the tomb of king You of Chu, who reigned from 237 to 228 BC), excavated in rock or earth and covered with hollow bricks or carved or painted stone slabs. The practice of raising great mounds of earth

over the tombs, first seen in the Zhou period, continued. Some mounds are veritable hills surrounded by protective walls, inside which wooden or stone structures and lush parks were built.

A fairly clear picture of life in the Eastern Zhou period is gained from numerous finds. Over 50 fortified towns and cities dating from the Warring States period have been located, most of which were protected by a double wall. Some were the political and religious capitals of kingdoms and principalities engaged in a constant battle for supremacy. Luoyang was the site of the Eastern Zhou court, while Linzi and Wuyang were the capitals of Qi and Yan.

At least 600 of the over 6,000 tombs dating from the Eastern Zhou period identified to date are located in the Luoyang area, in the territory of the Wei kingdom, and 500 are in Shaanxi, which was dominated by the Qin in ancient times. Over 4,000 tombs have been found in the vast area of the magnificent Southern Chu culture: no fewer than 1,800 of them are situated in the area of Changsha (Hunan), and 851 near the ancient capital Ying, at Jiangling and Dangyang (Hubei).

Among the most interesting sites of this period are the last Qin capital at Xianyang (Shaanxi), where the ruins of an impressive palace still retain fragments of the delicate, coloured murals that once decorated its plastered walls. At Houma (Shanxi) the remains of a huge foundry have been discovered, and at Jincun, Sanmenxia, Xiasi and Xinyang (Henan), some exquisite grave goods have survived. Pingshan (Hebei) was the capital of the small Zhongshan

kingdom. The first bronzes cast by the lost-wax technique were found at Xiasi. Finally the tomb of the Marquis of Cai is at Ximennei (Anhui), and the tombs of the rulers of the Southern Dian kingdom, which flourished between the Warring States period and the Western Han dynasty, are at Shizhaishan (Yunnan).

The tomb of Marquis Yi of Zeng at Leigudun (Hubei), dating from 433 BC, is representative of the great ideological changes that took place during the Zhou dynasty. Excavated vertically in a small hill to a depth of 13 m (43 ft), it consists of four adjacent, intercommunicating chambers 3 m (10 ft) high. The walls were wood panelled and probably draped with magnificent tapestries. Each chamber had a specific function, as demonstrated by the objects found there. The central room, which was also the largest, with an area of over 46 sq. m (495 sq. ft), reproduced the audience and ceremonial chamber of the Marquis' palace on a small scale. It contained household furnishings, magnificent bronzes for ritual use and musical instruments, including the most impressive set of bronze bells found so far, consisting of 64 bells arranged on a wooden stand in decreasing order of size. The private apartments of the Marquis were reproduced to the east, in the chamber containing his body, which was buried in two magnificent lacquered coffins, one inside the other. The coffins of 8 women, the remains of a dog and musical instruments probably played at private entertainments were found in the same room, while the instruments found in the central room were used for official ceremonies. The western room contained

the coffins of 13 girls, and the northern room was a very detailed reproduction of an armoury and contained over 4,500 weapons of various kinds, shields, breastplates and trappings for carriages and horses.

Finds from the first imperial period demonstrate the popularity of new architectural concepts. In addition, several factors combined to produce increasingly magnificent funerary art. The religious beliefs and philosophical ideas that permeated life in the Han age and the conviction that techniques used to preserve the body could achieve immortality meant that tombs and grave goods became ever more impressive and magnificent, made possible by the huge wealth of some aristocratic clans. Members of the imperial family, the aristocracy, large landowners, ministers, officials, army officers and wealthy merchants flaunted the privileges of their rank, which they retained after death. Tombs began to become the focus of devotion and piety towards the deceased, whose religious and cosmological beliefs were reflected in the grave goods and the murals on the walls.

Although vertical-pit tombs began to disappear as the horizontal chamber type became increasingly common in ever larger areas of the empire, they were still numerous in the Western Han period. Examples of tombs in this tradition are found at Mawangdui near Changsha (Hunan), Fenghuangshan, near Jiangling (Hebei) and Dabaotai near Beijing. The three Mawangdui tombs, belonging to Li Cang, Marquis of Dai (died 186 BC), and his wife and son (died 168 BC), contained exquisite lacquerware, elegant garments, silk books and Lady Dai's funeral banner, of incomparable beauty, which depicted the deceased's journey to immortality and illustrated a concept of the cosmos that unified the worlds of the living and the dead.

Various types of horizontal chamber tomb are known. The tombs of Liu Sheng (died 113 BC), son of emperor Jingdi (157–141 BC) and prince of Zhongshan, and his wife princess Dou Wan, found in

1968 at Mancheng (Hebei), were tunnelled into the rock of the mountain. The entrance corridor leads to various chambers: first are two side rooms, the southern one serving as stables and a carriage store, as shown by the presence of wooden shelters with tiled roofs, and the northern one serving as a storeroom. Following on from this is a large central room used for ritual activities and containing a great wooden structure, also tiled, underneath which tents were set up. Beyond this was the burial chamber with finely carved walls and elegant furnishings, to one side of which was a bathroom. The prince's body was covered with an exquisite jade suit made with 2,498 pieces of jade of various sizes sewn together with gold thread.

This kind of rock-cut tomb, which was later imitated by the Tang emperors, is known as an 'underground palace' (*dixia gongdian*).

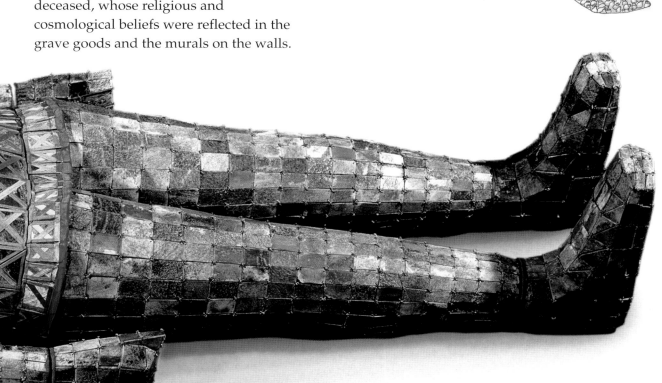

236–237 The jade suit of princess Dou Wan consisted of 2,160 pieces of jade, sewn together with 700 g (25 oz) of gold thread. In the Eastern Han period, gold thread was reserved for the emperor alone; silver thread was used for princes, and copper thread for aristocrats of lower rank. [Western Han]

237 (centre) This reconstruction of the tomb of prince Liu Sheng shows the arrangement of the grave goods typical of the eternal dwellings of the Han aristocrats, which consisted of a number of chambers, each of which had a different function.

237

Some tombs at Luoyang (Henan) are chamber tombs with walls and ceilings made of hollow bricks. The bricks were sometimes decorated with traditional subjects such as mythological characters, imaginary or realistic animals, and scenes from history or legend. The hollow bricks, usually large, were soon replaced by smaller solid bricks, allowing the construction of more complex architectural structures. The tombs of prince Jing of Pengcheng at Xuzhou (Jiangsu), prince Jian of Zhongshan at Ding xian (Hebei) and Marquis Fuyang at Wangdu (Hebei) belong to this type of structure.

So far 39 tombs of princes have been discovered, 34 of which date from the Western Han dynasty and 5 from the Eastern Han dynasty; all are organized internally in a fairly similar way. In the first imperial period the practice of plastering and painting the walls with multicoloured murals became common. In the tomb of the Marquis of Fuyang, people close to the deceased, probably attendants and officials in his service,

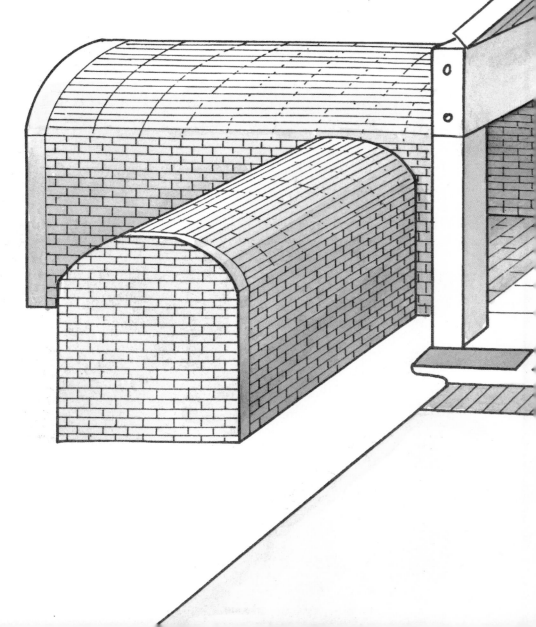

238

are depicted, so that the dead man was surrounded by familiar figures.

The tombs of Anping (Hebei), discovered in 1971, and Holingor (Horinger) (Inner Mongolia), discovered in 1972, both dating from the Eastern Han dynasty, are particularly fine. The former, made of fine clay bricks, covers an area of over 262 sq. m (2,820 sq. ft) and consists of a corridor, 2 niches and 10 chambers with arched doors and vaulted ceilings, up to 4.4 m (14 ft) high. The walls have magnificent paintings of the deceased, probably a high-ranking

army officer, leading a long procession of his troops, consisting of infantry, cavalry and no fewer than 80 chariots. Some short inscriptions can be read, one of which dates the tomb at 176.

A high-ranking army military officer stationed in the Wuhuan district was buried in the Holingor tomb, which consists of a number of vaulted chambers. The murals on the brick walls depict the main events in his life, the campaigns he took part in and the places where he served. The estate to which he probably retired at an advanced age is also portrayed, with vivid scenes of rural life.

Chamber tombs built of large blocks of stone, often decorated with scenes from everyday life or portrayals of historical or mythological events, became common during the Eastern Han dynasty. The tomb of a general who lived in the 1st century AD, found at Yi'nan (Shandong), is of this type. A painting on one of the walls of the deceased's home, shows that the tomb was designed as a model of it. Scenes

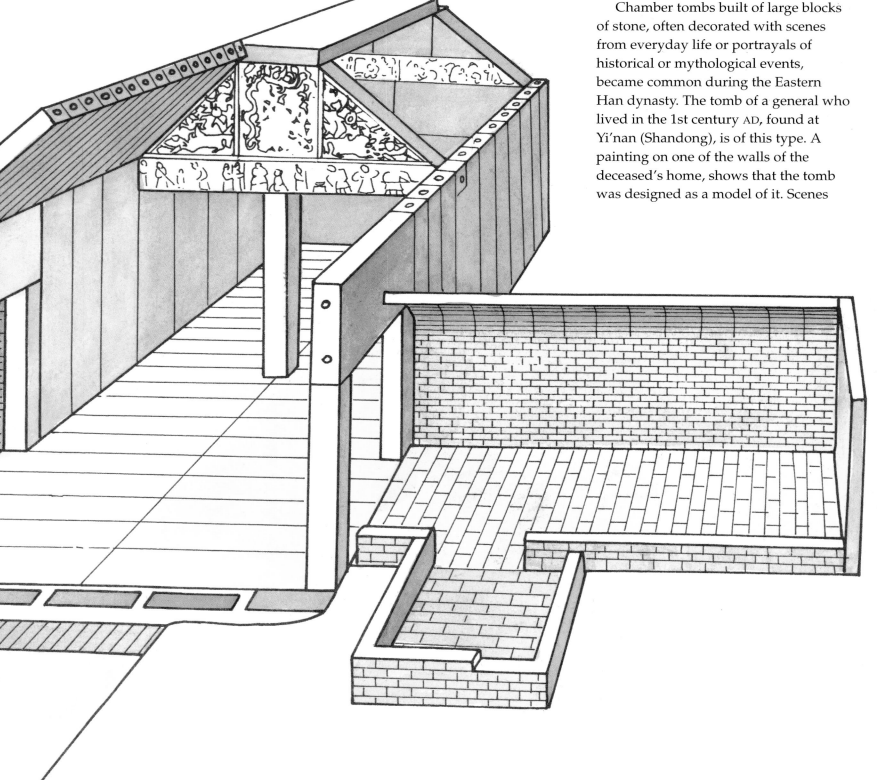

240–241 and 241 Most of the few surviving wall paintings from the Han period are fairly badly damaged. The tomb at Holingor in what is now Inner Mongolia, a reconstruction and interior view of which are seen here, provides a good idea of what the tomb of an important person must have looked like.
[Western Han]

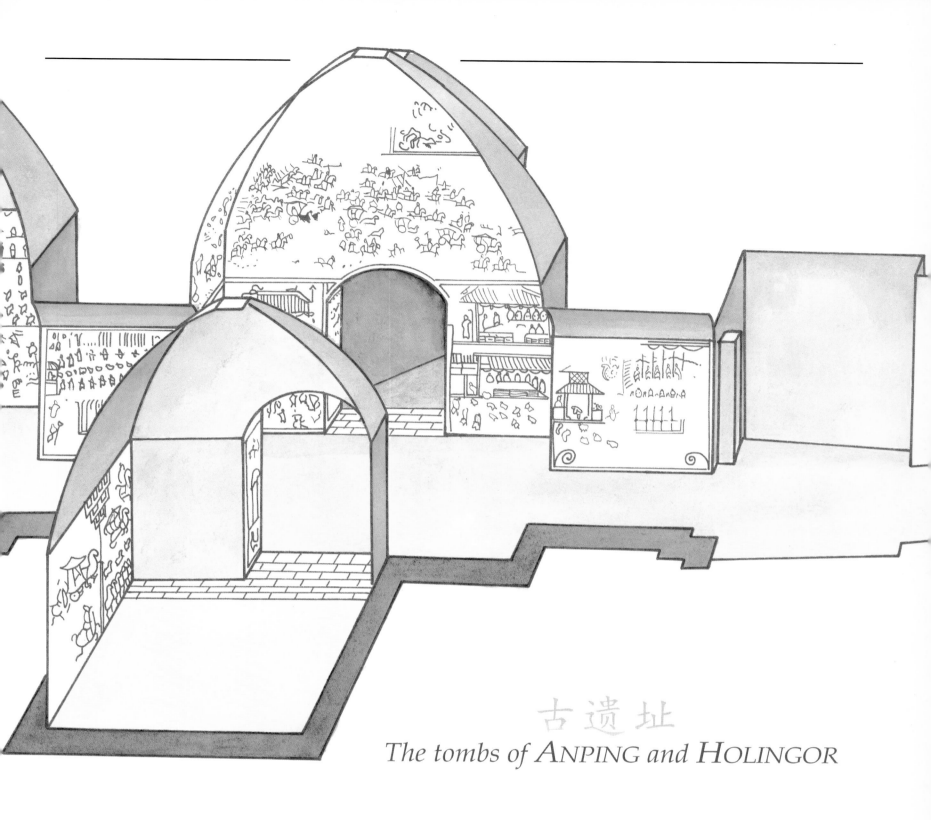

古遗址

The tombs of ANPING *and* HOLINGOR

illustrate events from his life and significant episodes in his career, one of the most important of which was a battle fought against the nomadic peoples of the north. The general is shown standing in his chariot, urging on his soldiers.

Tomb no. 1 at Yangzishan (Sichuan), north of Chengdu, the largest and best decorated of the over 200 tombs found in the area, also dates from the Han period, as do tomb no. 2 at Dongyuancun (Anhui) and tombs 1 and 2 at Mixian, near Dahuting. The Yangzishan tomb and tomb no. 2 at Dahuting were made of brick, while the others were built with great blocks of stone.

240 (opposite below) The rank of the person buried in the tomb at Anping tomb is demonstrated by the number of carriages and horsemen portrayed in the four parallel registers painted on the walls of the central chamber. These murals are believed to depict important episodes in the life of the deceased.
[Western Han]

241

242–243
The discovery of the tomb of the general Lou Rui was an outstanding event because of the many magnificent murals that it contained. A detail of the 28 constellations painted along the walls and arches of the central chamber can be seen here. [Northern Qi]

The decorations of these tombs are among the finest expressions of funerary art in the Eastern Han period. Such an outstanding technical and artistic level was not seen again until the Tang dynasty, with the exception of the magnificent murals covering the walls of the tomb of a Xiangbei general called Lou Rui, who died in 577 (Northern Qi), found in the suburbs of Taiyuan (Shanxi) in 1979. The paintings, cover a total area of 200 sq. m (2,153 sq. ft) and depict scenes of horsemen, caravans of camels, officials and the animal symbols of 28 constellations. The frescoes are innovative compared with the classic Han style: the rhythm and movement of the complex groups portrayed clearly demonstrate the influence of the art of the steppes. While the animal symbols of the constellations are majestic and static, the horses and camels, caught in movement, convey the impression of vibrant energy. Clever use of shading gives the images a depth rarely seen in the paintings of earlier periods, and this was to become a feature of Tang pictorial art.

242 (opposite below right) The entrance to the tomb of Lou Rui gives on to a corridor painted with scenes of riders, soldiers and caravans of camels ready to set off on a journey. [Northern Qi]

243 (centre) Groups of horsemen in dress uniform gallop towards the exit of the tomb. They were probably the general's escort to accompany him on his long journey to the afterworld. [Northern Qi]

243 (bottom) The animals symbolizing the 28 constellations are drawn in the baimiao (line drawing) technique, characterized by clean, sharp lines and delicate chiaroscuro effects. [Northern Qi]

242 (opposite below left) This painting from the tomb of Lou Rui depicts a banquet in honour of an important foreign dignitary. [Northern Qi]

The Tomb of the FIRST EMPEROR

While noblemen and other dignitaries dedicated increasing resources to building their tombs, there was no limit to the imagination and wealth lavished on the dwellings designed for the afterlife of the emperors. Court architects and artists were commissioned to satisfy their every desire, and put even the boldest designs into practice. Unfortunately, many tombs have been destroyed, and those which have not been raided have not yet been entered by archaeologists.

One such tomb is the mausoleum of the First Emperor, Qin Shihuangdi, who

244

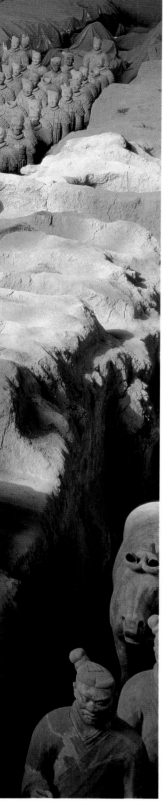

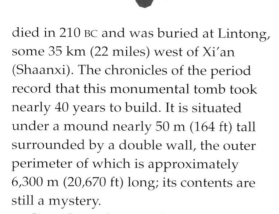

秦

died in 210 BC and was buried at Lintong, some 35 km (22 miles) west of Xi'an (Shaanxi). The chronicles of the period record that this monumental tomb took nearly 40 years to build. It is situated under a mound nearly 50 m (164 ft) tall surrounded by a double wall, the outer perimeter of which is approximately 6,300 m (20,670 ft) long; its contents are still a mystery.

Sima Qian, the great historian who lived in the 1st century BC, just over a century after the death of the First August Emperor, recounts that in the huge underground palace, built using the forced labour of over 700,000 men, the ceiling of the main hall faithfully reproduced the heavens, while the empire was depicted on the floor. Rivers of mercury instead of water flowed into a model sea, thanks to ingenious mechanical devices. The tomb's huge treasures may have been robbed a few years after the emperor was buried, when the dynasty was overthrown and the capital Xianyang destroyed by rebel troops commanded by Xiang Yu.

Twenty-two centuries later, in March 1974, 1,225 m (4,020 ft) from the First Emperor's tomb mound, farmers digging a well uncovered the head of a terracotta warrior. Investigations conducted by a team of archaeologists who immediately rushed to the site confirmed the theory that it was part of the legendary army that defended the First Emperor, buried in the huge mausoleum, whose position was thus clearly identified.

Four burial pits have so far been opened. Pit no. 1 was the one found by chance by the local farmers; nos. 2 and 3 were found in 1976 and 1977 after scientific survey operations. A fourth pit, which proved empty, was discovered in 1995. Some 8,000 statues were buried, just over 1,300 of which have so far been recovered. The entire burial complex

244–245 The First Emperor's terracotta army makes a tremendous impression on those who visit pit no. 1 for the first time; the thousands of soldiers, lined up in an orderly way, represent a magnificent symbol of strength and power. [Qin]

covers an area of about 0.025 sq. km (0.0096 sq. mile). Some of the pits contained the skeletons of horses, birds and wild animals. Tools of various kinds have also been found, together with numerous statuettes portraying attendants and servants and two magnificent painted bronze horse-drawn chariots, perhaps intended to convey the emperor to the legendary land of the Immortals. The finds are now displayed in a museum near pit no. 1; permanent roofs have been built over pits 1, 2 and 3 to ensure that the work of excavating the statues can continue under the best conditions, and to facilitate public access to the site.

The terracotta warriors are slightly larger than lifesize – the standing statues are 2 m (6½ ft) tall while the kneeling archers are 1.20 m (4 ft) tall and weigh around 150 kg (330 lb). As befits the members of an imperial army, they have a very solemn, martial deportment. Made with great attention to detail, the facial features, expressions and hairstyles are so perfect as to indicate the ethnic origin of each soldier. While there was a limited number of moulds for various elements of all the statues, the features of each were individually modelled, and the military equipment

244 (opposite below) The burial mound of the First Emperor, beneath which the tomb may still be intact, is 50.5 m (165 ft) high; but this is only a third of its original height. Associated burial pits have been excavated over a wide area around it. [Qin]

245 (above) It took years of patient work to reconstruct the bronze chariots and terracotta horses of the First Emperor from thousands of fragments; they had been crushed by the collapse of the wooden structures that protected the pit. [Qin]

and horses' trappings are equally realistic. The statues were originally painted, but only a few traces remain.

The manufacture of the terracotta army required huge resources; it is estimated that at least 85 master sculptors (whose names are engraved on the statues) worked on the task, each helped by 18 assistants, making a total of over 1,500 craftsmen. From the location of the pits and the equipment of the warriors found so far, it is clear that the statues were deployed according to the principles of military tactics in use at the end of the Zhou period and the beginning of the imperial period.

Pit no. 1, the largest, is rectangular, with an area of 14,260 sq. m (153,500 sq. ft). So far 1,087 warriors, 32 horses and the remains of 8 wooden chariots have recovered from it, but it is estimated that a total of over 6,000 warriors, 160 horses and 40 chariots, making up infantry legions with all the necessary combat equipment, deployed in tight formation, are buried there. The central nucleus comprises nine columns of four rows of infantry, and two side columns consisting of a single row. At the head of the army are 210 archers in close formation, three rows of lancers and four-horse wooden chariots, each carrying a charioteer and two soldiers. The formation is protected on either side by an outward-facing column of men. The rearguard consists of three rows of warriors; the soldiers in the last one have their backs to the rest of the army.

Pit no. 2, with an L-shaped plan, is situated some 20 m (66 ft) from pit no. 1, and is smaller, covering an area of some 6,000 sq. m (64,585 sq. ft). Around 70 crossbowmen, kneeling and standing, numerous cavalrymen, 50 horses and the remains of various wooden chariots have been recovered so far. It is estimated that some 1,300 warriors, 450 horses and 89 chariots are buried there. The soldiers are deployed more compactly in this pit, reflecting the striking force of cavalry units protected by archers.

Pit no. 3, the smallest, covering an area of scarcely 500 sq. m (5,382 sq. ft), is believed to have been the army's headquarters. Sixty-eight unarmed warriors, comprising officers and attendants, not deployed in precise ranks, have been found there, together

246 (above) Only part of the huge terracotta army has so far been uncovered. Here, two archaeologists are at work on the site, which has been turned into a museum. [Qin]

246 (below) The discovery of two unique bronze chariots of the First Emperor is considered almost as significant as the finding of the terracotta army itself by Chinese archaeologists. [Qin]

247 (opposite) Standing calmly in ordered lines, these infantrymen seem to be awaiting orders. The workmanship of the statues and the chariots is so detailed and on such a scale that it has no equal anywhere in the world. [Qin]

with four horses and the remains of a chariot. A large amount of animal bones suggests that the commanders made propitiatory sacrifices before engaging in battle. Deer horns and numerous bronze weapons have also been found.

Pit no. 4 covers an area of 4,608 sq. m (49, 602 sq. ft) and is 4.8 m (15–16 ft) deep, as are the others. Its function is a mystery, as it was found completely empty. Among the various theories put forward to explain this puzzle, the most plausible is that proposed by Yuan Zhonyi, Director of the museum in Xi'an. In his opinion pit no. 4 should have contained the central corps of the army; the units deployed in pits 1 and 2 represented the right and left wings of the army respectively, while pit no. 3 contained the high command. The entire legion for which pit no. 4 was prepared would have consisted of real soldiers, probably the recruits who had worked on the construction of the mausoleum, destined to be sacrificed on the spot in accordance with an ancient practice that had not yet been abandoned.

Information contained in the writings of the historian Sima Qian supports this theory, and explains why the mass sacrifice never took place. In his work *Shiji* (Memoirs of a Historian), Sima Qian states that, following the suggestion of one of his ministers, the August Emperor decided to save the men and send them to fight against populations in various parts of the empire who were rebelling against subjugation by the Chinese empire. The soldiers would thus defend their emperor on the field of battle instead of being at his disposal for the glories of the afterlife. Pit no. 4 has now been filled in, except for the northwest corner.

Another pit measuring 3,025 sq. m (32,560 sq. ft), containing two bronze carriages complete with driver and horses, about half lifesize, was found in 1980, some 20 m (66 ft) west of the tomb. The smaller of the two (*gaoche*),

in which the traveller stood upright, had a parasol. It preceded the larger carriage, called the 'carriage of tranquillity' (*anche*), in which the passenger travelled seated and was thus used for pleasure journeys. The first carriage is 2.25 m (7 ft) long and weighs 1,061 kg (2,340 lb); the second is 3.17 m (10½ ft) long and 1.06 m (3½ ft) tall, weighs 1,241 kg (2,736 lb), and consists of 3,462 cast metal parts assembled by various techniques. Of the total parts, 1,742 are made of bronze, 737 gold and 983 silver. This unique find demonstrates the exceptional skill of the Chinese craftsman in the field of metallurgy.

The discovery of the army of China's First Emperor, considered by many to be the greatest archaeological find of the

20th century, caused a worldwide stir. The entire area of the tomb and the terracotta army has been placed under the protection of UNESCO, and declared a World Heritage Site.

Other terracotta armies, more modest than Qin Shihuangdi's, have been found in other tombs of the Western Han dynasty. Thousands of statuettes up to 47 cm (18½ in) high were found at Xuzhou, and 1,965 infantrymen and 583 cavalry at Yangjiawan, near Xianyang, in a tomb next to the tomb of the first Han Emperor (similar finds have also been made in the same area, at Langjiagou), while thousands of statues, some with jointed wooden arms attached to the torso, around 62 cm (24 in) high, have been discovered at Yangling (Shaanxi).

248 (opposite) The simple, strong features of each soldier were individually modelled, and are evidence of a striving after realism and great attention to detail. [Qin]

249 The skill of the Qin craftsmen is particularly evident in the modelling of the heads; the soldiers have a proud, martial air, high, wide foreheads, marked eyebrows, thick moustaches that softly follow the curve of their wide cheekbones, and elaborate but neat hairstyles. [Qin]

唐

As with the tomb of Qin Shihuangdi, the funeral dwellings of the Han emperors have not yet been opened. The most impressive belongs to emperor Wudi, who died in 87 BC and is buried at Maoling, near Xingping, some 40 km (25 miles) from Xi'an, which took 53 years to build. The rectangular mound, 480 m (1,575 ft) east–west and 414 m (1,358 ft) north–south, is surrounded by a rammed earth wall some 6 m (20 ft) thick. Contemporary sources say that it was situated in the middle of a huge park, which contained the residences of over 5,000 people – watchmen, servants and gardeners – who looked after the entire area. Members of the imperial family and particularly devoted attendants, officials and army officers were buried nearby.

Historical sources state that at least 20 tombs of this kind are situated near the remains of Wudi. Perhaps the most important of the dozen tombs identified nearby is the tomb of Huo Qubing (140–117 BC). A powerful general who won some glorious victories against the Xiongnu, Huo Qubing died at the age of only 24.

250 (top) Looters probably entered the tomb of princess Xincheng through tunnels above the entrance corridor to rob it of its priceless treasures. [Tang]

250 (centre) and 251 (opposite above right) Although damaged in places, the murals covering the plastered surface of the walls and ceiling are among the loveliest of the Tang period. Here, two

archaeologists are engaged in the patient task of recovery and restoration. [Tang]

250–251 and 251 (opposite above left) Funerary statuettes made of painted pottery were arranged in niches cut into the walls of the corridor to the central chamber. Their presence in the tomb was considered essential, as they were designed to assist and amuse the princess after her death. [Tang]

The tomb of princess XINCHENG

Some large statues depicting a human figure and various animals, and two great stelae with inscriptions, were found near the tomb. These statues, standing in the park or in the small buildings now used as museums, are the most important evidence of sculpture in the Western Han period. Later, statues of this kind became increasingly frequent; they were placed outside tombs in order to ward off evil spirits and indicate the sanctity of the place. Statues lined the avenue leading to the tomb, forming the 'spirit road' (shendao), which became an imperial prerogative during the Tang period.

If the tomb complexes of Qin Shihuangdi and Wudi appear incredibly large, we can only imagine how impressive the Tang mausolea must have been in the eyes of the vassal populations taken to them to pay homage to the ancestors of the imperial family. The tombs of the Tang rulers were built inside mountains; the most famous are those at Zhaoling, where emperor Taizong was buried, and the one at Qianling, belonging to emperor Gaozong and his concubine Wu Zhao, who became empress in AD 690 as Wu Zetian.

Sadly, all 18 tombs of the Tang rulers were raided and largely destroyed shortly after the fall of the dynasty, and little now remains of their former splendour. The burial complex of Zhaoling is certainly the most impressive, covering an area of 200 sq. km (77 sq. miles), with an outer wall roughly 60 km (37 miles) long. The cemetery contains the tomb of emperor Taizong and 167 satellite tombs belonging to princes, princesses, consorts, high officials and generals who had distinguished themselves for their loyalty and zeal to the point of meriting burial alongside their lord.

position, while those of the noblemen, concubines and dignitaries were ranked in order of precedence.

The building of the complex began in 636 and ended in 649, when the emperor died. Contemporary sources recount that famous artists such as the painters Yan Lide and Yan Liben were involved in its design and construction. The tomb mound was an actual mountain, and a stairway with 230 steps led to the entrance of the underground palace.

The 'spirit road' leading to the tomb was 1 km (0.6 miles) long, and at least 68 statues, on average 4 m (13 ft) high, were erected along it. The burial chamber within the palace excavated under Mt Jiuzong, was reached by a tunnel 230 m (755 ft) long. A veritable city was built around the entrance, reproducing the capital on a small scale, with temples and palaces, fortifications and a city wall with access gates surmounted by guard towers. According to the chronicles of the period, no fewer than 378 rooms were repaired or totally rebuilt in AD 798 when five of the tombs were restored.

253 (below) One of the most striking characteristics of the wall paintings of the Tang period is their accuracy in reproducing the smallest details, both in depictions of people and representations of objects. [Tang]

253 (bottom) Today, the heavy stone door that once protected the eternal dwelling of the princess, and the tombstone engraved with a long epitaph dedicated to her, lie on the ground inside her funerary chamber. [Tang]

One of the most interesting satellite tombs is that of princess Xincheng, excavated between 1994 and 1995. Attendants and courtiers accompanying the deceased on her last journey are portrayed on the walls of the long corridor that leads to the burial chamber. Ox-drawn carts, servants, a military escort and a palanquin in which the princess probably lay are depicted. The funeral chamber is magnificently painted with scenes illustrating episodes from everyday life in the women's quarters – elegant ladies converse, and serving-girls arrange items to meet their lady's needs, such as precious caskets containing cosmetics, musical instruments and flowers.

Some of the commanders of ethnic groups subjugated by the Tang who had rendered important services to the empire were also buried at Zhaoling. Taizong's tomb occupied the dominant

252 (opposite) and 253 (above) The delicate images decorating the walls of the tomb of princess Xincheng appear to bring the visitor into the princess's private rooms, in the company of her maids and ladies-in-waiting. [Tang]

The necropolis of QIANLING

The necropolis of Qianling, built on the highest peak of Mt Liang (1049 m (3,441 ft) high), covered an area of around 40 sq. km (15½ sq. miles). The inner wall, excavated along with the ruins of four access gates and a sacrificial temple, encloses a huge area. Gaozong's tomb, its entrance closed by a huge stone door, is still intact. Along the majestic 'spirit road' leading to the tomb stand two octagonal columns of dressed stone, one on either side, numerous impressive stone statues of soldiers and wild beasts

who guarded the tomb, and two stelae, one of which is inscribed.

Other sculptures portray saddled horses, magnificent winged steeds and benevolent and auspicious birds; 61 statues portray foreign ambassadors and the commanders of ethnic minorities who were present at the funeral of Gaozong. The emperor died in December 683 at the age of 56 and was buried at Qianling in August 684. Wu Zetian died in 705 at the age of 82, and was buried at Qianling in May 706.

254 (above centre) The ostrich, an exotic animal for the Chinese, was often depicted in the statues erected around Tang imperial tombs. Its presence was intended to arouse the surprise and admiration of visitors, and was also an allusion to the empire's many contacts with distant, unknown countries. [Tang]

254 (opposite centre and below) Visitors are constantly amazed by the size and majesty of the stone statues lining the 'spirit road' leading to the tombs of Gaozong and Wu Zetian. [Tang]

254–255 (above) Statues of 61 kings and ambassadors from nearby countries who had been awarded prestigious honorary titles by the Tang court stand in two separate groups at Qianling. The statues, now headless, have inscriptions on the back that have long been illegible; however, the recent discovery of ancient paper copies has enabled many of the personalities portrayed to be identified. [Tang]

Seventeen tombs, all of similar structure, have been found near the tomb of Gaozong. Some have not yet been excavated, but others which have can be attributed to princesses Yongtai, Xue Yuanchao and Li Jingxing and princes Zhanghuai and Yide, members of the imperial family. The tombs, enclosed by walls, have a south-facing access route lined with stone columns and statues. Inside, they take the form of underground palaces, with a tunnel leading to antechambers and the burial chamber. The walls of the corridors and halls are magnificently painted, with subjects including scenes from court life, the amusements of the nobility and processions. The human and animal figures are portrayed lifesize in the elegant, courtly Tang style, and set amid landscapes similar to those depicted in paintings on paper and silk. Similar paintings, with fresh, bright red, ochre, green and blue colours, undoubtedly also covered the walls of the palaces and mansions of the period.

The most important tombs belong to three members of the royal family who met the same tragic fate. Li Xian (654–684), prince Zhuanghuai, was the son of emperor Gaozong and Wu Zetian. Li Zhongrun (682–701), prince Yide, and his sister Li Xianhui (684–701), princess Yongtai, were all murdered on the orders of Wu Zetian.

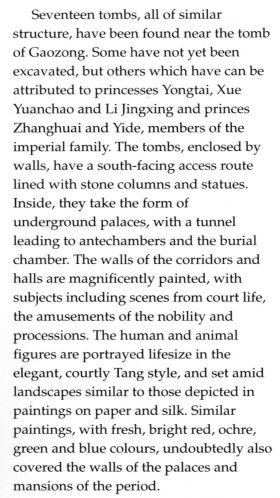

Over 4,300 finely made luxury objects, including pottery statuettes and precious jade, gold and bronze items were placed among their grave goods as a sign of mourning by those who had looked on powerless at their ruin. They were rehabilitated some time after their death, following the demise of Wu Zetian.

The tomb of Li Xian (Zhanghuai), who was forced to commit suicide at the age of 30, is the most spectacular. The murals, which cover some 400 sq. m (4,305 sq. ft) contain 130 male and female figures, in 50 pictorial groups. The most attractive scenes depict a polo game, a procession of foreign guests and hunting.

256–257 In the Tang period, hunting parties organized for members of the imperial family involved huge numbers of people, rather like the great fox-hunts of the English aristocracy in past centuries. [Tang]

257 (left) A detail of polo players in action: Li Xian's enthusiasm for this game is apparent from the murals decorating the west wall of the corridor leading to his funeral chamber. [Tang]

The tomb of Li Zhongrun (Yide), murdered at the age of 19, contains 40 magnificent paintings. Of the 27 tombs with murals dating from the Tang period found in the Chang'an area, these are some of the finest, best preserved and the most representative of the taste and style of the Tang period. Some of the wall paintings at Qianling have been detached from the walls and restored, and are now on display in the Shaanxi museum. In addition to 10 murals from the tomb of Li Xian and 6 from the tomb of Li Zhongrun, another 23 wall paintings from the tombs of various members of the imperial family and high dignitaries are on display.

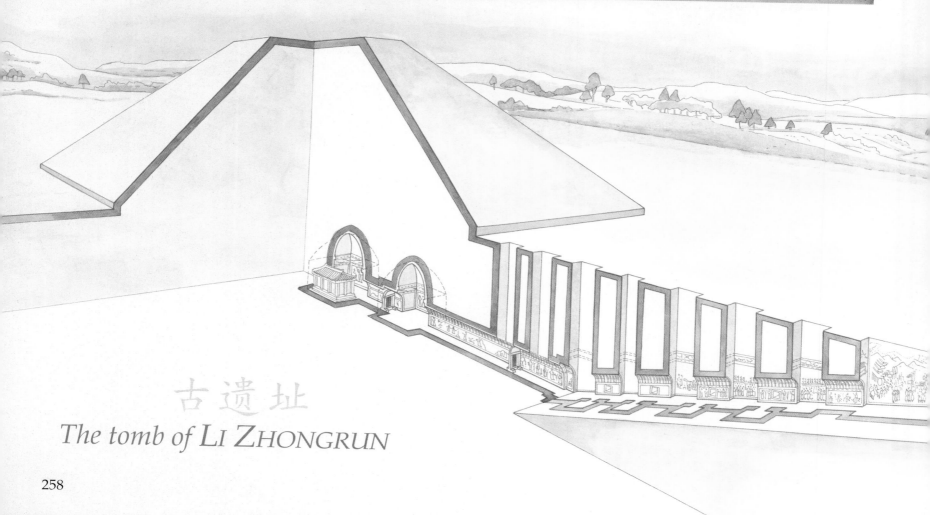

古遗址

The tomb of LI ZHONGRUN

258 (opposite above left) Delicate and supple as reeds in the wind, the women shown here seem to move, as if to the slow rhythm of music. These graceful figures are from the tomb of Li Zhongrun. [Tang]

258 (opposite above right) The paintings on the wall of the corridor leading to the burial chamber of Li Zhongrun include portrayals of the impressive towers built along the defensive walls and on either side of the gates to the capital, Chang'an, the most populous city in the world in the Tang period. [Tang]

258–259 (below) A reconstruction drawing of the tomb of Li Zhongrun, with its entrance tunnel, various chambers and magnificent wall paintings. [Tang]

259 (above) Eunuchs, seen here in a tomb painting, were highly influential at court, especially towards the end of the Tang dynasty when a series of child emperors succeeded to the throne, and their intrigues often caused serious political crises. 'They were like the most lethal poisons and as ferocious as wild beasts', so said Huang Zongxi, one of the leading Confucian intellectuals of the 17th century. [Tang]

The GREAT WALL

260 The Great Wall is still very well preserved over large stretches of its length, with battlements, thousands of steps and square towers.

This brief review of the most important archaeological sites in China cannot ignore what is perhaps the most grandiose work ever constructed: the Great Wall or *wanli changheng* (The Wall of Ten Thousand Li). Thousands of Chinese and foreign visitors travel the 65 km (40 miles) from Beijing to Badaling, the section of the wall nearest the capital, which dates from the Ming period (1368–1644), or 80 km (50 miles) to Mutianyu, where the Wall winds along a route dating from the 6th century, though restored at a later period.

The Great Wall now covers a length of 2,950 km (1,830 miles), running from the east coast of China to the Gobi desert. It varies in size from section to section, but for much of the route it is between 7 and 8 m (23 and 26 ft) tall, while in thickness it narrows from 6.5 m (21 ft) at the base to 5.8 m (19 ft) at the top. Construction began in the 5th–6th centuries BC, when China was divided into kingdoms

but in time the Wall lost its defensive function, and was left to decay. The first emperor of the Ming dynasty, Hongwu (1368–1398), however, began an impressive and systematic project of restoration and enlargement.

Today, the Great Wall is not as large as it once was, and has only been restored and made accessible to the public in some sections; the final section of the wall at Jiayuguan (Gansu), dating from the Ming period, stands in a particularly lovely and remote setting.

260–261 The Great Wall, designed as a defensive barrier against the threat posed by nomadic peoples (China had never feared attack from the sea until modern times), still represents a symbol of national unity and identity.

constantly fighting one another for supremacy. The principalities of Qin, Zhao and Yan erected the first fortified barriers to protect their territories against continual incursions by the nomadic populations of the northwest. The First Emperor of the Qin dynasty consolidated and unified these defences.

Legend has it that 300,000 men were employed for over 10 years on building the Wall. The Han emperors undertook major extensions of the original structure.

261 (left) The section of the Wall that winds past Mutianyu was of great strategic importance, as it was designed to stop continual incursions from nomadic populations from the lands to the northeast of the empire, especially the Ruzhen (Jurchen), a race of Manchurian origin who were particularly powerful under the reign of Aguda (1068–1123).

TESTIMONIES TO A PROFESSED FAITH: BUDDHIST CAVE TEMPLES

For centuries, trading centres along the Silk Route were meeting points for various populations who gathered not only for the purpose of financially advantageous trade but also because distant echoes of exotic splendour aroused a genuine curiosity about unknown civilizations, attracting merchants and others from far and wide. In the Han period Buddhism arrived

262 (above) Xinjiang province is studded with the remains of the important religious centres that sprang up along the northern part of the Silk Route, especially in the Turfan area. These photographs show the ruins of Jiaohe (top), an ancient town dating from the Han period, and Gaochang (bottom), from the Tang period.

from India along the Silk Route, bringing with it its doctrines, writings, rituals and pictorial traditions already centuries old. In the western provinces of Xinjiang and Gansu there is ample evidence of incessant migrations in both directions; monks from India and other parts of Central Asia travelled to the Chinese empire in search of converts, while Chinese monks and disciples made pilgrimages to visit the places where Buddhism originated, in search of sacred scriptures to translate and disseminate at home. As Buddhism gradually spread throughout the empire, major centres of worship developed in the central regions, in what are now Henan and Shanxi provinces, and in the south, especially Sichuan.

Kucha, Khotan and Karashahr, founded as independent kingdoms on the Silk Route in present-day Xinjiang, became important Buddhist centres and were a major destination for pilgrims for centuries. Splendid cave temples were built here and at the oases in the nearby desert areas, at Turgan, Kizil and Miran.

The most important complex is in West Gansu, 25 km (15½ miles) southeast of the Dunhuang oasis, an ancient trading post. The magnificent Mogao Caves (Mogao ku) at Dunhuang, known in China as the Caves of the Thousand Buddhas (Qianfodong), are situated along the edge of the immense sandy wastes of the Gobi Desert, near the Yumen Pass, where the northern and southern sections of the Silk Route converged.

Beginning in AD 366, around a thousand caves of various sizes were excavated in the friable rock of Mt Mingsha, in the cliff overlooking the muddy waters of the Dachuan river.

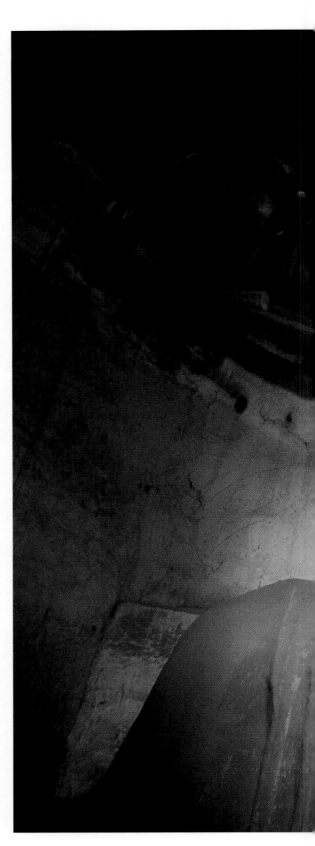

262–263 Of the 670 statues from the Tang era in the religious complex at Mogao, Dunhuang, many are of enormous size, such as this Buddha which is 33 m (108 ft) tall.

263 (right) The Mogao cave complex, near Dunhuang, stretches for over 1.5 km (around 1 mile) in the cliff side of Mt Mingsha. Because of its geographical position, Dunhuang was the ideal meeting point between the Chinese civilization of the imperial age and the populations who had settled to the west of its borders.

264–265. The Mogao Caves, decorated with thousands of statues, altars and columns, are painted with murals illustrating episodes from the life of the Buddha and sacred Buddhist texts. This cave (no. 285), for meditation, is 4.3 m (14 ft) high; an inscription dates its painting to AD 538/9.

264 (opposite below) The Mogao Caves were painted in rich colours, including some pigments that had to be imported over long distances.

These paintings depict the feats of a group of 500 brave men, called brigands by some, who fought against injustice in the world and became Buddhas.

265 The statue on the left is Kāśyapa, shown here at an advanced age to emphasize his wisdom and proverbial prudence; a bodhisattva of almost feminine beauty and elegance

appears at his side. This image emanates such sweetness and serenity that it represents one of the most outstanding expressions of religious art of the Tang period.

This is the most impressive Chinese religious complex carved completely from the bare rock. Many of the caves have been destroyed by erosion or human action, but 492 have survived (not all can be visited). Some of the oldest caves now date from the early 5th century: 23 of them, in the centre of the rock wall, were constructed in the Northern Dynasties period, 95 in the Sui dynasty, 213 in the Tang dynasty, and the remaining 161 between the 10th and 14th centuries. Many of the older caves have been rebuilt or extended.

One of the interesting aspects of this religious complex is the unusual but harmonious combination of different architectural, sculptural and pictorial styles. The caves have a fairly simple structure: some, usually the older ones, consist of a single chamber, while others have a sort of antechamber leading into a hall richly decorated with paintings, statues, columns, altars and niches of various sizes. They range in area from 9 to 70 sq. m (97 to 753 sq. ft), and in height from 1.5 to 5 m (5 to 16 ft). The oldest caves show influences from

Central Asian and Indian religious architecture (for instance the pillar in the middle of the hall), but this influence gradually declined, and disappeared entirely in the Sui and Tang periods.

As the rock was too gravelly to be carved, the Mogao complex contains 2,400 painted clay statues of individual deities or groups of deities and saints belonging to the extensive Buddhist pantheon. The oldest works usually consist of a figure of Buddha in the centre with a bodhisattva on either side, while others feature up to nine characters. The

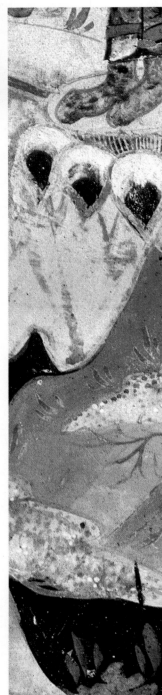

266 (above) Two
Buddhist monks sit
rapt in meditation on
lotus-shaped thrones;
an antelope, a hare
and a gazelle gambol
amid the greenery in
the background,
completing the
atmosphere of peace
and tranquillity with
which the composition
is imbued.

sculptures are displayed along the walls
or in niches of varying elaboration. Some
are of majestic proportions, such as the
magnificent 26-m (85-ft) high sculpture
of Buddha Maitreya (cave no. 130),
attributed to Ma Sizhong, an artist of the
early 8th century, or the statue in cave
no. 96 which is 33 m (108 ft) high.

The paintings in the Mogao Caves are
equally magnificent. Images of deities,
holy places and places of worship,
scenes illustrating parables and
anecdotes belonging to Buddhist
tradition cover the walls and ceilings.
Rural landscapes sometimes appear in

the background, with ordinary people
going about their everyday tasks:
peasants working in the fields, craftsmen
carving and casting, fishermen and
huntsmen, and tumblers entertaining
onlookers with acrobatic performances,
music and singing.

The oldest frescoes, painted before the
Sui period, depict stories taken from
famous *sutras* or *jātaka sūtras*, recounting
the laudable actions performed by
Sākyamuni in lives prior to his
reincarnation as a prince. These tales
offer the faithful an example of humble
behaviour, based on generosity and the
highest sacrifice. Paintings from
subsequent periods, especially the Sui
and Tang dynasties, illustrate theological
disputes, often enlivened by magical
events and fantastic transformations, or
portray magnificent Buddhist heavens:
the one presided over by Maitreya
Buddha is illustrated on 64 walls, while
125 frescoes tell stories about the
paradise of the West, *Sukhāvatī*.

The pictorial styles vary a great deal,
reflecting the developments that took
place over the centuries not only in tastes
and techniques, but also in religion.

After the 16th century, the Mogao
Caves lost their importance as a religious

centre, because of the decreasing flow of Chinese worshippers who visited them.

More recently, the caves became famous as a result of an event that took place centuries later. In 1899, a Daoist hermit called Wang Yuanlu, who lived in the caves, discovered by chance the entrance to a stone chapel which contained over 40,000 manuscripts and several thousand paintings, in an excellent state of preservation due to the dryness of the caves.

This priceless treasure consisted of religious texts, mostly Buddhist, although there were also some important Confucian and Daoist documents, and texts on historical, legal, literary, astronomical and medical subjects. All trace of some of these works had previously been lost for centuries.

266–267 (below) A detail from the story of the 500 brigands who became Buddhas: an archer is about to shoot an arrow at a gazelle leaping among the hills.

267 (left) This scene, from the sūtra of Vimalakirti, shows Mañjuśri seated with his hand raised, intent on conversation. Opposite him is Sāriputra, a disciple of Buddha; celestial flowers rain down on him to induce him to break once and for all with earthly cares.

Over 80 per cent of the manuscripts are written in Chinese, while the others are in Tibetan, Turkic, Sogdian, Khotanese, Uighur, Runic and Brahmi, the languages spoken by the merchants and adventurers who travelled the Silk Route. The texts, paintings and fabrics found at Dunhuang date from between 406 and 1004. At first, the discovery attracted the attention of Chinese scholars, who collected a number of paintings and manuscripts. The importance of the find then attracted Western scholars (the Russians Obruchev and Sergei Oldenburg, the Englishman Aurel Stein, the Frenchman Paul Pelliot and the American Longdon Warner) and Japanese experts (Tachibana Zuicho and Yoshikawa Koichiro), who managed to acquire much of the secret library, often for virtually nothing. The finds are now on display in major museums and cultural institutions in Beijing, London, Paris, Saint Petersburg, Kyoto and Delhi.

268–269 (top) Celestial musicians with strong, agile bodies float in the air amid swirling flowers. Moving in the wind, they display great dynamism compared to the static composure of the seated Buddhas.

268 (above) This painting of Buddha riding an elephant, followed by two musicians is part of the representation of a new incarnation of Buddha.

268 (left) Floral motifs and garlands of leaves are painted in bright colours on this coffered ceiling. The colours of the paintings in the Mogao Caves are extremely well preserved due to the dryness.

268–269 (below) This impressive painting illustrates an episode from the Jātaka of Sāmaka, a story that tells of the love of a young man for his blind parents. The love of the son was rewarded by divine compassion when he was restored to life after dying from a wound.

270 (opposite) A system of wooden walkways has been installed on the steep side of the rock to allow access to the caves, which cannot be reached in any other way. The caves have remained isolated for long periods in the past when these walkways became unsafe through lack of maintenance.

271 (above) This statue of Buddha, dating from the Sui period, is the most impressive in the entire complex. It dominates the entire rock face, and can be seen from a distance.

Other sites of particular interest in Gansu province are the cave temples of Wenshushan, (some 15 km (9 km) from Jiuquan), Maijishan (around 50 km (31 miles) from Tianshui), Wushan and Qingyang. Ten caves, two of which are in a good state of preservation, have survived at Wenshushan, a very important religious centre from the 4th century. The oldest is the Cave of the Thousand Buddhas (*Qianfodong*), which contains clay statues and murals dating from the Northern Wei period.

The most important complex, at Maijishan, consists of 194 caves painted and decorated with niches and sacred images made mostly of clay, as the rock was unsuitable for carving. The caves, on a steep, almost inaccessible face of a cliff, can be reached by a series of wooden walkways.

Maijishan was a place of worship at the crossroads of numerous cultures, and contains works of art dating between the 5th and 11th centuries, which display a perfect, original blend of different styles and influences. The oldest statues, dating from the Wei period, are of elegant characters wearing ample draped garments according to the custom of Gandhara, in a particularly relaxed attitude which inspired the attainment of inner peace in the faithful.

The largest cave, no. 4, has a complex architectural structure which is certainly of Indian derivation: seven square niches are situated along a corridor that leads to a large room lined with pillars carved from the rock. Images of Buddha, surrounded by bodhisattvas and disciples, decorate every niche.

Cave no. 30 is also of great interest. It consists of three chambers, each of which contains a niche with a seated Buddha and six assistants and has a vault supported by four pillars with the characteristic octagonal shape. Particularly elaborate stone stelae depict scenes from the life of the historical Buddha, with references to episodes and personalities appearing in famous sutras such as the *Lotus Sūtra*.

271 (above and left) The isolated location and difficulty of access to the outcrop of rock on which the Maijishan cave complex stands have helped preserve the magnificent statues, which were mainly modelled in clay on a framework of wood or stone. In the 5th century, over 100 monks lived permanently in the caves.

272 (left and centre) These views of the Yungang cave complex show a barren landscape. However, ancient texts describe pavilions and monasteries by rivers surrounded by lush vegetation, and the name Yungang (Hill of Clouds) suggests a climate that was anything but arid.

272 (below right) Natural erosion in this desert area, has caused less damage than the neglect, looting and vandalism perpetrated by man.

Perhaps the finest sculptures are to be found in Shanxi and Henan provinces. The Yungang cave complex (*Yungang shiku*), the Hill of Clouds, was excavated in a sandstone crag on the south side of Mt Wuzhou, 15 km (9 miles) west of Datong in Shanxi. This was one of the most important centres of Buddhist worship in imperial China, and contains significant evidence of the development of Buddhist sculpture in the early centuries of the religion's spread. The Yungang complex was constructed under the rule of the Tuoba, an ethnic group of Turkic origin whose rulers reigned over Northern China in the 4th–6th centuries under the dynastic name of Northern Wei. They established their capital at Pingcheng (now Datong).

Work on the cave complex began in 460, by order of emperor Wen Cheng, who intended it as a symbol of repentance and expiation for the terrible persecution perpetrated against the Buddhist religion by his predecessor in 446. The project was facilitated by the presence in Pingcheng of families of craftsmen who had been deported from Dunhuang in 439 after working on Mogao, and were consequently familiar with the traditional Buddhist iconography of Central Asia and India.

The cave complex was mainly carved between 460 and 490, and its splendour began to decline in 494, when the capital of the empire was moved to Luoyang.

272 (right) This impressive seated Buddha is considered to be one of the best examples of sculpture from the first Yungang period, which reached the height of its glory in the Caves of Tan Yao (nos. 16–20), named after the monk who persuaded emperor Wen Cheng to carve them. The face of this Buddha probably reproduces the emperor's features.

273 (opposite) The gentle, serene features and sweet smile on the closed lips of this Buddha transmit a sensation of profound tranquillity to the faithful who contemplated it.

Many of the over 50,000 statues that decorated the caves were made in just a few decades; some sculptures were added and partial restoration work performed under the Sui and Tang dynasties, while further small-scale work took place under later dynasties. Over the centuries many caves were destroyed or irretrievably damaged by erosion, sandstorms and repeated sacking, especially in the first half of the 20th century. Numerous pieces from Yungang are now in private collections and museums all over the world.

The caves are divided into three separate groups: four situated to the east (nos. 1–4), nine in the centre (nos. 5–13), and forty to the west (nos. 14–53). A very large number of niches, varying in size and decorated with thousands of sacred images, contribute to the atmosphere of religious devotion. The influence of

274 (opposite) In architecture and sculpture, as well as iconography, some of the Yungang caves seem to derive ultimately from Western models, mediated through Gandharan influence.

275 (below left) Pillars carved with religious images on all sides stand in the centre of the largest cave temples. This allowed the devotees to walk around the images in an act of worship.

275 (top) Sacred images and scenes from the life of Buddha, depicted alone or with bodhisattvas and worshippers, decorate the numerous niches found everywhere.

275 (above centre) Large colonnades carved in the cave temples allowed the construction of a sheltered, open room which acted as a vestibule to the central chamber.

275 (above) The spread of Buddhism was facilitated by the fact that the new doctrine could be reconciled with ancestor worship. Commissioning a statue in honour of an ancestor, an expression also of devotion, brought the worshipper closer to salvation.

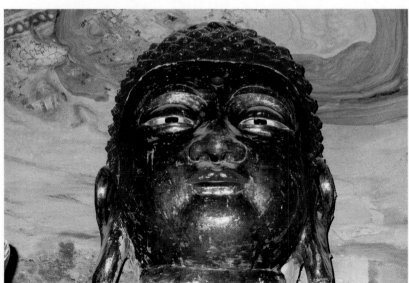

Central Asian religious art is evident in many of the statues and reliefs which, especially the early ones, were based on Sassanian or Parthian models, while themes of ultimately Ionic or Hellenistic derivation can also be recognized.

The oldest caves contain statues of exceptional size, some of which (nos. 16–20) are thought by some to be portraits of the first Wei emperors who supported Buddhism. The statues of Buddha in caves 5, 16, 17, 18 and 19, perhaps inspired by the sculptures of Bamiyan in Afghanistan, are between 13 and 17 m (43 and 56 ft) tall. Gandharan and Indian influences are also evident in cave no. 8, where there are images of Vishnu with five heads and six arms, riding a peacock, and Shiva with three heads and eight arms, riding a bull.

Wutaishan, a religious site on a plateau in Shanxi, 240 km (149 miles) from Taiyuan, contains wooden temples from the Tang period, the oldest still surviving in China. The Tianlongshan caves, Shanxi, are some 25 km (15 miles) from Taiyuan.

277 (below) Many of the statues at Yungang are painted in a range of often bright colours, sometimes in unusual combinations. The spectacular, vivid chromatic effects tend to soften the severe, intensely religious atmosphere of the places of worship.

276–277 The influence of Indian sculptural style is clear in the statues at Yungang, for instance this colossal painted Buddha.

276 (opposite below left) A round head and full face are typical of the iconographic style in sculpture from the second half of the 6th century. The serene yet severe expression of the deity radiates great authority and spiritual force.

276 (opposite below right) The depiction of Buddha in peaceful conversation with his disciples is a recurrent theme in the Buddhist art of the cave temples and in sculptures commissioned for private worship.

278 (below) A view of Fengxian temple: the magnificent, imposing image of Buddha is flanked on the right by his disciples Ānanda and Kāśyapa.

278–279 A standing bodhisattva wearing a garment with rich drapery that falls in regular folds and adorned with numerous jewels in the Indian tradition, is accompanied by a pair of menacing celestial guardians: a lokapāla supporting a pagoda and subjugating an evil demon, and an imposing, severe dvārapāla.

278 (below right) Tens of thousands of statues had their heads removed or were stolen to supply the profitable trade in artifacts, especially in the 19th and 20th centuries.

In 494, when the imperial court moved to Luoyang, work began on the construction of a new cave complex not far from the city walls. Over 2,000 caves, some of them vast, were carved in the rock walls along the river Yi where it forms a narrow canyon (hence the name Longmen, meaning Dragon Gate). The complex contains no fewer than 97,300 statues of Buddha, bodhisattvas and celestial guardians ranging between 2 cm (under 1 in) and 17 m (56 ft) tall, and some 40 pagodas and pillars; 3,608 inscriptions have been recorded.

The oldest caves, dating from before the Sui dynasty, recall those at Yungang in architecture and artistic style. Those made under the Sui and Tang dynasties present a more mature style, no longer influenced by Indian and Central Asian art and they can be described as wholly Chinese.

The Fengxian temple, carved in 672–3 by order of emperor Gaozong and empress Wu Zetian, is perhaps the most spectacular cave. Now open to the sky as the wooden roof has disappeared, it is 35 m (115 ft) long; the focal point is a colossal Buddha, over 11 m (36 ft) tall, whose rounded form can be discerned

279 (opposite below) The Longmen cave temples were only rediscovered relatively recently, even though they are close to Luoyang. This site, which was once the the capital of ten dynasties, is now an ordinary industrial city, its illustrious past forgotten.

through the drapery of his garments. He sits with an imperturbable expression on a throne in the shape of a lotus flower consisting of thousands of petals. Each petal represents a separate universe with its own Buddha, which in turn contains other universes. This is Vairocana, the Buddha of Endless Light, the first cosmic principle from which all things originated. On either side are his loyal disciples and two bodhisattvas. Majestic, threatening pairs of celestial guardians line the end wall. A *lokapāla*, portrayed in the act of trampling on a demon, supports a votive pagoda, the symbol of the north.

The Cave of the Ten Thousand Buddhas (*Wanfodong*) contains portrayals of Guanyin, the female version of Avaloketesvara, the Buddha of Compassion, and the Buddha Amithaba who sits, composed and serene, on a throne in the shape of a lotus flower, surrounded by disciples, bodhisattvas and celestial guardians. In the background are 54 bodhisattvas on lotus flowers, and all around the walls are lined with ten thousand small Buddhas and a group of musicians and dancers. The Cave of the Ancient Sun (*Guyangdong*), famous for a statue of Buddha which is compared with Laozi, the legendary founder of Daoism,

because of his serene expression, contains some reliefs which are a very useful source of information about the costumes and architecture of the 5th century.

The Xiangtangshan caves, where the most representative sculptures of the Northern Qi period were carved, are on the border between Henan and Hebei provinces. There are also interesting and spectacular places of worship in Sichuan, including Bamiaoxiang, some 40 km (25 miles) from Anyüe, Dazu caves, and the temples near the towns of Jiajiang and Chengdu. Other well-known cave complexes include Shizhongshan, 100 km (62 miles) from

280 (opposite) A detail of the celestial guardian responsible for protecting the temple of Fengxian against demons and evil influences. His fierce, threatening expression was intended to terrify visitors.

281 (above) Sculpture of the early Tang period features full forms and great attention to the details of costume and jewelry, which sometimes show the strong influence of Indian art. This is clearly evident in the diadem and necklace of this bodhisattva.

281 (above left) The simple drapery of the garments emphasizes the powerful, harmonious form of this seated Buddha, which seems to emerge from the bare rock.

281 (above right) The naturalism characteristic of many of the different sculptural styles found at Longmen is completely lacking in some statues. For instance, the hands of this statue are out of proportion with the rest of the body.

281 (left) The calm, reassuring gaze characteristic of images of Buddha and the bodhisattvas contrasts with the terrifying eyes of the celestial guardian shown on the opposite page; the gaze is made even more frightening by the hollow pupils.

282–283 (above) The guardians standing on either side of the entrance to this cave are intended to protect Buddha, his teachings and the sanctuaries dedicated to him against the forces of evil, and also to instil respect and awe in onlookers.

Dali in Yunnan which, as well as religious images, contains depictions members of the local Nanzhao royal family in magnificent garments, and the Xumishan complex, some 55 km (34 miles) from Guyuan in the Ningxia Autonomous region.

All of these cave temples, which bear witness to the depth of religious devotion of the Chinese people over the centuries, have known times of great splendour, followed by decline and oblivion. As a result of the interest they have aroused in scholars from all over the world and in the general public, the authorities have performed some major restoration work, which has gradually restored these treasures of immense historical and artistic value to their original state.

283 The seemingly endless repetition of the image of Buddha represents the philosophic concept of 'a thousand Buddhas'. The terms 'a thousand Buddhas' or 'ten thousand Buddhas' are also often used in the name of a temple.

282 (opposite below left) This Buddha is flanked by two bodhisattvas in accordance with the iconography of the period. One of his hands is facing upwards with the palm open in the sign of protection (abhayamudra) while the other faces down in the sign indicating charity (varadamudra).

282 (opposite below right) The inner and outer walls of sacred caves were often carved in relief with rows of tiny images of Buddha to show that he is ever-present in time and space.

284 (below) Buddha, seated on a throne, is flanked by his disciples and bodhisattvas standing on pedestals in the form of an open lotus.

This flower is the symbol of the greatest purity and considered by the Buddhists to be one of the eight most precious things in the world.

284 (left) Although the myriad sacred images and symbols forming complex themes on the walls of cave temples may seem to follow no particular arrangement, they are in fact ordered in a precise way, according to Buddhist beliefs and the sacred texts by which the artists were inspired.

284 (top) The scale of some of the Longmen caves and many of the statues contained in them can be seen in this photograph, which shows a worshipper at the feet of one of the finest statues in the entire Longmen complex.

284 (above) The pattern visible on the side walls of this

cave consists of an apparently infinite number of representations of Buddha.

285 (opposite) This decorated rock wall in the Guyang cave features numerous inscriptions left by worshippers as well as religious images and portrayals of Buddha.

GLOSSARY

BI: circular jade discs with a hole in the centre. Their function remains a mystery, but they are believed to have been used in religious practices during the Neolithic period.

BIXIE: fierce mythological animals resembling winged lions, believed to have the power to ward off evil spirits; for this reason they were often placed in tombs for protection.

BODHISATTVA: followers of Buddha who have achieved enlightenment but choose to remain in the world to help others on the difficult path to sanctity instead of reaching eternal beatitude and sharing in Nirvana.

CELADON: ceramics fired at high temperatures (1,260–1,310°C / 2,300–2,390°F), coated in a translucent glaze in various shades of green based on iron oxides.

CELESTIAL KINGS: the Celestial Kings were placed in the most important tombs, to protect them from evil influences. Complete with weapons and clad in heavy armour, the Kings have a truly fearsome and warlike appearance.

CONG: jade rectangular blocks , perforated by a tubular vertical hole, often decorated with human and animal motifs. Their function, which remains a mystery, seems to be related to the religious and spiritual practices of the Neolithic period.

DI or SHANGDI: the Lord of the Heavens, the most powerful god of the Shang epoch, held by some to be the Supreme Ancestor of the royal clan, and by others a deified totem figure.

DAO (TAO): lit. the 'Way'; to the Daoists this is the primary source of the Universe and of life, which permeates and transforms every living being and leads them back into their original state of non-being. A silent, immaterial entity, unchangeable and mysterious, superior to all, constantly in motion, with a vastness that makes it inexpressible in words, and therefore indefinable. In Confucian belief, it corresponds to the moral ideal which man incarnates through education and inner training, as well as to the teachings of the ruling sages of ancient times; it is the master Way that must be followed in order to find social peace.

ERCENTAI: a terrace of beaten earth, built on different step-like levels and set in one of the tomb walls, where, during the Shang period, a part of the funeral treasure was placed

GUAN: wooden sarcophagus containing the body of the deceased.

GUO: wooden funeral chamber, in which the coffin, or *guan* was placed.

HANGTU: embankment used as the foundations of palaces and houses since the Neolithic period.

HUANGDI: *Huang* and *Di* were honorary titles assumed by the mythical rulers and founders of the civilisation. In 221 BC, the year of the founding of the Empire, the First Emperor, Zheng of Qin, conferred upon himself the title Huangdi, 'August Emperor', to emphasize the birth of a new era which was supposed to last forever.

GLAZE: thin, glassy coating, usually shiny and translucent, which covers the surface of certain ceramics. It is formed during the process of oxidation of certain minerals in the course of firing. The different colours depended on the minerals used.

JIAGUWEN: lit. 'inscriptions on bone oracles ', the prophetic instrument used by the court shamans of the Shang period to consult divinities and ancestors of the royal family in the Other World.

JATAKA: anecdotes and proverbs about the life of Buddha that were often depicted in the mural paintings in cave temples.

LEIWEN: spiral geometric motifs used mainly during the Shang and Zhou, periods, found predominantly in the decorations of bronzes, lacquerware and ceramics.

MINGQI: lit. 'numinous articles', manufactured artifacts of great symbolic value, mainly made of terracotta or wood but occasionally also of metal, placed inside the tomb to recreate a familiar atmosphere for the deceased and to satisfy his or her needs in the afterlife.

MUDRĀ: position of the hands of Buddha or the Bodhisattva: abhayamudra – the hand open, facing upwards, with the palm forward in sign of protection and varamudra – the hand turned downwards in sign of charity.

NIRVANA: fusion of virtue and wisdom, well-defined and supreme, attained by putting an end to suffering and to the cycle of births, thus realizing the human potential for goodness and happiness which leads the individual into a state of eternal beatitude. It is imagined as a kind of paradise.

PINGTUO: decorative technique consisting in the application of thin gold or silver leaf on a support of lacquered wood, which is then covered with a transparent coating.

RHYTON: drinking utensil in the shape of a curved horn, usually made from worked jade. Such vessels often end in the head of an animal.

SANCAI: lit. 'three colours', polychrome glazed ceramics in the characteristic lead-based colours which were fashionable during the Tang period.

SANDAI: lit. 'Three Dynasties', referring to the three pre-imperial dynasties Xia, Shang and Zhou.

SANJIAO: lit. 'Three Doctrines', the syncretism of the three Chinese 'religions': Confucianism, Daoism and Buddhism.

SHENDAO: lit. 'Spirit Road', the avenue often lined with impressive stone statues which led to imperial and noble tombs.

SŪTRA: sacred scriptures, composed of aphorisms of a religious, ritual and philosophical nature, accompanied by short comments.

TAOTIE: iconographic motifs found mainly in the bronze decorations of the Shang and Zhou periods, consisting in the face of a mythical animal seen from the front, characterized by large eyes and a body which, split in two, spreads out symmetrically on either side of the head.

TIAN: lit. 'Heaven', the greatest divinity from the Zhou period onwards. Its will was known as *Tian dao*, 'the Way of Heaven', or Tian Ming, 'the Law of Heaven', or 'Mandate of Heaven' in the cases where great power and responsibility was conferred on those deemed worthy and deserving of it. Tian Zi, lit. 'Son of Heaven', was one of the emperor's names.

TIANXIA: lit. 'all that is under the Heavens', indicates the civilized world.

WANG: noble title, roughly translated as 'king'. The prerogative of the first king of Zhou, the title was usurped by the royalty of the principalities into which China was divided before the founding of the empire.

PRONUNCIATION OF CHINESE TERMS

For the transcription of the Chinese terms, the official system adopted by the People's Republic of China (commonly known as *pinyin*) has been followed. This is mostly pronounced as it appears, but some general indications concerning pronunciation are as follows, as given in C. Blunden & M. Elvin, *Cultural Atlas of China*, Oxford, 1983.

c	ts, as in 'cats'
j	as r
q	ch, as in 'cheek'
x	sh, as in 'sheen'
z	dz, as in 'adze'
zh	j, as in 'jar'
ian, yan	'yen'
ui	'way'

also, e and i after c, s, z, and ch, sh and zh, as in 'serve' and 'shirk'.

An apostrophe separates syllables where the break is not clear, as in Xi'an.

INDEX

BIBLIOGRAPHY

Allan, Sarah, *The Shape of the Turtle: Myth, Art, and Cosmos in Early China*, Albany, 1991.

Bagley, Robert W., *Shang Ritual Bronzes in the Arthur M. Sackler Collections*, New York, 1987.

Baker, Janet (ed.), *The Flowering of a Foreign Faith: New Studies in Chinese Buddhist Art*, New Delhi, 1998.

Barnes, Gina, *China, Korea and Japan. The Rise of Civlization in East Asia*, London and New York, rev. ed. 2000.

Berger, Patricia Ann *et al.*, *Tomb Treasures from China: The Buried Art of Ancient Xi'an*, San Francisco, 1994.

Birrel, Anne, *Chinese Mythology: An Introduction*, Baltimore and London, 1993.

Blunden, Caroline and Elvin, Mark, *Cultural Atlas of Ancient China*, Oxford, 1983.

Caswell, James O., *Written and Unwritten: A New History of the Buddhist Caves at Yungang*, Vancouver, 1988.

Chang Kwang-chih, *Shang Civilization*, New Haven and London, 1980.

Chang Kwang-chih, *Art, Myth, and Ritual: The Path to Political Authority in Ancient China*, Cambridge, Mass., and London, 1983.

Chang Kwang-chih, *The Archaeology of Ancient China*, 4th edition, New Haven and London, 1986.

Chang Kwang-chih, (ed.), *Studies of Shang Archaeology*, New Haven and London, 1986.

Chase, William T., *Ancient Chinese Bronze Art: Casting the Precious Sacral Vessel*, New York, 1991.

Cheng, Anne, *Histoire de la pensée chinoise*, Paris, 1997.

China Cultural Relics Promotion Centre (ed.), *Treasures: 300 Best Excavated Antiques from China*, Beijing, 1992.

Ciarla, Roberto and Lionello Lanciotti (eds.), *I bronzi del regno di Dian, Yunnan, Cina (secoli VI/I aC)*, Modena, 1987.

Clunas, Craig, *Art in China*, Oxford, New York, 1997.

Debine-Francfort, Corinne, *The Search for Ancient China*, London and New York, 1990.

Debine-Francfort, Corinne, *Du Néolithique à l'Age du Bronze en Chine du Nord-Ouest: La culture de Qijia et ses connexions*, Paris, 1995.

Dunhuang Institute of Cultural Relics (ed.), *Art and Treasures of Dunhuang*, Hong Kong, 1983.

Falkenhausen, Lothar von, *Suspended Music: Chime-bells in the Culture of Bronze Age China*, Berkeley, Los Angeles, Oxford, 1993.

Fong, Wen (ed.), *The Great Bronze Age of China: An Exhibition from the People's Republic of China*, New York, 1980.

Fu Tianchou (ed.), *Les fresques de Dunhuang*, Bruxelles, 1989.

Gray, B. and Vincent, J. E., *Buddhist Cave Paintings at Dun-Huang*, London, 1959.

He Li, *Chinese Ceramics. The New Standard Guide*. London and New York, 1986.

Hsu, Cho-yun and Linduff, Katheryn M., *Western Zhou Civilization*, New Haven and London, 1988.

Keightley, David N., *Sources of Shang History: The Oracle-Bone Inscriptions of Bronze Age China*, Berkeley, Los Angeles, London, 1978.

Keightley, David N., (ed.), *The Origins of Chinese Civilization*, Berkeley, Los Angeles, London, 1983.

Kuttner, Fritz A., *The Archaeology of Music in Ancient China: 2,000 Years of Acoustical Experimentations, 1400 BC–AD 750*, New York, 1990.

Kuwayama, George, *Ancient Ritual Bronzes of China*, Los Angeles, 1976.

Kuwayama, George, *The Great Bronze Age of China: A Symposium*, Los Angeles, 1983.

Lam, Peter Y. K., *Jades from the Tomb of the King of Nan Yue*, Hong Kong, 1991.

Lawton, Thomas (ed.), *New Perspectives on Chu Culture during the Eastern Zhou Period*, Princeton and Washington, D.C., 1991.

Lee, Sherman and Rogers, Howard (eds.), *China 5,000 Years: Innovation and Transformation in the Arts*, New York, 1998.

Li Chi, *Anyang*, Seattle, 1977.

Li Xueqin, *The Wonder of Chinese Bronzes*, Beijing, 1980.

Li Xueqin, *Eastern Zhou and Qin Civilizations*, New Haven and London, 1985.

Loehr, Max, *Ritual Vessels of Bronze Age China*, New York, 1968.

Loewe, Michael, *Way to Paradise: The Chinese Quest for Immortality*, London, 1979.

Loewe, Michael, *Chinese Ideas of Life and Death: Faith, Myth and Reason in the Han Period*, London, 1982.

Loewe, Michael and Shaughnessy, Edward L. (eds.), *The Cambridge History of Ancient China: From the Origins of Civilization to 221 B.C.*, Cambridge, New York, Melbourne, 1999.

Paludan, Ann, *Chronicle of the Chinese Emperors*, London, New York 1998.

Pelliot, Paul, *Mission Pelliot en Asie Centrale. Les Grottes de Touen-Houang*, Paris, 1914-24.

Pirazzoli-t'Serstevens Michèle, *The Han Dynasty*, New York, 1982.

Pirazzoli-t'Serstevens Michèle, (ed.), *L'arte della Cina*, Torino, 1996.

Powers, Martin J., *Art and Political Expression in Early China*, New Haven and London, 1991.

Rawson, Jessica M., *Chinese Bronzes: Art and Ritual*, London, 1987.

Rawson, Jessica M., *Western Zhou Ritual Bronzes in the Arthur M. Sackler Collections*, Washington, D.C., 1990.

Rawson, Jessica M. with Carol Michaelson, *Chinese Jade from the Neolithic to the Qing*, London, 1995.

Rawson, Jessica M. (ed.), *Mysteries of Ancient China: New Discoveries from the Early Dynasties*, London, 1996.

Rawson, Jessica (ed.) *The British Museum Book of Chinese Art*, London, 1992.

Rawson, Jessica M. and Bunker, Emma C., *Ancient Chinese and Ordos Bronzes*, Hong Kong, 1990.

Sabattini, Mario e Santangelo, Paolo, *Storia della Cina. Dalle origini alla fondazione della Repubblica*, Roma e Bari, 1986.

Scarpari, Maurizio (ed.), *Le fonti per lo studio della civiltà cinese*, Venezia, 1995.

Segalen, V., *The Great Statuary of China*, Chicago, 1978.

Shaughnessy, Edward L., *Sources of Western Zhou History: Inscribed Bronze Vessels*, Berkeley, Los Angeles, London, 1991.

Shensi Provincial Museum and Commission for the Preservation of Archaeological Monuments of Shensi Province, *Murals in the Tomb of Li Hsien and Li Chung-jun of the T'ang Dynasty*, Beijing, 1974.

So, Jenny F., *Eastern Zhou Ritual Bronzes from the Arthur M. Sackler Collections*, New York, 1995.

Stein, Aurel, *The Thousand Buddhas: Ancient Buddhist Paintings from the Cave-Temples of Tun-huang on the Western Frontier of China*, London, 1921.

Sullivan, Michael and Darbois, D., *The Cave Temples of Maichishan*, London, 1969.

Thorp, Robert L., *Son of Heaven: Imperial Arts of China*, Seattle, 1988.

Tregear, Mary, *Chinese Art*, London and New York, 1997.

Twitchett, Dennis (ed.), *The Cambridge History of China. 3: Sui and T'ang China, 589-906, Part 1*, Cambridge, 1979.

Twitchett, Dennis and Loewe, Michael (eds.), *The Cambridge History of China. 1: The Ch'in and Han Empires (221 B.C.-A.D. 220)*, Cambridge, 1986.

Wang Zhongshu, *Han Civilization*, New Haven and London, 1984.

Watson, William, *The Arts of China to AD 900*, New Haven and London, 1995.

White, Julia M. and Bunker, Emma, with contributions by Chen Peifen (eds.), *Adornment for Eternity. Status and Rank in Chinese Ornament*, Hong Kong and Seattle, 1994.

Withfield, Roderick (ed.), *The Problem of Meaning in Early Chinese Ritual Bronzes*, London, 1993.

Withfield, Roderick and Farrer A., *Caves of the Thousand Buddhas. Chinese Art from the Silk Route*, London, 1990.

Wu, Hung, *Monumentality in Early Chinese Art and Architecture*, Stanford, 1995.

Wu, Hung et al., *3,000 Years of Chinese Painting*, New Haven, 1997.

Yang, Xiaoneng, *The Golden Age of Chinese Archaeology: Celebrated Discoveries from the People's Republic of China*, New Haven and London, 1999.

ILLUSTRATION CREDITS

The Editor wishes to thank the Cultural Relics Publishing House of Peking, without whose valuable co-operation this book could never have been realized. Special thanks to Art Exhibitions China, Eskenazi Ltd., Christian Deydier, Francesca Dal Lago, Davide Cucino and all those who gave their kind permission to publish the pictures in the book. Extra special thanks also to Cristina Biondi and Stefania Stafutti for her endless assistance.

中國古代文明

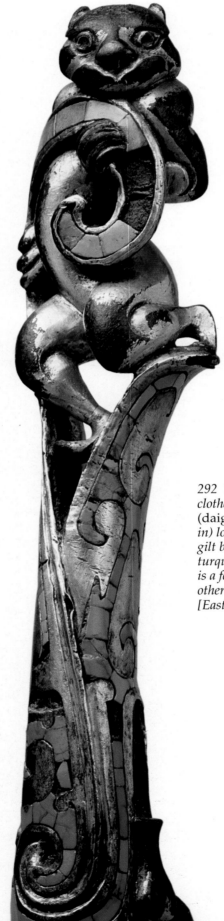

292 This curved clothes-hook (daigou), 16.5 cm (6½ in) long, is made of gilt bronze, silver and turquoise. At one end is a feline, and at the other is a dragon. [Eastern Zhou]